Soccer's Neoliberal Pitch

Rhetoric, Culture, and Social Critique

Soccer's Neoliberal Pitch

The Sport's Power, Profit, and Discursive Politics

John M. Sloop

THE UNIVERSITY OF ALABAMA PRESS | Tuscaloosa

The University of Alabama Press
Tuscaloosa, Alabama 35487-0380
uapress.ua.edu

Typeface: Arno Pro

Cover image: Nashville Soccer Club player celebrates with the supporters fan section after the final goal of a game at First Tennessee Park in Nashville, Tennessee; photograph by Casey Gower, Caseysphotography.co
Cover design: Lori Lynch

Cataloging-in-Publication data is available from the Library of Congress.
ISBN: 978-0-8173-2160-4 (cloth)
ISBN: 978-0-8173-6102-0 (paper)
E-ISBN: 978-0-8173-9454-7

Contents

Acknowledgments

Several years ago, reflecting on the depth of my passion for soccer in general and particular teams in specific (e.g., Chelsea FC, Nashville SC, the United States Men's National Soccer Team [USMNT], and the United States Women's National Soccer Team [USWNT]), I realized that I should take the advice I have given to many junior scholars over the years and utilize that passion to launch a larger critical investigation. After all, our choice and drive to pursue particular passions must necessarily get bound up with our identity(ies) and therefore with a vast array of intersecting cultural meanings. This manuscript represents my attempt to take a personal passion and utilize my intersections with soccer fandom and public argument to think through some of the tensions of contemporary culture.

I want to begin my list of thanks/inspirations with my Vanderbilt colleague Lutz Koepnick. For the last several years (and, hopefully, for the next decade or so), Lutz and I have team-taught an undergraduate course at Vanderbilt entitled. "Soccer: Media, Art and Society." Lutz had at first designed this course on his own and then invited me to teach with him. I absolutely cannot thank him enough for doing so. Because we come from different academic traditions, our conversations with each other and with the class are lively ones. As a result, I have been introduced to new ways of thinking about soccer and have taken fresh eyes to old, familiar material. Not only have I benefited from the lecture and discussion sections, I also learned a great deal on a trip we took with a half dozen of the students to London, Liverpool, and Manchester to watch games, tour a variety of stadiums, and meet with journalists and fan groups. Thanks, then, is also due to the College of Arts and Science at Vanderbilt for providing an Immersion Grant that allowed that trip. I also am grateful for the conversations with, and support of, Abby Trozenski and Vivian Langer, the graduate students who assisted in the course. We were teaching this course in the first stages of the pandemic, narrowly making our trip to Europe before the world came to a halt. I was on research leave the following year (again, thanks to the College of Arts and Science at Vanderbilt), and the thinking initiated in that course prepared me well for kicking off several chapters of the book. And finally, teaching this course has allowed me to have a course listed in the German department. I never saw that coming.

There are a number of friends and scholars in the academy with whom I have both bantered about soccer and traded ideas over the years. I am thankful for each of those conversations and the many "academic" panels we have shared. This group includes but is not limited to Kendall Phillips, Fernando Delgado, Michelle Ramsey, Michael Janus, Divine Narkotey Aboagye, Brian McNelly, Lillian Feder, Abraham Khan, Leslie Rossman, Daniel Kim, Colleen English, Randall Monty, Jim Jasinski, and Michael Butterworth. While it has only on rare occasion led me to discussions about soccer, I want to thank the scholars who compose the Facebook group Communication Scholars for Transformation. The conversations and topics raised there have led me down many a self-reflective path and have made a better, and more humane, scholar.

When you are tackling a topic like soccer, there are large numbers of individuals outside of the academy who shape your understanding of the game and its culture. First and foremost, I want to thank my colleagues at Speedway Soccer, a Nashville SC–focused media group that publishes content through Broadways Sports Media. This group, including Ben Wright, Jonathan Slape, Chris Ivey, Casey Gower, Anderson Simmons, Lucas Panzica, and Davey Shepherd, have pushed me to rethink aspects of soccer harder than any other conversations. Part of it is simply because I'm in constant contact with this group; part of it is that they are a belligerent bunch. At any rate, I cannot thank them enough for this multiyear conversation. In 2013 I helped cofound the Music City Blues (the Nashville-based Chelsea FC supporters group under the Chelsea in America umbrella) with Ryan Green and David Bone. From 6 a.m. Saturday games, in which we would struggle to get ten people to the pub, to championship games with hundreds of fans, to road trips for Chelsea tours in the States, this group has put up with a great number of my anxieties, my pacing, and my ridiculous celebrations. It all hurts, but it's all good. I also want to raise a pint in the direction of the Bayou City Blues and the Chicago Blues, two groups that helped shepherd the Nashville group and have been welcoming during road trips. I also acknowledge all the members of the Middle TN Premier League fan community; we all get along fairly well. Finally, I want to thank all of the members of the local fan groups (virtual and IRL) for Nashville SC and the Nashville members of the American Outlaws. My world would be impoverished without all of you. I give special acknowledgments to capo Stephen Robinson and the omnipresent Soccer Moses (Stephen Mason).

Across the pond, I need to give special thanks to three different people who gave me very different ways of understanding the game and its history. First, and certainly foremost, Spurs supporter Neil Rebak has shown extraordinary patience with me, as I asked him question after question early in my fandom. I first met Neil three decades ago on an internet-based backgammon site. Sharing a sense of humor, we talked music and politics for years while I still thought of soccer as the dullest sport on earth. When I feel in love with the game and with Chelsea, I wrote Neil to let him know. "Brilliant," he responded, "I despise Chelsea." Thus began several years of him hosting me in London, attending Chelsea matches with me at Stamford Bridge and inviting me along to White Hart Lane to watch his beloved Spurs. I will never know how to thank him enough for a virtual friendship that turned very real. Secondly, Chelsea super blogger Chris Axon not only answered numerous questions for me about fandom over the course of his life but also answered my questions about the casual movement, his memories of hooligan culture, and soccer style in general. In addition he met with the traveling students from my soccer class and talked to them about fan culture. He's aces. Finally, I must thank Jen Abergel. Jen and I first met when she was handing off some volunteer data entry work for Chelsea in America that I was taking over. During our one session of Skype training, I decided we were going to be friends. Luckily, she agreed. While she seems to be moving all over the globe, we had the chance to go to both Stamford Bridge and Birmingham on one of my trips over. Her love of the game is infectious.

Compared to what I hear from others via social media, I feel extraordinarily fortunate to be at Vanderbilt. My colleagues in the Department of Communication Studies are amazingly supportive and collegial in all ways. I want to especially highlight Isaac West, with whom I coauthored the chapter on Robbie Rogers (thank you for making me better), as well as Paul Stob and Jeff Bennett, both of whom served as chair of the department during the writing. Bonnie Dow has been a very supportive colleague and friend, even when I wasn't deserving. Her sense of professionalism and "adulting" will forever astound me. I thank the College of Arts and Science for the research leave and research funds that supported the time writing and researching this book. The Vanderbilt Library staff was simply amazing in their ability to quickly find material for me, even in the midst of a pandemic.

The original version of chapter 2 was published as John M. Sloop and Isaac West, "Heroism's Contexts: Robbie Rogers and the Ghost of Justin Fashanu," *QED: A Journal of GLBTQ Worldmaking* 3 (2016): 1–28. I thank *QED* (and editors Charles Morris and Thomas Nakayama) for their work on the essay. That version was also originally presented as the keynote at the Sam Becker Memorial Conference, University of Iowa, Iowa City, April 1, 2014, and as keynote address for the *Rhetoric in Contemporary Culture* Spring 2017 Honors Lecture Series, Middle Tennessee State University, Murfreesboro, January 31, 2017. Versions of chapter 3 were presented at the University of Utah, Salt Lake City, March 20, 2017, and at the University of Colorado, Boulder, on April 6, 2017. Versions of chapters 5 and 6 were presented at the November 2021 meeting of the National Communication Association in Seattle, Washington.

In addition to soccer, my daily life is enhanced in a number of avenues, and I want to acknowledge each. Too often, scholars forget the way their lives are enriched by pursuits that have little to do with their "work." First, I want to thank my normal running group, the Righteous Possum Eaters. My Tuesday and Thursday mornings are blessed—through snow, rain, wind, and heat—as a result of more than a decade of its existence. I could not be more grateful for the many versions of the Couch Bats, the relay running team that has pounded the streets of the Bourbon Chase, Hood to Coast, the Smoky Mountain Relay, and Ville to Ville. I seriously love my excursions with the many manifestations of this group, most notably, the stable members of Van 1. John Jordan, who makes an appearance in the introduction, is also the only other member of the World's Worst Book Club. I will forever be grateful for the deep dives we make into each book we choose. It's a lot of work, a lot of talking, and even more laughter. The TenX9 Nashville storytelling community has been an ongoing life stream for me; we live in the shelter of others, indeed. The Belcourt Theatre and its supporters give me new hope for nonprofit arts with community support. My friends in the 12SBS club have become a necessary foundation for me to renew my sense of life excitement each month. Robert Huffman and Daniel Conover were my college roommates. Who knew that Robert would eventually infect Daniel and me with the soccer disease? Thanks a lot, Robert (really). Finally, the regulars at Smokin Thighs (James Hedges, Kristian Booth, Kevin Polk, and Danny Lacouture), my local watering hole, are more important to my non-Vanderbilt life than I would have ever expected.

The "Introduction" to this book was the last thing I wrote, and while I knew what I wanted to say and how it connected to the chapters that followed, something about it made me feel uncomfortable. Jenny Rice was the first, and only, person I trusted to read it and give me advice. While, of course, any and all weaknesses of that chapter remain mine, her advice changed so much for me that I had to dig back into the chapters that followed and rethink parts of the entire project. And that's something of a metaphor of what she's done for me in general. Her presence in my life not only improves everything in the here and now but forced me to rethink my past and future. My faults remain my own, but knowing her has improved me in numerous ways. I am forever tangled up.

Soccer's Neoliberal Pitch

Introduction

> Some people—and many Americans, it must be said—find football boring. This is wrong. And they are boring for believing it.
>
> —Simon Critchley, *What We Think about When We Think about Soccer*

> The fact that US soccer culture has in many ways lived, and thrived, on the margins of mainstream sports is part of what has made it a vector for different ways of thinking about what this country is and can be, and what role sports can play in that.
>
> —Laurent Dubois, *The Language of the Game*

> Rather, the argument is that nothing is untouched by a neoliberal mode of reason and valuation and that neoliberalism's attack on democracy has everywhere inflected law, political culture, and political subjectivity.
>
> —Wendy Brown, *In the Ruins of Neoliberalism*

A Diaspora without Origin

In early summer 2015, I contacted my friend and colleague John Jordan, who is a professor at the University of Wisconsin, Milwaukee, and tried to talk him into meeting up with me in Indianapolis during the summer to watch Chelsea FC play Inter Milan at Lucas Oil Stadium in the Guinness International Champions Cup. While being billed as a tournament that was "more than friendlies," it was simply a different guise by which European teams could carry out one of their normal summer tours. The tours and this tournament make immediate profit, but they are also more of a long-term investment as the teams grow their global brands. Honestly, I didn't care what the team's purpose was; I unabashedly love Chelsea and thought it would be a good occasion to visit with a friend who described himself at the time as, at best, a "casual soccer fan."

One of the benefits of going on these summer tours is that you get a chance to meet up with other (in my case) Chelsea fans throughout the nation who have traveled to the game. For me, this means meeting up with folks I knew previously only through the Chelsea in America umbrella group, or through other digital connections. While I revel in being surrounded by hundreds of friends wearing Chelsea gear and waving scarves while drinking and chanting, that was my only qualm about inviting Jordan. Would it be fun for him once we were all wound up in the collective hysteria of a supporters section? Would this trip end up being a bust for him?

With those concerns (but really, I was too excited to entertain them for long), Jordan and I arrived separately in Indianapolis, meeting up at the hotel and then at the bar that was acting as a host for the Chelsea faithful. The afternoon had many of the normal activities of these events: day drinking, raffles, shopping for Chelsea gear, and then a very strange march to the stadium that seemed to involve going up and down the same street rather than directly toward Lucas Oil. Throughout it, there were the cheers and chants familiar to the Chelsea faithful (e.g., "Carefree," "Celery"), the shouting at people wearing the jerseys of other clubs ("Who are ya? Who are ya?"), and the general sense of joy of being part of a mob.

Jordan and I arrived at the game now loosely knowing a good number of the Chelsea faithful. While I honestly cannot tell you who won the game (I could easily look it up, but it's absolutely beside the point in these friendlies), I do know that both of us found the experience fascinating and fun. From listening to the Chicago supporters' group leading the cheers for Branislav Ivanović (to the tune of "Manamana," a song most of us had learned from *Sesame Street*) to watching the singular Chelsea supporter who would yell "Left, Right, Left, Right, Left, Right, Now Die" at the Inter players who were warming up, we were giddy with enthusiasm.

Back at the bar later, we sat around drinking beer and musing with other supporters late into the night. While we would talk about the game, the upcoming season, and so forth, we also spent a lot of time in what I can best describe as a rhetoric of romance. "How do you come to Chelsea?" "I freaking love this team." "I lose sleep just thinking about them." While we learned a lot about each other's backgrounds, we spent a great deal of our time simply confirming each other's love for the team. Jordan enjoyed his time, I believe, but, not being a Chelsea fan in general, he was more observant of our behavior than a participant in it.

Perhaps because of his status as an outsider, his observations later struck me hard when he was able to articulate something I couldn't see myself: "You guys act like you're part of a diaspora, coming back together after having been distributed throughout the globe. But it's strange, because it's an imagined diaspora, a diaspora without origin." On the one hand, as anyone who has had a cursory acquaintance with Benedict Anderson's concept of "imagined communities" as a starting place for nations, or of constitutive rhetoric more general, would tell you, all communities are, in some sense, imagined communities.[1] Yet Jordan was identifying something else; we all appeared as if we somehow came from a tribe housed at Stamford Bridge in London, that our ancestors must have lived there. Indeed, when several years later, I ran across Michael Silk and Emma Chumley's essay "Memphis United? Diaspora, S(t)imulated Spaces and Global Consumption Economies," in which they investigate how both real and imagined diasporas form in "third spaces" (digital spaces, as well as bars) away from a club's home stadium, I could agree with it on both an intellectual and an emotional, felt, level.[2] Most of us were first-generation fans of Chelsea who had no—or little—geographic connection to London, and yet we felt as if we were reconnecting to some fundamental aspect of our lived experience or spiritual makeup.

I tell this story here, and the one that follows below, because while the case studies that constitute this book cover topics such as gender equality, sexuality, race, violence, globalism, memory, and, importantly and interconnectedly, the logic of neoliberal values, the starting point is the way that soccer (and I will rely on the term "soccer" rather than "football" for the most part[3]), fandom often takes hold of us, provides us with new constitutions, and hence forces intense reflection about meaning, about culture, and about politics as players and teams we know act and react to political and personal circumstances. Many fans care so deeply about their teams that these reactions to political and personal circumstances become topics of deep discussion and conflict among those of the imagined diaspora. While there are in fact people who find soccer boring, soccer is anything but boring. It is also often "about" anything but soccer. It is not just the game but the community, the arguments, the meanings. To experience soccer is to experience what Simon Critchley refers to as "sensate ecstasy," and to experience that is to provide entirely different insights into our shared world, and our struggles over this world.[4]

My love affair begins. In 2010, I was in Portland, Oregon, visiting my close friend Robert. We had been college roommates and were both in our mid-forties but had remained in close touch throughout the years. Our interests had developed in many different directions, but generally we found a way to share those interests. On this particular trip, however, Robert surprised me by asking if I would like to go with him to see a soccer game. Portland had the Timbers, then a United Soccer League (USL)–level[5] club that had quite a following. This, however, was not the Timbers proper but their Professional Development League (PDL) team who were in the finals against the Tampa Bay Chill.[6]

I had no interest in going; it wasn't because it was the youth team, but because I was one of those boring Americans Critchley refers to who find soccer shockingly dull. A good southern boy, my (only half-) joking line was that the only way to make soccer interesting would be to give the players guns. And yet, Robert promised me, this being Portland (and this being before craft breweries were in every US city), the beer would be magnificent. So, I went, despite the fact that I would have to sit through a few hours of a ball randomly bouncing around between grown men.

Two hours later everything had changed. It was, using that old chestnut, as if the world went from black-and-white to color. I was completely seduced. It's not so much that I fell in love with the game itself—it still appeared to me to be grown men randomly running around until the ball luckily fell into the net. No, it was the crowd that got me: thousands of people standing the entire time, chanting endlessly, hugging madly when the Timbers scored, reacting with energy even during the brief period when the Timbers were losing. And unlike any professional sporting event I had attended before, this was all done by the crowd alone, without piped music or sound effects, without any announcer saying a word. There were fans who served as capos[7] helping energize the crowd, but they were fans, not club employees, and they did so with only their bodies and voices. I felt suddenly alive when a player from the Chill scored and began taunting the crowd. The reaction was loud and magnificent. Again, I can't say I loved, or even liked, soccer as a sport at that moment, but I loved the crowd; I loved being part of it. Maybe *that* was loving soccer, I thought, or at least part of it.

I was recently reading James Montague's account of the game-day experience at Borussia Dortmund in the first decade of this century and discovered a passage that reflected my first real exposure to soccer in Portland. He notes: "Against the corporate excess of Bayern, Dortmund felt like a rock and roll underdog that provided the best fan experience of any club in Europe. Cheap tickets. Cheap beer. Standing. Pyro. Choreography. Incessant chanting no matter the score. The experience was so focused on the supporters that thousands of foreign fans flew to Dortmund every weekend to marvel at what football might have been for them had their own clubs not sold their soul."[8] That rang true. While I knew nothing of clubs selling their souls, that day in Portland, I felt I was witnessing what must surely be the greatest fan experience in history. It was otherworldly. "What we have here," Critchley writes, "is what [William] James calls one of the holidays of life, something like an experience of enchantment, where we are lifted out of the everyday into something ecstatic, evanescent and shared, a subtly transfigured sensorium. It is what I call *sensate ecstasy*."[9]

The experience of the crowd produced a surge of endorphins, and I was quickly an addict.[10] Over time, of course, my experience and my knowledge have changed. Over the next decade, I attended multiple US men's and women's games as a member of the American Outlaws,[11] became a Chelsea FC supporter above all other identities, went to Brazil to watch the USMNT during the 2014 World Cup, made multiple trips to the mother church of Stamford Bridge, cofounded the Music City Blues (Nashville's Chelsea supporters group), began reading books about history and tactics (starting, of course, with Jonathan Wilson's ubiquitous *Inverting the Pyramid*),[12] got a Chelsea tattoo upon their winning the Premier League in 2015, become a founding member of Nashville Football Club, and a season ticket holder each year as the club changed to USL side Nashville Soccer Club and then received a Major League Soccer (MLS) franchise. I started a podcast and news service about local soccer with some local friends,[13] began teaching courses about soccer, took a field trip to London, Manchester, and Liverpool with a group of students from the soccer class just before the pandemic. In other words, my life had become soccer-ized. It was with great understanding and sympathy that I read Nick Hornby's classic *Fever Pitch*.[14]

I had found soccer boring, and I was boring for finding it that way. That is, I was boring relative to my life after finding it. Now, it had affected me so much that my identity was bound up in an imagined diaspora. I was fundamentally changed, defined in large part by soccer.

In some ways, this book has nothing to do specifically with sensate ecstasy, although the concept will always be lurking in the background because it is important to the way meanings become agreed upon in soccer culture. I will be spending very little time on my own fan experience or on philosophical thoughts about the crowd in what follows. The chapters that make up this book each take on a case study of mediated coverage of a variety of soccer-related issues. One need not be a fan to read these chapters or even to have written them (although that may be a stretch). One could find soccer boring and still draw from the chapters. And yet, still, I think it wise to linger on this larger concept of sensate ecstasy for a number of reasons, primarily of which, one could argue, and I certain believe this to true, that each of the cases I write about takes on additional impact, additional ideological meaning, because of fan investment in this powerful, entrancingly beautiful game and, importantly, its communities. Critical work involving soccer, and sport in general, is not dismissive of sport or sport fandom; indeed, it takes rabid fandom as an additional (affective) reason why a connection to sport is such an important site for thinking about meaning and culture.

Attempting to write in an almost colloquial philosophical style, Critchley works to have non-soccer-fans understand that the experience of fandom, similar to particular religious experiences, is one that creates that sense of *ecstasis*—of being outside oneself. There are three aspects of the ecstasy of soccer fandom that he firmly underlines. First, in referring to it as sensate ecstasy, Critchley confirms that the experiences, when they come, are very bound up in the senses one engages as part of the crowd. He mentions the term four times in his book. In the first he is describing the events surrounding a goal being scored: "A flare detonates . . . red smoke scatters over the heads of jubilant fans. People—proper, grown-up, intelligent, thoughtful people, some of them with careers and deep into middle age and even beyond—kiss, high-five and hug each other in delight."[15] In the second he highlights the sensorium that is the football stadium. He describes the concrete halls, the seats under floodlights, the pitch, and the entire stadium: "shining, gleaming. It is real, but too real, hyper-real, almost too much. . . . It is the empire of the senses, the realm of the in-between."[16] In the third, a short review of the movie *Zidane,* Critchley discusses the sound of the stadium and Zidane's observation that in soccer one becomes engulfed by the "sound of noise," and being engulfed and lost in that sound is to be in ecstasy.[17] In his final reflection on the term, Critchley again describes those moments of sensate ecstasy as "magically irresponsible moments . . . a dynamic figuration of beauty, the dramatic mobility of play, the movement of free association between players and amongst fans."[18] Communication scholars would find interesting parallels in H. Lloyd Goodall's equation of moments of "sports ecstasy" and the loss of a sense of self.[19] These are brief but powerful moments, then, sensory-induced moments, in which we find ourselves briefly outside of ourselves.

Secondly, and partially assumed by the first point, sensate ecstasy is public and communal. To be engulfed by the crowd, to be outside oneself with others, to be lost in the noise of sound, to be involved in the free association between players and amongst fans, creates an ecstatic public that is made possible through the experience/feeling among individuals-as-not-individual.

When Critchley notes that a game without fans is a category mistake, an "exercise devoid of sense,"[20] he is clear that sensate ecstasy is allowed only by the coming together of this type of public. Indeed, his claim is similar to that made by Michael Serazio about sport fandom in general when he observes, "In an era of cultural fragmentation, political polarization, and the relentless distraction that comes with living amidst media abundance, sport represents one of the last institutions of unifying mass ritual—bringing together enormous audiences, focused on the present, live moment."[21]

Thirdly, and Critchley perhaps rightly ends on this point—one that proves foundational to my own project—while (or, because) these moments of delight and ecstasy are only fleeting, they do not save fans "from the horrors of the neo-liberal, globalized world," nor do they abstract fans out of the world of public and political problems. If anything, those moments of ecstasy only provide emphasis to the problems of the world. "Beauty," Critchley notes, "is nothing but the beginning of terror."[22]

Ultimately, then, the sensate ecstasy of soccer fandom makes possible a public of individuals not as individual. And the moments of ecstasy are not escapism and are not moments that encourage this public to be passive. Yet the consequences of this public encourage a flattening of discourse toward the center to the degree that in order to maintain the sense of being one out of many, the public discourse of soccer almost necessarily tends back toward the center, where there is more of a chance of mob ecstasy. The sound of noise is to be lost in the crowd (and to agree with it); the sound of rational argument is to fracture the sense of ecstatic public. As a result, cases of argument or public discussion in/about soccer do, to some degree, necessarily reconfirm some of the "horrors of the globalized world." That is, if we are to be "as one," there are going to be agreements and assumptions that meet in popular culture and therefore, as Wendy Brown notes in one of the opening quotations, reconfirm the logics of neoliberalism. It is this somewhat unique creation of an ecstatic public that gives "good reasons for spending time and labor within the context" of sports studies.[23]

Neoliberalism and Cultural and Rhetorical Criticism

The last decade has seen a proliferation of discussion concerning "neoliberalism" throughout the critical cultural community, including rhetorical studies. While I see no need to rehearse the entire body of discourse about neoliberalism here, I do want to set out very briefly my assumptions and point in the direction of neoliberalism and its intersections with sports and rhetorical/communication studies. In *The Burnout Society*, Byung-Chul Han suggests, as have others, that we have moved ideologically to a space beyond Foucault's disciplinary society.[24] However, rather than the pivot to a discussion of a society of control that many have taken, Han diagnoses contemporary culture as a "society of achievement," with a fixation on the individual as an "entrepreneur of self."[25] While Han is driven in large part by media ecology in his overall body of work, he sees this move to positivity and production as ideologically overdetermined. The difference he sees is between being motivated by "should" to being more internally motivated by "can." The achievement-subject is not passive; rather, standing free from external instances of domination forcing it to work, "the achievement-subject gives itself over to compulsive freedom—that is, to the free constraint of maximizing achievement. Excess work and performance escalate into auto-exploitation."[26] What is important here is the description of human subjects who have internalized norms enough that their actions toward achievement and flexibility are publicly described as internally motivated, rather than motivated by a sense of surveillance or top-down control, and that the achievements lead to a subject with the flexible skills to be successful in the marketplace. These are subjects who have assumed a logic of neoliberalism.

The subject who is compulsively driven to achievement fits snugly within any thesis concerning the neoliberal marketplace (e.g., labor, social, political). Multiple critical/cultural scholars have illustrated a variety of ways neoliberalism as an ideology is underlined in mass-mediated texts and hence operates as a script for behavior. In a landscape overview that fits my purposes well, Robert Asen notes, via Benhabib, that public conversation takes place through an interlocking set of associations, networks and organizations.[27] Drawing on Wendy Brown, he argues that the current public conversation situates all social actors as working within markets, *whether or not money is at stake*.[28] As a result, "public goods" disappear, and the means for redressing inequality and mobilizing diversity are obfuscated.[29] Because of the emphasis on the individual and of working "on oneself constantly to survive competition," neoliberal logic must deny the ways racism, sexism, classism, etc. work against individual actors.[30] By "flattening difference and discounting inequality, a neoliberal public assumes that everyone can adopt the position of *homo oeconmicus*."[31]

As I pointed out above, the logic of neoliberalism has become so pervasive that it can be found throughout culture, not simply in labor, but in all markets. Again, quoting Brown, "Nothing is untouched by a neoliberal mode of reason and valuation."[32] Aligning herself with the Foucault of *The Birth of Biopolitics*,[33] Brown sees neoliberalism as "an order of normative reason that . . . takes shape as a governing rationality extending a specific formulation of economic values, practices, and metrics to every dimension of human life."[34] While the effects and outcomes of this neoliberal shift are widespread, one overarching change is that we see commitments to equality, liberty, and inclusion become subordinate to a logic of the market,[35] and a commitment of individual resources and risks into almost intractable faith in the neoliberal system as a whole.[36] This, for example, will become especially clear in the arguments over equal pay for the US Women's National Team in soccer. In what follows I investigate numerous conversations and public discussions that emerge around various elements of soccer culture as a way of bringing those logics into relief, acting as an intervention or reflective moment about the ways we assume discourses that might not work in our own interests. In short, lost in the throes of a culture and with a discourse driven toward commonsense assumptions, we find ourselves replicating and reaffirming logics; in this book I find different ways to critique these assumptions while acknowledging the way that the unifying fandom of "sensate ecstasy" often acts as an implicit endorsement of these assumptions. As Andrei Markovits and Steven Hellerman put it in their overview of soccer and neoliberalism, "hegemonic sports cultures are very 'sticky' and 'path dependent' and cannot be acquired through intellect but only through emotion and identity, which is what ultimately sustains them in a historically lasting way."[37] Or, perhaps more pointedly, as David Andres and Michael L. Silk observe, "Sport serves as an economy of affect through which power, privilege, politics, and position are (re)produced."[38]

In addition to those who have discussed the connections among politics, ideology, neoliberalism, and soccer, a number of scholars in rhetoric and communication studies have stressed that, in fact, the rhetorical study of sport is never just about the sport; rather, it is always the study of ideology. For instance, in Abraham Khan's analysis of the discourse surrounding baseball player/free agency advocate Curt Flood, he notes that all institutions—including those of sports—"and the political practices they make possible are not only shaped by ideas and arguments but are also constituted in part by the rhetoric through which those ideas are rendered."[39] More specifically invoking neoliberalism, Dan Grano argues that the discourse around "brain banking" in the NFL works to "reify neoliberal conceptions of personalized risk management and informed choice."[40] In his pointedly titled essay "Ideology Doesn't Just Happen," Jay Coakley observes the interconnection between discourse about sports as an institution and contemporary discussions of ideology. Looking at sports as a cultural practice and form of social organizing, Coakley claims that sport reinforces the neoliberal ideology requiring the use of competitive reward structures, the alignment of merit with market values, and a focus on individual responsibility.[41] Grano and Butterworth begin with the assumption that "sport—like other prominent culture institutions—both reflects and mobilizes political commitments, ideologies and antagonisms."[42] This, despite the communication studies disciplines' tendency to mobilize sports studies as being merely about sport.[43] Ultimately, I want to stress here, along with Michael Serazio, that "sports are, in many ways, the least interesting thing about sports."[44] As every rhetorical and cultural critic who approaches sports (and there have been a great number of them) could attest, the study of sport is always a displaced study of something else. Because sports are meaningful sites of emotive attachment, spaces that maintained some sense of metanarrative, they are spaces that urgently call out for investigation of all aspects of cultural ideology. This book will join these others in providing something of a cultural snapshot of meanings.

The title of the book, *Soccer's Neoliberal Pitch,* is meant to play in at least two different ways in guiding this argument. First, the book is in part an analysis of the ways neoliberal arguments pervade each of the case studies. Again, given that neoliberal modes of thinking are pervasive culturally, it is no surprise to see that the arguments in the case studies employ them. Hence, on the one hand, this book is a way of understanding how various "events" in soccer are understood through neoliberalism. Secondly, the arguments made in these case studies represent "neoliberalism's pitch" (as in a sales pitch). In essence, through the arguments made or assumed in each chapter, we see the type of world that neoliberalism as a political philosophy is pitching us, and what its influence might be across some identity markers and behaviors. While neoliberalism is not the sole, or even primary, logic at work in the arguments in each chapter, it does intersect with all of them through its intersection in discourses of gender, sexuality, race, nationalism, class, and labor.

Overview of Chapters

What you will read over the following pages are six case studies of "public arguments" that take place in the context of soccer culture. In each chapter I attempt to outline the "commonsense" ideological commitments of (primarily) US mainstream culture—many of which are based in neoliberalism—and illustrate the ways arguments allow for transition and change within a context of ideological constraint. I want to make two assumptions clear: first, while I understand that there are multiple networks of communication that are always ongoing, my focus will be primarily, although not exclusively, on fairly central news sources and columns, rather than social media platforms or other forms of digital discourse (e.g., blogs). While I assume, along with Robert Asen, that there are multiple networked publics that can create resistant discourses to those in the particular public discourse I investigate, these discourses are the ones against which we all react.[45] Secondly, I assume that these discourses constrain public discussion and do so with an accent thoroughly versed with neoliberalism. Neoliberalism obviously highlights individual responsibility and self-improvement over forms of coalition or programs that provide support across the board. While resistance to neoliberal logic is possible, it must take place with purposeful attention to relationships and respond to the types of discourses I investigate here.

While my primary focus is on discourse about US soccer (both league soccer and national team soccer, both men's and women's teams), I also touch on other leagues (especially the English Premier League) to provide some of the background for understanding the context of the discussion of soccer in the United States. Hence, because many nonfans often came to understand soccer as a professional sport (as opposed to what their children do on weekends) through the hooligan movements in Europe, especially England, at the end of the last century, I begin the first chapter, "When Career Opportunities Finally Knock: Addiction, Displacement, and Hooligan Memoirs," with an analysis of hooligan memoirs. The question here is, "How does a game that was known for crowds of unruly (white, male, racist, sexist) fans prone to violence get re-presented as a more genteel sport with potentially, albeit muted, progressive politics?" Through a reading of more than a dozen books by former hooligans (so-called hooli-lit, written at the turn of the century), in addition to a discussion of material changes (e.g., ticket prices, "no standing" policies), I offer an explanation for the ways that economic and material changes "encouraged" a change in the ideology of soccer and of the former hooligans who offer their memories and explanations of fandom as something more familiar, more central, than was ever the case. Hooliganism becomes a form of neoliberal training in which politically offensive behavior (e.g., racism, sexism) is displaced. It is not that such behaviors did not take place; it is more that they are civilized in memory as soccer is structured as part of the neoliberal lifeworld in which people can act without systemic racism, sexism, etc. as constraints. And to maintain a more contemporary sense of the ecstatic public of soccer fandom, these hooligan memoirs reflect contemporary shared understandings of public value.

Chapter 1 can be seen as loosely coupled with the second chapter as two different cases of the development of the "self" in neoliberal culture. Hence, I follow up the discussion of hooli-lit with "Heroism's Contexts: Robbie Rogers and the Ghost of Justin Fashanu," a reading of the discourse that emerged in the wake of Robbie Rogers's coming-out story. When Rogers initially came out as gay, he retired from playing soccer (he was at the time playing in England at Stevenage), citing the ontological impossibility of being a soccer player *and* gay. When Rogers then returns to the US to play for the LA Galaxy of Major League Soccer, a discourse celebratory of homosexuality emerges. I discuss the ways the discourse operates to provide new spaces for changing the popular understanding of sexuality while simultaneously cordoning off the range of behaviors one should publicly exhibit. Moreover, I look at the way Rogers begins to take it upon himself to have acted differently, ultimately ignoring the weight of cultural logics upon him, and encourages others to understand that each person needs to take individual responsibility for coming out, each person needs to see their economic and social lives as ultimately unconstrained by any form of social discipline.

The following two chapters focus on the cultural and commercial translation of neoliberalism via soccer. Chapter 3, "Soccer in the Mirror World," investigates a period almost a decade ago when NBC bought the rights to show all English Premier League games on US television. Given the large outlay of capital to purchase these rights, NBC had incentive to encourage multiple news outlets to help bring new fans (viewers) to the game. As a result, dozens of formal and informal guides to choosing a favorite Premier League team appeared that year. Invoking the concept of the "postfan," I provide an analysis of these guides as cultural artifacts that reflect the ideological values of US culture (in this way, constraining meaning, making what might be different into something more familiar). This chapter, then, illustrates the ways US soccer, even if marginal in Dubois's meaning, is ideologically constrained by the economic need to center it, bring it to the nonmarginal or mainstream. In doing so, the possibilities of marginal or oppositional values are far more limited.

In the fourth chapter, "Liga MX, MLS, and the Neoliberal Corporate Politics of 'Othering,'" I look at the landscape of the competitive relationship between the United States' Major League Soccer and Mexico's Liga MX. By drawing upon both "print" publications and websites, some originating in the US and focusing on MLS, and some originating in Mexico and focusing on Liga MX, I draw out different ways the popularity of the leagues is covered and then underline the arguments that have led to a partnership between the leagues. Ultimately, I argue that the discourse works upon what I refer to as a logic of "corporate neoliberalism" that erases the ways that European familiarity and US capital operate to provide MLS with advantages over Liga MX.

The remaining two chapters are studies of neoliberal culture and social movements, investigating the way soccer and soccer journalism work to reinforce neoliberal logics within arguments over race, gender, sexuality, and nationality. Chapter 5, "What Is American Exceptionalism Doing in a Place like This?" is a reading of the news coverage and public arguments surrounding "equal pay" for the USWNT. While seeing great possibilities in how some of the arguments for equal pay operate on a universalizing principle, I offer concerns about the ways that many of the arguments more directly reaffirm some of the economic and neoliberal arguments that had earlier worked against the women's teams. While not taking neoliberalism down to the individual actor, the logic of the arguments in favor of equal pay are often driven by neoliberal logics at the level of the team. The soccer public that produces these arguments relies on something of a shared, communal logic.

In the sixth and final chapter, "'Black Lives Matter' Matters: Soccer, Slogans, Spectacle, and the Shape of Meaning," I provide a reading of the public arguments about the Black Lives Matter (BLM) movement and soccer, both in the US and in the Premier League. In tracing out these discourses, I again discuss many of the transformative possibilities of the visibility of BLM within the sport but also offer a critical reading of the many ways that the more radical potential meanings of Black Lives Matter are slowly massaged into a much softer argument concerning racial equality, a logic that works much more smoothly with neoliberal logics. To a degree, the counternarrative to Black Lives Matter works to lessen any acknowledgment of the role of race or racism on the formation of identity and agency, as well as erasing BLM's concerns with gender, sexuality, and creativity.

In short, then, I take the discourse around soccer as a location for potentially radical, or at least progressive, cultural politics, put those arguments into relief, and highlight the ways they are disciplined or constrained, both by the general draw of economic incentives and by the draw of the ecstatic public. The politics of constraint and discipline are ones that I hope readers may take into other arenas of popular culture. Again, I wish to stress that while the concept of "sensate ecstasy" will not be drawn forth in each chapter, I take the communal needs of the ecstatic public for soccer to be ones that lead toward common understanding rather than critique. Finally, I want to stress that the motivation for highlighting such constraint is to provide those involved in these public arguments helpful ways to engage in arguments and discussions that alter and shift such disciplining discourses.

Soccer and Writing

Finally, before I move on to the cases themselves, a few brief words about some recent and canonical writing about soccer are in order. Like the game itself, many of the people who are writing about soccer seem to be inspired to alter their aesthetic.[46] While I do not hope to provide a comprehensive collection of soccer writing here, I do want to gesture to some of the work that is influential in how I understand the game and our collective connection to it. These texts, as well as others, help nuance my thinking. In a way, this is a thank-you to those authors.

A pause first, however, as I think it is important to get one critique at least partially off the table before one reads the remainder of this book. While some forms of fandom are tied to the radical Right and others to the radical Left, nothing about it is predetermined, except for the need to find compromised meanings for the community as a whole. While compromised meanings blunt the radical edge of politics at times, it is an active rather than a passive ecstatic public that continues to have potential for change.

Most modern writing about soccer, especially beautiful writing about soccer, is inspired by the poetic history written by Uruguayan author Eduardo Galeano—*Soccer in Sun and Shadow*[47]—and English author Nick Hornby in his breakout novel/personal exposition, *Fever Pitch*.[48] In each we are provided different ways of understanding the positions in which fans find themselves: in a seemingly predestined manner, articulated to teams and to the game. While Galeano provides delightful and poetic descriptions of players, positions, and individual goals, he ultimately sees soccer as the most important venue for human discussion today. For Galeano, "these days, soccer fanaticism has come to occupy the place formerly reserved for religious fervor, patriotic ardor and political passion."[49] For his part, Hornby, after exploring the absolute fanaticism soccer fandom inspired in him, concludes by discussing his love for, and the importance of, the "communal ecstasy" (interesting how often that term arises in these discussions) of soccer: "So, please, be tolerant of those who describe a sporting moment as their best ever. We do not lack imagination, nor have we had sad and barren lives; it is just that real life is paler, duller and contains less potential for unexpected delirium."[50]

While the work I carry out in the pages that follow relies on the work of numerous scholars—some focusing directly on soccer, some on sport, some on culture in general—it is the work and worldview that I see as having origins in works like Galeano's and Hornby's that I want to highlight here, because it is the sense of the importance of soccer for identity and for the imaginary that I need in order to underline the fundamental reason the cases I point to matter, culturally and politically. While Galeano, as I have shown, thinks soccer fanaticism has come to occupy the place formerly reserved for religious fervor,[51] Simon Critchley perhaps takes it a step further and argues, "Football is about so many things, so many complex, contradictory and conflicting things: memory, history, place, social class, gender in all its troubled variations . . . family identity, tribal identity, national identity."[52] In his attempt to develop a "poetics of soccer," what Critchley ultimately does, with the founding principle being the way we create an understanding of ourselves within a diaspora without origin, is to come to understand soccer as a fundamental form of identity. Hence, for Critchley, soccer fandom creates something of a "sacred canopy," to use Peter Berger's phrase,[53] an identity that protects us from the existential crisis provoked by death or meaninglessness. "The experience of football," Critchley notes, "can save us from death, giving us a sense of continuity with the past and the possibility of posthumous survival through the words and lives of future fans."[54] Michael Serazio confirms that sport fandom in general is driven by a hope to find those shared sensations that have been lost to the fragmentation of culture. He observes, "So, perhaps it is that—the most basic of human dreads, mortality—which drives us into the arms of the sports community."[55] Overstated? Not at all in my experience. The "sensate ecstasy" of soccer fandom alters everything.

One of my absolute favorite works about soccer is Laurent Dubois's *The Language of the Game: How to Understand Soccer*.[56] Dubois begins with the somewhat audacious claim that "the ball is unnecessary, in the end, because soccer, more than anything, is an idea."[57] Dubois's point, as it unfolds, is that while we may get addicted to soccer for some of the same reasons offered by Hornby (i.e., "the thrill of seeing someone do something that can only be done three or four times in a whole game if you are lucky," the small margins for error, the human elements, the way the best team doesn't always win[58]), once that identification takes place, it notches up the import of every single aspect of the game, even those that take place outside the game itself. Ultimately, as with Hornby, the reason the ball is unnecessary is that once we identify with a team, we are there forever, longer than anyone who could possibly play for the team. As a result, Dubois points to a "sensual intensity"[59] to fandom, something akin to Bill Buford's discussion of "an experience of absolute completeness."[60] Again, then, while Dubois's book ultimately moves in and out of discussions of a variety of issues, including gender, race, and politics, he does so by underlining this poetics of identity that soccer encourages.

In addition we have been gifted with a number of wonderful works regarding the role of soccer on the global stage, from Franklin Foer's *How Soccer Explains the World* to David Goldblatt's *The Age of Football* to Simon Kuper and Stefan Szymanski's *Soccernomics,* as well as many more.[61] They are absolutely essential to my understanding of the importance and role of soccer in culture. While my perspective, as a cultural and discourse critic, is very different than each of these others, I rely heavily on, and am indebted to, their empirical and philosophical work that ultimately guides me here. But it is imperative that the idea of this identity-transforming power of soccer fandom underlines the import of the discourses I analyze in the chapters that follow. As Dubois notes, "In the end, it is that search for beauty, for transcendence, for communication with others in moments of joy, that keeps people returning to this game."[62] And, in the midst of this search for transcendence, fans encounter and transform the discourses I investigate here (even if only marginally so), and, in so doing, maintain a challenge or change in the meanings and social situations for themselves and for others, while also resisting that change in the interest of community.

1

When Career Opportunities Finally Knock

Addiction, Displacement, and Hooligan Memories

> I am addicted to it and have sought professional help to try to get to the bottom of my problem. Because that is what it is—a mental problem that needs addressing. Had I been a flasher, an alcoholic or a drug addict, the courts would have got me counseling or medical treatment. As a football hooligan, they just want to lock you up. . . . By seeking help from a psychiatrist, I hope that I will be able to pack it in.
>
> —Andy Nicholls, Scally: Confessions of a Category C Football Hooligan

Of the many experiences of being a soccer fan in the United States, one of the slightly annoying ones is when someone who knows very little about the sport will jokingly refer to you as a "hooligan." This person knows a few names—David Beckham, Lionel Messi, Manchester United—and also knows vaguely that at some point in the past soccer hooligans in England wreaked havoc at games by fighting, burning, and looting. They will at times mention that they once read Bill Buford's *Among the Thugs*[1] or have seen the film *Green Street Hooligans*. Regardless of how they have arrived at their idea of hooligans, they vaguely know of them as racist men involved in physical violence at soccer games. As Franklin Foer observes, the fact that this particular type of soccer fan does in fact come to mind so easily is evidence that in memory "the English hooligan . . . has become a glamorized, commodified criminal."[2] It is indeed telling that the spectacle of the hooligan continues to stand in—sometimes completely—for soccer for many nonfans, especially given its relative demise in the English game, and the way it has arisen and taken form differently in leagues all around the globe. More, it is interesting to see how the story of the hooligan has played out in England, once the hotbed of hooliganism, since the demise of the phenomenon itself. While the "hooligan" has remained a viable narrative in US culture, the story of the hooligan as adult (the post-hooligan) is, I will show, the story of the rise of neoliberalism.

While I explore the memories of English hooligans exclusively below, I want to be clear that I recognize it as a very particular type of "extreme" fandom and one that had its height in a particular period of time. The fact that it remains a conversational meme for those in the US not interested in soccer only affirms both how invisible soccer is for some and how relatively visible this one representation was. In his recent pictorial celebration of the genre around the globe, Patrick Potter makes it clear that while there is overlap between hooligans and "ultras" (another type of extreme fan), he draws a fine line between the two, as ultras are more involved in the celebration of the game itself and are more often involved in real politic.[3] More recently, James Montague provides a comprehensive look at the phenomenon of extreme football fandom around the world: "the ultras, the hooligans, the *barras bravas*, the *torcidas*, the maniacs, how the most passionate and extreme supporters have become known in their home countries."[4] As both authors make clear, unlike English hooliganism, a great number of the more recent ultra movements—including those in Serbia, Cairo, and Ukraine—have been actively (and physically) involved in politics on both the Right and the Left, for instance, serving as shock troops for Slobodan Milošević and providing the basis for some Arab Spring protests.[5]

Ultra groups cover a wide range of political positions, then, from far left to extreme right to having no political intent whatsoever. Their practices vary from the production of *tifos* and cheers led by capos to smoke bombs and face paint. The common denominator is the collective identity that binds those fans. Indeed, as Potter notes, "the joy of expressing your identity collectively is enough of a reward in itself. . . . Obviously, fans are happier when their team wins, but there is also an emotional zeitgeist that develops among spectators that can even overrise the outcome of a game."[6] Nonetheless, it is the memory of English hooligans that shapes much of the US notion of ultra fans.[7]

While entire "schools" attempt to explain or understand the phenomenon of hooliganism, and while others have looked at hooligan biography (or "hooli-lit," as the genre came to be known) as a potential way of archiving the period (and I will touch on these below), I want to take hooligan memoir seriously as just that—a re-membering of the hooligan phenomenon, a rhetoric of values. That is, memoir is always fiction, as Keith Richards and numerous public memory scholars tells us,[8] so regardless of how "honest" memoir is, it always provides details, creates details, leaves out details, and identifies its world in accordance to what is valued and what is not in the present. Any story could be told differently. As a result, rather than looking toward the memoirs of hooligans as a way of understanding "what happened," I want to look at memoir as a way of seeing the values of the present being written into stories about the past. These stories, even when focusing on potentially transgressive values and movements, get clawed back or translated into the values and language of the present, hence, ultimately working to reinscribe existing values.[9] While the politics of hooliganism were dubious at best (and quite clearly accented with shades of nationalism and racism), the way the story is retold is relevant to any "movements" from the past and the ways they are tamed by, and consequently reinforce, the values of the present, values and logics shaped in part by neoliberal modes of thinking.

Hooligan Memoirs in Context

While hooliganism in the form of crowd fights and pitch invasions might be said to have been loosely in existence as long as the game itself, the period of mass-mediated fascination with the so-called English disease ran from the late 1950s through the 1990s.[10] Again, while a number of forms of ultra groups and behavior exist worldwide, it often is remarked now that outside of a small number of clubs (e.g., Millwall), changes in stadium attendance (e.g., seating required, no standing terraces), alcohol policies (consumption allowed only in bar areas away from the game itself), large increases in ticket prices (changing the composition of the audience), and the use of cameras to record fan behavior, led to the overall demise of hooligan behavior in the United Kingdom. Moreover, and as I illustrate below, the Heysel Stadium disaster—in which Liverpool and Juventus fans rushed each other during a 1985 European Cup Final, leading to thirty-nine people dying and six hundred injured during the confrontation—is often cited as the beginning of the real end of hooligan behavior, as the government, the police, and the hooligan groups themselves were forced to begin to take the behavior more seriously. Tim Crabbe and Adam Brown provide an excellent analysis of the ways both material changes in the stadia and in pricing and marketing systems worked well by the turn of the century to "socially exclude" working-class people and aesthetics from the game.[11]

Throughout the period of its height, however, there was a great deal of both journalistic and academic study of the phenomenon. From the academic perspective, the primary focus was on explaining why hooliganism was occurring. For example, the so-called Leicester School of thought published a great deal of material that attempted to explain the history and root causes of hooliganism; this work has been contested and reworked by others.[12] Because I am not interested in explaining the sociological or psychological reasons behind hooligan behavior, I am not going to take up that work here (as important as it might be for other purposes). Again, I am interested in how hooligans understand or explain their own pasts, including their explanations for the phenomenon, regardless of how "right or wrong" they are. That said, and as Shaun Best illustrates in a review of the sociological and psychological work surrounding the Leicester school and others associated with that era of work, the root causes of hooliganism were often reduced to the failure of education programs and high rates of unemployment.[13]

For those of us interested in public logics and struggles over cultural values, we were blessed when something of a cottage industry of hooligan memoirs and hooligan representations appeared in books, film, articles and other media at around the turn of the millennium. Emerging during a period when the "hooligan" looked to be largely a category of the past (and while the neoliberal policies of the Clinton and Blair eras had been in place long enough to take further hold of popular discourse), it was seemingly natural that those who were now "former hooligans" by choice or by force (i.e., they had been imprisoned or given stadium bans for hooligan crimes) would now romanticize their past for those willing to pay the price of a paperback. Hence, accounts of hooliganism were written seemingly by the "top lads" of almost every firm across the country. The books I mostly focus on here were published by a wide variety of presses of different caliber (including a few that were either vanity presses or close to it).

Academics being academics, a small number of essays have already taken a look at these books from different disciplinary angles. Joe Dart, whose interests lie in sport and leisure studies, criticizes almost the entire lot of books for not providing accurate historical representations of events.[14] Dart approaches the texts in order to assess how well they help him confirm the theses of the Leicester school in terms of the causes of hooliganism, but he ultimately finds that "one of the disappointments when reading most of these accounts was their unashamedly biased approach."[15] Dart argues that the books have little value beyond memorializing the past for the authors themselves, because each account is "extremely dubious with extensive levels of self-absorption."[16]

In another review essay, Steve Redhead argues that while the memories may in fact have some minor use as a way filling in some historic holes, in general the books offer little of academic value. That said, according to Redhead, the fact that scholars have not been able to grapple with the memoirs points out an overall failure to theorize soccer culture and its modernities.[17] Redhead's interest in these books emerged after coverage of Euro 2000 and Euro 2004 zeroed in on "soccer thugs" appearing at the games, claiming that this marked the return of hooliganism. Hoping to find discussions that would help make sense of this "return," Redhead comes back empty-handed. While coming to no conclusions beyond the need for more theorizing, he does make the interesting observation about the pride with which hooligans remember their past, and he points to this pride as a potential area of inquiry.[18]

The final "essay review" I turn to, and the one that begins to hint at my interest here, is Anthony King's "Violent Pasts."[19] While writing it prior to Redhead's review, King is himself most interested in the pride one finds in "hooli-lit" concerning the fact that informal and unwritten rules are followed by hooligans, underlining a shared sense of values.[20] Observing that most of the literature about hooligans has focused on the causes of football violence (again, this focus concerns the Leicester school), King is more interested in understanding collective memory as a way hooligans affirm internal group solidarity. In effect, King investigates the ways shared memory works to provide an "ego function" within hooligan groups.[21] While King does not go far beyond group affirmation, he does make an interesting claim about the importance of these affirmations as public memory: "It is through this re-creation of past memories within the horizon of the present that the future is formed. . . . The future of hooligan gangs and the form which their violence will take is substantially determined by the common values upon which they agree and which they establish through their public affirmation for shared memory in their interaction with each other."[22]

While King too seamlessly connects hooligan memoirs with hooligans in the present (globalism indeed creates a very mixed bag of behaviors and adaptations), it is the case that hooli-lit as a whole reaches a number of shared themes and shared values. Moreover, the memoirs often engage in a collective conversation, referring to one another, rehearsing similar stories of similar games from different perspectives. And while winners and losers of particular battles may differ in these accounts, the sense of a shared memory of values, of cause, of relationships, becomes clear.

Rather than read these books for shared internal group affirmation, as does King, I am more interested in the way these memoirs are read into the language of the present and of the non-hooligan reader, thereby reflecting the values and modes of thinking of mainstream culture. Hence, how do carriers of the "English disease," of behaviors that were rejected by mainstream politics, justify and discuss their own past actions in the present? What are their collective values? How to understand themselves? Their entry points? How do they understand those who set out to judge them? What is the story of hooliganism, and in what ways does it continue to affect or shape our present? What does it say about the strength of dominant values in a culture? In short, I am less interested in "internal group affirmation" than in the ways the memoirs work with cultural affirmation at large.

Given the large number of volumes and memoirs that exist, I chose to read ones that appeared routinely in the reviews above. While I made some exceptions in order to not have multiple volumes from single firms (e.g., rather than five from the Chelsea Headhunters and two from the Inter City Firm of West Ham, I kept the numbers equally the same). And while I did include some classic fiction (e.g., *The Football Factory*)[23] and Bill Buford's classic bit of gonzo journalism,[24] I will carefully point out those as somewhat different than the others when I discuss them. My interest is not in being comprehensive but in getting a large enough sample of the mosaic to provide the overall picture. Ultimately, hooli-lit not only acts as a shared memory and justification of values that sets the horizon for the present and future but also tells us something about the way memory reinscribes itself over dominant values. To look ahead, I will suggest that while hooliganism to a large degree gets tied down as an addiction, as Andy Nicholls notes in the epigraph with which I start this chapter, the journey each man takes through this addiction becomes a neoliberal path in which each must find their own resources to craft more traditional forms of social and economic success. More, it is a journey that ultimately dilutes the nationalism and racism of the past, providing a somewhat level playing ground for everyone (i.e., racism and nationalism are erased as constraints on success). In each section below, I trace out different dimensions of the collective memory of the hooligan past.

Apologia Rather than Apology

By definition, hooligan behavior was always in opposition to dominant values. That said, these books are all written by *former* hooligans; given stadium bans, jail sentences, and changed lifestyles, few of the authors are allowed to even attend games, much less engage in hooliganism. It is an interesting rhetorical position from which to write. The authenticity of the author demands evidence of their "hard" past and proud present, while the values of readers—those who will purchase the books—demand or encourage some sense of dominant values. Moreover, each author positions himself as a person who has made a transition to productive citizenship. As a result, almost every memoir positions itself not as an apology for past behaviors but rather as an apologia or explanation. In this way, the authors are able to stand on the ethos of hooliganism while leaving space for a reaffirmation of cultural values as their lives unfold.

Examples of this form of apologia are both overt and plentiful. For example, Mickey Francis, a former top lad in the Guvnors, a Manchester City firm, states early and explicitly, "Well, I'm not sorry. I make no apologies because I don't regret what I did. . . . The people you will read about on these pages, the ones I attacked and what attacked me, were as up for it as I was. They loved it."[25] Tony O'Neill, labeled as the Red Army [Manchester United] General, similarly begins: "I have been asked how I justify the things that we did. Well, why should I? . . . Football brought an excitement into our lives that we couldn't get anywhere else."[26] In *Hoolifan,* former Chelsea Headhunter Martin King announces that his book is not meant to "justify or condemn, just tells the truth."[27] The wording is profoundly similar throughout hooligan discourse—the testimonials are not apologies; these men are proud of their lives. When first encountering this discourse, the reader finds the voice of a countercultural movement that ran against dominant civil society. This is made even more profoundly so because the "authenticity" of the voices is consistently forefronted with a statement both of their past violence and of the time they have spent imprisoned as a result.

Just who are these men who refuse to apologize? By what actions, what discourse do they establish the authority to speak to us? In almost every instance, the author establishes both visually and discursively his interactions with the criminal justice system. For example, in his author bio, Mickey Francis is described thus: "Mickey Francis, thirty-seven, was born and raised in Moss Side, Manchester. A football hooligan since his youth, he has numerous convictions for violence-related offences, has served two prison terms and is currently banned from every soccer ground in Britain."[28] The entirety of his biography consists of establishing the "rough" neighborhood from which he emerges, his convictions and prison terms of his hooligan behavior, and the fact that he is no longer allowed to even attend games. Moreover, the prologue of the book begins with a scene of him in court, being called "the hooligan in chief" by a judge and sentenced to jail.[29]

Regardless of the order in which you read hooligan literature, you would not be blamed for finding yourself thinking that the first one set a pattern for the rest. The need to establish a criminal record is so powerful as to be a defining generic constraint. In the introduction to his book, for example, Tony O'Neill tells the reader that he began writing his book while an inmate in Sudbury Open Prison.[30] Similarly, Cass Pennant, one of the leaders of West Ham's Inter City Firm, begins his autobiography describing his life of violence and the consequences: "I've been involved in more violence than most people will experience in a hundred lifetimes. I've been shot, I've been stabbed and I've dished it out. . . . I probably brought brutality and bloodshed to the streets of your town. I paid a heavy price when an Old Bailey judge made an example of me in an attempt to rid football of the cancer that was destroying the game."[31] Jason Marriner, one of the Chelsea Headhunters who was prosecuted as a result of a BBC undercover documentary, is described in the sleeve author note as a lifelong fan of Chelsea who was thrust into the spotlight as a result of his "high profile court case and prison sentence."[32]

Visually, Martin King's book cover is graced with the image of a hooligan (presumably King himself) being led off the grounds by police.[33] A very similar image graces the Mickey Francis book.[34] The cover of the edited interview volume, *Terrace Legends,* consists of a blurred image of what appears to be a fight between hooligans while a police officer steps in.[35] The back cover of Andy Nicholls's memoir is a picture of a letter addressed to Nicholls from the Merseyside police. In part it reads, "I write in reply to your enquiry regarding travel to the FIFA World Cup 2002 being held in Japan & Korea. *The National Criminal Intelligence Service (Football Section) informs me, that the Japanese Immigration Service would refuse you entry to their country should you decide to travel there during this event.* I believe this decision has been made in view of your previous history of involvement in football disorder."[36]

As a whole, then, these memoirs present men who, while past their hooligan years, are unapologetic, indeed are proud of their behavior, wearing the badges of their imprisonment. At first blush in the tellings, hooligans are positioned as counter to dominant values. Indeed, the fact that they do not apologize for their violence, even after having been punished for it, is an anchor of authenticity, prior to the road of redemption. This realignment of hooligan values takes place not in a step-by-step fashion but in an overall mosaic involving the "causes" of hooligan behavior, the displacement of negative values associated with hooliganism, and the perhaps not-before-seen prosocial and proeconomic skills developed through a life of hooliganism. As a result, the stereotypical understanding of the hooligan as a violent, racist, uneducated blight, part of the "English disease," becomes instead something quite different: a figure who, while forced or pushed into forms of violence, develops rules and skill sets that curtail the behavior into a set of games, from which, ultimately, the individual recrafts himself into a practitioner of neoliberal values. Not to be criticized, then, for violent antisocial behavior, the hooligan is to be praised for his ability to fight against seemingly predetermined behaviors and ultimately realign himself with English society.

The Seeds of Addiction

As with the Nicholls quotation that heads this chapter, hooliganism is reconfigured as a literal addiction, with the violence of hooligan fights providing the types of thrills one associates with drugs, sex, and alcohol. As Mickey Francis stands in front of the judge to be sentenced, the judge says to him that of Francis's actions, "the common denominator is the thrill of violence," to which Mickey thinks silently, "Now you're talking. It is a thrill. It's a fucking buzz like nothing."[37] Later, as he recounts how his firm[38] slipped and did not notice the undercover cops that had infiltrated them, he notes, "We were spinning out of control. The violence was too addictive. We were too into it to stop."[39] After his first couple of games hanging around with hooligans, Tony O'Neill similarly says, "I couldn't do without it: the roar of the crowds and the way they moved as one was an unbelievable buzz."[40] Later, O'Neill notes that he never was a drinker and never needed to be: "I didn't even smoke cigarettes, and it was the same with the other lads. The football got us high."[41] In his fictional account *The Football Factory*, John King would agree with O'Neill: "You shit yourself inside but the rush is so good you love it more than anything. . . . They say it's adrenalin and that may be true, but all I know is that nothing compares. Not drugs, sex, money, nothing."[42] Matt King observes that hooligan violence is "a great feeling, it must be a chemical thing,"[43] while Cass Pennant tells the reader that the violence "was a buzz that gripped you just like a drug."[44] In a collection of interviews with hooligans, Lee "Oathead" Owens observes, "Rucking at a football is a buzz. You can't get the same buzz from drugs as you do at football,"[45] and Pat "Fat Pat" Dolan notes that his desire for the "buzz" of football violence caused him to lose his girlfriend and daughter, but he couldn't get over it.[46] The addiction is that compelling.

While coming down solidly against hooliganism, given a more journalistic approach, Bill Buford understands the hooligan love of violence in very similar terms: "This, it would seem, was neither natural nor logical. It was, I see now on reflection, not unlike alcohol or tobacco; disgusting, at first; pleasurable, with effort; addictive, over time. And perhaps, in the end, a little self-destroying."[47] In describing a hooligan riot, Buford notes that one of the hooligans standing near him "said that he was happy. He said that he was very, very happy, that he could not remember ever being so happy."[48] Indeed, Buford slowly becomes somewhat addicted himself; he describes watching a match with hooligans: "It was involving so many aspects—what I saw, smelled, said, sang, moaned, what I was feeling up and down my body—that I was becoming a different person from the one who had entered the ground: I was ceasing to be me."[49] At a different match, surrounded by violence, Buford describes the way his perceptions were heightened and notes, "I realized later that that I was on a druggy high, in a state of adrenaline euphoria. . . . An experience of absolute completeness."[50] Ultimately, while he critiques hooligan behavior, he understands it as addiction: "Violence is their antisocial kick, their mind altering experience, an adrenaline-induced euphoria that might be all the more powerful because it is generated by the body itself with, I was convinced, many of the same addictive qualities that characterize synthetically produced drugs."[51]

James Bannon, who worked as an undercover police officer infiltrating the firms at Millwall, describes a similar addiction, as he finds himself charmed by the very behaviors he was supposed to help stop: "Yes, there were many times I was scared shitless, but the adrenalin and the buzz were amazing . . . that rush can be addictive."[52] Indeed, one of the major narrative themes of his memoir is the way his colleagues continue to warn him that he is enjoying being a hooligan "too much," and Bannon slowly realizes he is becoming addicted to the buzz in the same way the "real" hooligans do: "I was without a doubt enjoying myself. Maybe a little too much."[53] "I was getting off on the whole experience . . . I felt alive."[54]

Buzz. Drug. Chemical. Addiction. The theme, the metaphor, is ubiquitous. It occurs in every account, in every memoir, in fact and in fiction. While we would help an addict overcome their addiction, as Nicholls notes at the start of the chapter, social programs never helped these guys. Addiction, we might say, displaces their responsibility, and yet, one might argue, they chose to take this first step, just as one chooses the first drink, the first snort, and one should bear responsibility for that. And yet, for the football hooligan, it's not that simple; the first decision at football violence, they both imply and overtly state, was itself almost predetermined by external and internal causes. While ultimately they must be rugged and strong enough as individuals to free themselves of the plight, their first steps toward addiction, as with all addiction, are both genetic and social.

The Roots of Addiction

The authors' involvement with hooligan behavior and firms, then, is the result of addiction, a buzz, fueled by adrenaline, almost impossible to stop. And yet the desire for this addiction itself has roots, in almost the same fashion as does alcohol or drugs. In essence the authors map the logic of alcoholism onto the logic of football violence. In turn they see the desire for the buzz of violence to be genetic or "in the blood" and to be encouraged or fostered by such environmental factors as economic deprivation and violent environments. Given the absence of women in these discourses, each is also articulated onto a particular form of masculinity.

Early on in his work, Mickey Francis observes that the reader may well wish to know why he was violent. Francis recalls a conversation with his Jamaican father when he was young, when his father told him that violence "was bred into you. A lot of Jamaicans like to fight."[55] Chelsea Headhunter Jason Marriner expands this from Jamaicans to the English when he observes that there is no way to really end hooliganism, because there's "something in the British breed . . . it's a part of what makes you."[56] When Bill Buford asks one of the supporters why the hooligan scene was so violent, he is informed that it is not the "scene" that is violent, in that the violence would take place if there were no football, because "it's what's in us, init?" Asked to clarify, he notes that supporters have all got the violence "in us. It just needs a cause. It needs an acceptable way of coming out."[57]

The repetition of the genetic "in your blood," "in your genes" is nowhere more apparent than in the collection of interviews Cass Pennant and Martin King conducted with top lads[58] from firms all over England. In their introduction to the collection, Pennant and King note that hooliganism is unstoppable, because "it's in the blood—in the genes."[59] From there, one of the questions they ask every subject is "What would have made you stop life as a hooligan?" While there are a few exceptions, for the most part, the same genetic line is given. Hence, Andy "The Bear" Phillips notes that nothing would stop it, "nothing at all—it's in the blood."[60] David "Skeeny" Skeen reads from what seems a similar script: "Nothing. What's in your blood is in your blood."[61] The repetition of this occurs so often as to seem agreed upon by the community loosely. It's an addiction, it's in the blood, nearly impossible to avoid.

Like alcoholism or drug addiction, however, sometimes this addiction takes the combination of genes and environmental factors to manifest.

Hence, while Mickey Francis notes above that his father said the violence was bred into him ethnically, he observes that his father also beat him and his brothers, teaching them to be violent. Hence, what he remembers of growing up "was the violence. My dad was violent to his sons and we were violent to each other."[62] More, it is not simply the violence of the home but the violence of the larger world that encouraged the addiction to grow. Tony O'Neill observes, "Through the sixties we saw the race riots in American cities and the student riots in Paris in 1968. The Vietnam War fed us uncensored images of killing day in day, day out, something that had never happened before. How could people not be affected by this?"[63]

Another factor cited as inducing violent behavior is the poor economic environment of the late seventies and early eighties. Mickey Francis says that the mass unemployment meant that "a lot of bored young men [. . .] looked forward to the weekend as the only excitement in their lives."[64] Red Army General Tony O'Neill points out that football was the only entertainment and sense of relief for working-class and unemployed youth: "If you wanted to escape a life of council estate drudgery, that's how it was."[65] He clarifies later, "I never saw myself as a radical in any way. I just looked at my surroundings and thought, fuck this, there's no way I'm going to listen to this bullshit about work and saving up for retirement, what a joke that is."[66] Part of the significance of this attitude comes later in each of the memoirs, as these former hooligans become invested in economic and career success.

Several of the characters in John King's *Football Factory* observe the class dimensions of hooliganism by noting that the clubs are raising prices because they know hooligans come from the working class and that football violence gives the poor something that the wealthy cannot have.[67] In *Road End Hooligans,* Rob Randle observes that the fights always pitted the disadvantaged against the disadvantaged, because this was a form of escape for working-class lads.[68] Millwall's Frank Harper observes that the most extreme hooligans came from rough areas because "tough areas breed tough people."[69] Jason Marriner claims that coming from the rough side of town somewhat "forced" you into such behavior. On stand during his trial, Marriner announced, "Let me tell you something. I come from the rough side of the road, I'm council, I've lived on a travelers' site for years, so don't you worry about my swearing because that's just the way I am."[70]

In short, then, it is difficult to put much blame on the hooligans if you affirm the logic of the "argument." Football violence is addictive, and the tendency toward violence is a combination of genetics and impoverished and violent lived environments. No one in such a configuration, the logic implies, really stood much of a chance. That said, the addiction metaphor has far more ideological importance than simply shifting the blame off the hooligans. Rather, the addiction metaphor ultimately works to reify the neoliberal market and the idea of a sovereign free acting subject competing in the marketplace. In *Scripting Addiction*, E. Summerson Carr investigates the language of addiction and recovery and argues that addiction is always discussed in ways that "resonate with broader cultural narratives, and thereby appeal to powerful, institutional audiences."[71] More, addicts going through treatment learn the language to discuss their addiction and ultimately learn to rely on a language that emphasizes "lasting sobriety and self-sufficiency."[72] In effect, those recovering from addiction learning to speak in terms of "anticipatory interpellation," illustrating that in recovery they are responsible individuals who have overcome addiction and its root causes to participate in mainstream values (hence, the values of the neoliberal citizen).[73] Whether or not addicts believe the script, they know to use it because they are rewarded for it in multiple ways. Hence, as I show later in the chapter, the addiction metaphor is important because it explains antisocial behavior at one point and the lessons learned that allow triumph and success within the economic marketplace as a sign of recovery.[74]

Ownership of Values, Protection of the Innocent

While displacing the ownership of violence through a rhetoric of addiction and environment, none of the hooligans distance themselves from the violence itself. That said, the violence is seen as enacted within a value system that respects the larger social order. If the discourse of addiction temporarily displaces responsibility for actions, the discourse below embraces responsibility because the hooligans had a system of ethics and principles that guided behavior.

A primary and repeatedly stated ethic of hooliganism is to engage in battle only with other hooligans, the ones up for the fight. I cannot stress enough how often this issue is raised throughout the literature. Cass Pennant very simply puts it this way: "It wasn't pretty stuff but we only ever targeted those who wanted to hurt us."[75] Returning again to Mickey Francis, just after telling the reader that he will explain his actions but not apologize for them, he goes on with "I fought with those wanted to fight with me. I didn't beat up parents with their children. I didn't batter little old ladies. The people you will read about on these pages, the ones I attacked and who attacked me, were as up for it as I was. They loved it."[76] Later, Francis stresses, "If you see a bloke with two kids and a scarf on, you're not going to batter him. If you do, you're a cunt."[77] In different words, Tony O'Neill provides the same reason for his lack of apology for the violence: "My thing was smacking people in the face who wanted it. If they didn't want it, there was no problem."[78] And while "observer" Bill Buford[79] and undercover cop James Bannon both note times when violence against non-hooligans occurred (Bannon: "Like the time I witnessed a Millwall fan stamp on an innocent bystander's head while his wife and daughters looked on"),[80] the hooligan authors position such behavior as not only abnormal but far outside the ethical boundaries of the hooligan community. Even undercover police officer Bannon defends the large majority of the hooligans he was hanging around. Of his friend Paul, "Yes, he was a hooligan, and yes, he was the first up the front if it kicked off, but I had never seen him carry out any acts of gratuitous violence or applaud anyone who did."[81] Andy Nicholls firmly states that the use of fists or "weapons against innocent or 'normal' fans was and is inexcusable."[82] Again, Jason Marriner notes, "It's an unwritten rule. Believe me, no dad just taking his kid to watch the game has *ever* been in any danger."[83]

Terrace Legends, the book of interviews with former hooligans, stresses the point repeatedly. Millwall's Frank Harper: "If innocent people get caught up, then that's wrong";[84] Wolverhampton's Gilroy "Gilly" Shaw: "Rules of combat apply: only fight like-minded people";[85] Mr. B, a Barnsley supporter: "We only fight lads who want to fight us Muppets. Whoever gives an innocent person a crack gets one back."[86] One of the standard questions each one is asked is "Have you ever been sickened by something you've witnessed at a game?" Without exception, when they do have a response to this question, it refers to a time an innocent fan who was not part of hooligan culture was hurt. Again, while hooligans admit there were rare occasions when the rules were broken, they were never broken by the authors and were always criticized.

Chelsea Headhunter Martin King stresses the multiple "unwritten rules" of hooliganism and then provides a metaphor that professionalizes the behavior and justifies it within ethical boundaries. The analogy, for King, "is boxing. Two opponents willingly and knowingly fight each other. They badly want to win and keep their reputations intact, but they definitely don't want to kill one another. Boxers do it for money. We do it for the buzz. And the buzz is addictive. But it is nothing personal."[87] While King later in the book refers to a few scenes where "innocents" were hurt, he makes it clear that these were the exceptions and not accepted within the group, much like how it would not be accepted for a boxer to start punching people in the street.[88]

The notion of protecting the innocent finds a galvanizing point among the memoirs with the Heysel Stadium incident. In the briefest terms, about an hour before kickoff at the 1985 European Cup final held in Brussels, a group of Liverpool fans crossed a fence separating them from a neutral area containing mostly Juventus fans. As they fled the threat, the fans were crushed together in a section of terrace hemmed in by a concrete retaining wall, which eventually collapsed. Thirty-nine people died. The incident was carried on the news and, along with the Hillsborough disaster four years later, is an oft-cited chapter in the demise of hooliganism, as stadiums were altered to no longer allow standing and to have a much greater degree of security and surveillance.

In the hooligan memoirs, Heysel stands out as an example of "innocent" people getting hurt. Even to the degree that this was not "caused" by hooligans, it is still cited as a way the unwritten rules were broken. While neither is a fan of former Prime Minister Margaret Thatcher, both Mickey Francis[89] and Tony O'Neill[90] cite the Heysel disaster as forcing the hand of the government to take some decisive action against hooligans and to establish safer crowd control. Richard Grey, a Derby County hooligan, notes that the Heysel incident was the one moment in all of football that sickened him the most.[91] Similarly, Steve "Wing Nut" Lyons of Charlton Athletic references Heysel as the most sickening moment of his "career" and reaffirms, "I can honestly say I only ever fought other geezers that were like me and wanted it."[92] Martin King acknowledges that something had to be done after Heysel, but he blames incidents like it and Hillsborough not on the hooligans but on the way they were disregarded and demeaned by the owners of the teams. He notes that he's surprised there haven't been more incidents like Heysel, because "football fans were treated like animals and with no respect," pointing to restrooms overflowing with urine, filth in the hallways, etc.[93]

Along the theme of Heysel as a personal stopping point, Cass Pennant explains: "No one was meant to get killed. . . . Heysel was the moment I realized it was time to give up hooliganism forever. Football violence was a drug and hard habit to kick but as I watched those fans dying before my eyes I vowed to turn my back on terrace violence for good."[94] Andy Nicholls, too, cites the Heysel incident as close to the end for him, explaining: "The next day, the full horror of it all was plain to see as the TV and papers carried images of people taking their last breath. It was horrible and I felt sick. . . . It was not what my notion of football hooliganism was about."[95] As a whole, then, hooligans never fought, and indeed see themselves as protecting, the innocent, going so far as to stop once it was impossible to offer such protection.

The Racist as Other

Before I attend to the cultural meaning of "kicking the hooligan habit," I want to address the ways other negative traits associated with hooliganism are "explained away" and how these explanations work within the neoliberal mode. One common understanding of hooligans and ultras is that they are often either casually racist or involved in something like the National Front, linking them to Nazis and far right politics. If we look at the fictional account included here (John King's *Football Factory*)[96] or the journalistic account by Bill Buford (*Among the Thugs*), we are presented not only with a number of racist incidents and language but also with encounters with the National Front, who use the terraces to recruit members.[97] That said, the memoirs consistently either attempt to undermine the idea that hooligans were racist or displace racism to a small minority who either existed only in other clubs or were so different as to not be considered under the same banner as "hooligan."

In Tony O'Neill's account of racism in hooliganism, it was not something seen in Manchester United's Red Army: "Another thing about United was that we never went in for any of that National Front stuff. . . . We have always had black, half-caste and Asian fans."[98] While he pushes off racism elsewhere (namely, toward Manchester City), Manchester City's own narrative, as I show below, makes that a very small part of the City following. Moreover, while O'Neill recognizes that the National Front was attempting to recruit from "the terraces for their marches and propaganda,"[99] he claims that there were very few of them; non-hooligans always assumed there were a lot of them, he says, because they were given disproportionate television time. Hence, O'Neill pushes racism away from his own group and diminishes its size.

Given the reputation of the Chelsea Headhunters as racist, Martin King's description of the era is especially interesting. He begins by noting that, historically, there was very little racism in football fandom: "In the '60s and early '70s, black kids and white kids played together, danced together, drank together and went to football together. We liked the same music, clothes and clubs. There was no animosity whatsoever."[100] While it is easy to challenge this racial utopia he remembers, he follows up by noting that by the late seventies, "far-right-wing groups began to attract a following at football."[101] King then goes on to minimize its existence both by seeing it as temporary and by pointing out the number of Black hooligans at Chelsea: "All the mobs went through a right-wing stage in the last '70s and early '80s, but Chelsea was no worse than anyone else. It was said in court that Icky and his gang hated blacks. Tell that to [Chelsea Headhunter and fan] Black Willie. . . . Racism was evident at Chelsea for awhile but it was not the cement that bound us together. The whole right-wing thing was a fad that passed."[102]

Jason Marriner, attempting to explain his behavior when he was caught on tape yelling at a Black West Ham fan—"Fuck off, you black cunt, I've had enough of you's lot around me today"—diminishes it by claiming it is a description, not a racist remark. As he notes, "It didn't matter to me if they were black, white, pink, or fucking blue, but it just so happens that they were black. Listen, if I have a row with a fat geezer, I'll call him a 'fat cunt,' if he's bald then I'll call him a 'bald cunt' and if he's black, yeah, I'll call him a 'black cunt.'"[103] Marriner goes on to explain that he's never been racist, and, while a loyalist, he's "not a member of the National front, Combat 18 or any other Far Right Group."[104]

Another uneasy apologia comes from Everton's Andy Nicholls, given the extreme racist reputation of the club and the hooligan culture around it. On the one hand, he attempts to minimize race as a cause of any action. When a "promising black boxer" with a Manchester United firm was cut and needed two hundred stitches after a fight with Everton, he notes, "There was a lot of racist bollocks about the cutting but it was nothing to do with color."[105] Simultaneously, however, he notes the threat faced by Blacks who came to fight. Because the city of Liverpool was so dominantly white, "It was always the same story at Everton: when it [the fighting] went off, there was no hiding place for black people."[106] Nicholls acknowledges that Everton "had some serious bad press for being a racist club," but he also doesn't "think we were as bad as was made out."[107] Nicholls notes, "In the Seventies and Eighties, if you were anything other than white you could be in for a rough ride when you came to Goodison. It didn't matter if you were player or fan, you got shit, and plenty of it."[108] However, despite this and despite his admission that the crowd used to chant phrases like "Everton are white" and "Liverpool is N——pool" when Liverpool began fielding Black players, he still denies that the fans were racist. Instead, many of the fans "started to act it, even though most really didn't' give a toss. . . . I don't think most of them really cared about race one way or another; it was just one of those things English football fans do to torment their opponents."[109] Nicholls finishes his discussion by noting that Everton actually never "had a big National Front following like some of the London clubs" and then, unironically, notes, "To the club's credit, we now have a couple of coloured lads who work for the Everton in the community."[110]

Two of the more interesting accounts, because they are authored by Black hooligans and top lads are Mickey Francis's *Guvnors* and Cass Pennant's *Cass*. Francis, who grew up in Moss Side, where there were a number of Black fans, begins by recalling the racism of the teachers and neighbors where he grew up. He makes note of how some of his teachers used to refer to him openly as "coffee-coloured boy."[111] Francis relays that the two firms he was involved in—the Cool Cats and, later, the Guvnors—began primarily as Black firms. While he notes that City did have a firm constituted by National Front members, the two firms had definite respect for each other.[112] Francis goes on to say that the firms to which he belonged became integrated with whites and Blacks and that Leeds fans—who were "notoriously racist"[113]—could never understand how that worked. He also notes that Liverpool was a bad place to go as a Black person: "You stood out a mile. There has always been a racist element there."[114]

In a similar manner, Pennant notes the racism of society (rather than hooligans) as he was growing up: "As I grew older we'd walk down the street, me clinging to Mrs. Chambers' hand, and kids would shout out, 'Blackie!,' 'N———,' 'Golliwog!'"[115] He also notes later, when he was imprisoned, that the prison environment, rather than football, was the most racist place he had ever experienced.[116] Pennant, who interestingly changed his birth name from Carol to Cassius in honor of Cassius Clay (Muhammad Ali), noted, "To my friends there's no colour—I'm just Cass. And when people—black or white—cross my friends, I'll show them no mercy."[117] One of his most interesting stories, because it puts into question the "true" racism of the National Front, was when one of his Black colleagues began to march with the National Front sector of the West Ham hooligan group. First, Pennant notes, "To the media, West Ham were the most racist bunch of supporters on earth. The reality is that the National Front lot were a tiny minority and they never had much influence."[118] Secondly, and importantly, when his Black friend began marching with the National Front, the leader of the group said he couldn't keep marching with them, because "nothing personal against him. It isn't me; it's the others."[119] Hence, even the National Front leader isn't racist, not overtly so. In these ways, Pennant, like Francis, flips the charge of racism to society at large, minimizing racism in hooliganism all together, and displacing it to other teams or to media fictions.

Across the board, then, racism and the presence of the National Front are minimized in each recounting. Not only were there fewer racists in each crowd than reported, but most racism was at other clubs. Moreover, even the racism that did exist was not meant as racism. It was either simply a tactic used to rile up the opponent or simply a description without derision. Hence, in line with a neoliberal logic, racism is not an active constraint toward individual success. In addition, the attempt to deny racism ever existed in hooligan culture only reaffirms the neoliberal logic.

Old Bill as Villain

In addition to representing themselves as protective of the innocent, there is a common motif of presenting the police (or "Old Bill") as villains, creating violent conditions rather than bringing it to a halt. On a trip to Liverpool with the Guvnors from Manchester City, Mickey Francis tells the story of a police officer approaching him and saying, "Hey you, fucking n———, don't hide yer fucking face here, we know who you are. Pull your fucking mask down, you," then leaving Francis to be beaten up by Liverpool fans.[120] In a parallel gesture, when Manchester United played Cardiff City away, Tony O'Neill joined the Red Army to fight with Cardiff fans. Because several police officers were standing nearby, O'Neill assumed the fighting would wait. When, instead, a Cardiff fan headbutted him right in front of the police, "the coppers grabbed me, not him, whacked me over the head and said, 'Go on, you English cunt, fuck off!'"[121] In John King's fictional account, he tells stories of police covering their badge numbers while beating up hooligans and claims that the police in Liverpool beat up any fans except for Liverpool ones.[122] Martin King makes a similar claim about all police in the northern portions of the country.[123] He also observes that police allowed violence to continue because they liked the extra pay for working security.[124] Finally, one of the questions put to the hooligans being interviewed in *Terrace Legends* is "Who are the fairest coppers you've ever come across in a match?" and the most common response indicates that there is no such thing as a fair cop.[125]

One of the great ironies of James Bannon's account of being an undercover cop acting as a Millwall hooligan is how often he reports that the police were out of line. He recounts the story of a game at Leicester away when, while simply marching and singing, he was grabbed by a police officer, "pushed against the wall and told to shut the fuck up. I tried to carry on singing but was then pushed to the ground and had my arm put up my back. I was hoisted to my feet and told that if I stepped out of line again, or opened my fucking mouth, it would be shut for me."[126] Later, after a hooligan skirmish at Coventry in which the police officers began beating fans, Bannon argues with his partner Chris that the report that they write for the police department that week needed to say, "The biggest hooligans at that match on Saturday were the fucking Old Bill. They waded into the crowd with their truncheons drawn for no fucking reason half the time."[127]

Hence, it is not simply that the hooligans themselves have unwritten rules and ethics that protect the innocent, but it is also the case that the police invert the values. Interested in extra pay, partisan toward the own favorite teams, and, in the case of Mickey Francis, racist, the police are unfair. They are the "real hooligans" who beat people with either no reason or unjust reasons. Hooligans walk on the right side of ethics; hooligans are fair. While "the prison" may capture bodies that fall outside of neoliberal freedom, as Stephen Dillon notes,[128] in this case, the hooligans were, in effect, neoliberal all along.

The Clobber: Hooligan as Style Guru

As police began to try to crack down on hooligan gatherings and the outbreaks of fights and riots, hooligans learned to stop wearing jerseys and waving scarves, and instead to dress "casually" in order to avoid surveillance. Hence, the casual movement, often attributed to fans in Liverpool (both Liverpool and Everton fans), spread across the country during this era. Now, what makes the movement interesting is that while casual clothing of course could have been almost any type of clothing, the style began to be based on middle-class and higher-end style and fashion (at different times LaCoste, Stone Island, Burberry, Harrington, Crombie). As a result, and despite the fact that the style is humorously attributed to Liverpool fans following their team to Europe and stealing stylish clothing,[129] higher-end fashion became an aspirational way to dress. In short, in attempting to be casual, the hooligan illustrates class aspiration.

This is such an important element of the way hooligans think about themselves that in *Terrace Legends*, a collection of interviews, two of the questions are "What's your favourite terrace fashion?" and "What's the worst fashion you've ever seen on the terrace?" While the answers range from an older generation still preferring the early skinhead outfits to younger types reeling off the names of designers, Steve "Wing Nut" Lyons provides his answer and adds, "Everyone wore their best clobber. If you didn't, you were looked upon as a mug."[130]

While the hooligans recognize the irony of such fashion, they take great pleasure in pointing it out. Tony O'Neill discusses the entire transition and observes, "It must have been a strange sight at the time. All these lads with smart haircuts and nice clothes, every one of them game as fuck."[131] In defending himself against charges made in a television documentary, Chelsea Headhunter Jason Marriner asserts, "It's true that I like my clothes and I spend a few quid on Prada and Armani, but so what? Surely a lot of people do, or am I the only one who likes nice clothes?"[132] Millwall's Frank Harper notes that he prefers Burberry above all else and observes that it's important to dress well because "football's such a big fashion statement."[133]

While the date is not always the same, hooligans remember different periods during the 1980s when style reached its peak. "Hoolifan" Martin King notes, "The early 1980s were arguably the years when soccer-related violence, or fear of it, reached its peak," and that it nevertheless was also the same time that "the boys were now dressing like tennis stars, sporting designer labels such as Ellesse, Tacchini, Fila and Lacoste. Terrace disturbances resembled clashes between armies of John McEnroe clones and hordes of Bjorn Borg lookalikes."[134] Referring to West Ham's InterCity Firm of 1981, Cass Pennant claims, "The ICF was at its peak—we were the toughest, meanest firm of football hooligans Britain had ever seen. We were also the best dressed,"[135] while Liverpool hooligan Rob Randles describes 1985 as the year when "the fashion, violence, and sheer ferocity was it its peak."[136] Reading these memoirs and these dates, one is prone to think of the hooligans in far different terms than before. Again, rather than for rogue lower-class villains, this becomes a game for those with aspiration for higher-class conditions.

Hooliganism as Training for Middle-Class Work

In terms of a capitulation to the norms of a business-driven society in which one must take responsibility for his or her own actions and behavior on the path to success within the open market, a major underlying theme of these memoirs is not only that these former hooligans are now often successful in business but that the work they performed as hooligans was in essence training for a middle- or upper-class lifestyle.[137] Again returning to the language of addiction, evidence that they have become "former" hooligans and have overcome their addiction comes in the form of how they used lessons from their past to become productive, ruggedly individualistic, neoliberal subjects.[138] Donald Francis, older brother of Mickey, and the former head of the Cool Cats, one of the original Manchester City firms, has a brief section in *Guvnors* in which he notes that while a Cool Cat, he was the one in charge of chartering buses to take everyone to away games. He was so successful at doing this that he founded a company that chartered buses for away supporters after he had been released from prison. Donald notes, "I was a lot happier making money than sitting in jail.... I'm squeaky-clean now. I would never go to a football match again. They would have to pay me."[139] While Mickey had worked at a scaffolding company prior to going to prison, upon his release he put the skills he learned as a hooligan to work, becoming a bouncer, then owning a security firm, and eventually purchasing his own scaffolding company. Ultimately, while he does not apologize for his hooligan life, his financial success makes himself "regret a little" the wasted years and the "failure to make something more of [himself]."[140] Andy Nicholls notes that, at this point in life, most of his friends are now making a lot of money, and that some former hooligans have now become teachers. Of himself, he notes that he had a "job paying [him] hundreds of pounds a week, living in luxury" and hopes to be finished with fighting and clubs.[141] The former hoolies interviewed in *Terrace Legends* all note the many types of successful businesses they own, including bars, financial services, and security firms.[142]

In perhaps less specific terms, but also stressing the types of skills required in the hooligan lifestyle, O'Neill notes that he feels as if he earned a master's degree in crowd control because he had to learn so much about how to organize people.[143] Of the several myths about hooligans, Martin King tells us, one is that hooligans are violent, mindless young men. This is not at all the case, King tells us, as the amount of planning and organization it took to pull off hooliganism required very bright people with managerial skills.[144] Not only does Cass Pennant express almost the same sentiment—"Critics and rent-a-quote pundits always branded us as mindless morons, but most of us had decent jobs. Organizing several hundred fans travelling on one train took special skills"[145]—but he also concludes his book with examples of how successful former hooligans are. He claims that "the leaders of the InterCity Firm had the brains and the determination to go to the top in whatever fields they chose" and provides examples of a radio station owner, a record label owner with a number one record, magazine photographers, and educators. They, he notes, "earned their money through enterprise and hard graft."[146]

Clearly, in the words of these former hooligans, the work they were doing in organizing and fighting was a type of alternative preparation for middle-class life. Many of them, now married, now with children, have found successful careers in middle-class society. As both Wendy Brown[147] and Melinda Cooper[148] have separately argued, neoliberalism helps produce a discourse in which the family, rather than the state, must be the economic umbrella that protects the individual and that imprisonment must work to help return individuals productively to the family unit. This is an overall narrative we see traced out in these memoirs. To underline, they do not see this as a conversion of their life; while hooliganism was an addiction that needed to be overcome, it also provided education and skills that prepared the former hooligan to succeed in the open market. It is not that they see themselves as redeemed from a life of hooliganism so much as that they took a different route to the same telos point—a successful middle-class life—shared by everyone else. Wendy Brown observes of neoliberalism that it not only privatizes the market for individual production and consumption but also "formulates everything, everywhere in terms of capital investment and appreciation, including and especially humans themselves."[149] Here the life of the hooligan is no longer seen as wasted years but as a form of investment and appreciation.

Hooligan Memoirs as Alt-Fairytale

In many ways, then, the story found here should not be surprising. Youth have always had more time for resistance and rebelliousness, as well as all types of recreational activities that lend themselves to group behavior and emotional release (think music). And it is certainly not unusual to see the stories of "successful" individuals include a youthful diversion. That said, given that I deal here with books not by simple members of hooligan groups but by supposedly "top lads," the expectations might not have been quite so clear. Nonetheless, given prison terms, stadium bans, and the pressures of family and friends, many of the men who wrote these books have indeed been "clawed back" into more traditional economic and familial pursuits. Ideology and economics are powerful pulls. Any cultural critic knows to expect that. "Discipline" is the general rule. So, one lesson we can learn—or rather, an old lesson we've learned multiple times but can underline again here—concerns the ways material and ideological change (both to the right and to the left) is difficult. The center always draws back in, even while struggles over meaning and behavior are ongoing. If hooliganism in part operated in a carnivalesque sense, allowing working-class youth a release from the pressures of labor, as John Clark contended at the time,[150] the "end" of hooliganism led to the individual redemption of former hooligans who then successfully perform within neoliberal constraints.

The particular discourse is interesting in these cases precisely because it simultaneously takes a stance that there will be no apology for past behaviors while the discourse reshapes those behaviors in ways that make them fit within dominant values. That is, of course, no apology is needed,[151] given that the hooligans (a) followed informal rules, (b) were not "really" racist, or only minimally so, (c) were addicted to the behavior but not even of their own volition, (d) behaved better than official protection (i.e., the police), and (e) ultimately, through individual work and determination, overcame their addictions and embraced the values of consumerism and employment within capital enterprise. If any group is a sign of neoliberal success, perhaps it is the hooligans.

While I, of course, am thrilled to see the racist discourses blunted through this discipline, in the larger picture this is another sign of the way politics by other means are often trampled down and fit into far more mainstream understandings. When the history of hooligan behavior is narrativized as it is in these memoirs, the ideology of contemporary neoliberal thought is not only underlined in the present but also situated as the driving force of the past.

This is not to say that these memoirs determine the future of all supporter groups. James Montague[152] and David Goldblatt[153] have each recently documented the exciting ways politics are enacted by ultra groups around the world. While each also understands the ways some ultra groups were ultimately "shut down" due to their political activity (e.g., in Turkey), they also note the remarkable way supporter groups have become political (discursively and, at times, physically) toward both the Right and the Left.

While US supporter groups seem to look far more to Italy for their cues on how to support (e.g., capos, *tifos*, organized chanting) than to the United Kingdom, the lessons learned here should be ones that make us look more closely at the rhetoric of the groups, at their official and unofficial links to the clubs, and at the multiple ways in which membership is involved in discussions. Indeed, the news in 2019 that MLS officials had worked with collective supporter groups to lift a ban on anti-Nazi symbols was an interesting moment of how supporter groups will function here.[154] As with the Premier League, balancing the desire for supporters who can spend money with supporter groups who provide atmosphere but often are driven by youth with less income but stronger politics, puts everyone in an interesting position. As we move forward, perhaps the lessons from hooligan memories here can help shape the creation of new discourses and new memories, setting different discursive conditions for the future.

2

Heroism's Contexts

Robbie Rogers and the Ghost of Justin Fashanu

> Rogers then became only the second gay footballer in Britain to come out in public. Justin Fashanu, his solitary predecessor, hanged himself in 1998 in Shoreditch, just a short walk from where Rogers now lives.
>
> —Donald McRae, "In Football It's Impossible to Come Out," *The Guardian*

> I don't know what I was so afraid of. It's been such a positive experience. The one thing I've learned from all of this is being gay is not that big of a deal to people.
>
> —Robbie Rogers, on the experience of coming out and playing for the first time.

A story, a context[1]: In 1981 Justin Fashanu made headlines as he became the first Black footballer in England to command a million-dollar transfer fee when Nottingham Forest Football Club (FC) purchased his rights from Norwich City FC. In 1990, as his career developed and after years of rumors, Fashanu gave a somewhat coerced interview to *The Sun*, in which he outed himself as gay.[2] The sensationalistic article detailed a secret relationship between Fashanu and a conservative member of Parliament, a claim Fashanu would later recant. Over the course of the next several years, Fashanu's life was a saga played out in the papers. For example, Fashanu's brother "disowned" him publicly—referring to Justin as a family outcast in a *Voice* article titled "John Fashanu: My Gay Brother Is an Outcast."[3] Fashanu's career stalled as he drifted from team to team, facing openly homophobic jeers from crowds (and teammates) as he moved from England to the US, then Canada, bouncing between teams and leagues. His best playing days behind him, by 1997 Fashanu settled in Elliott City, Maryland, to coach the

Maryland Mania, a new professional team in the (then) second division United Soccer League's A-League. In March 1998 a seventeen-year-old male informed police that he had spent the night at Fashanu's apartment and had awoken to Fashanu performing a sexual act on him. After an arrest on a sexual assault charge, Fashanu fled to England, where a month later he was found dead, having broken into a garage and hanged himself. In his suicide note, Fashanu claimed the sex act in question was consensual, but he feared he could not get a fair trial and did not wish to drag his family through additional pain and publicity.

A second story, to be read in context(s)[4]: After a successful start to his professional soccer career with Major League Soccer's Columbus Crew, Robbie Rogers fulfilled a childhood dream when he signed with English Championship side Leeds in 2011. After several injuries, Leeds FC placed Rogers on loan[5] with League One team Stevenage FC, a demotion of sorts, although it placed him in London, where Rogers increasingly accepted his sexual identity as a gay man. On February 15, 2013, Rogers announced via his personal blog and Twitter account that he was gay, retiring from soccer, and pursuing a degree in fashion in London. Despite his worst fears, Rogers's revelation garnered supportive tweets and public statements from professional soccer players in the US and abroad as well as from other sports stars. Upon Rogers's return to the United States to visit his family, he also attended a Gay, Lesbian & Straight Education Network—Nike Be True LGBT Youth Forum in Portland, Oregon, where he found courage and inspiration in the successes of the youth in their schools and communities. All of this provided Rogers with a newfound sense of what was possible for him and his career. After some contractual maneuvering, in May 2013 Rogers began training with the MLS team the LA Galaxy, where he could live and work close to his family. When he stepped on the field on May 26, 2013, in the seventy-seventh minute in a game against the Seattle Sounders, Rogers became the first openly gay male athlete to play in any of the five major North American men's sports.

A ghost story, providing context(s)[6]: Fashanu and Rogers share more than a common sport or an identity defined by same-sex sexual experiences. They are united by a spectral economy wherein Fashanu's presence as an iconic warning haunts the narrative landscape of Rogers's coming-out story, if not also Rogers himself. Fashanu's mode of haunting, however, like all hauntings, differs importantly by context.[7] In almost all of the commentary originating outside of the US, Fashanu's ghost takes on the form of an apparition. Fashanu's ghost does not hide in the shadows or make creaking sounds on the stairwell. To the contrary, almost without exception, Fashanu is front and center, visible through photographs and/or substantial prose, as a possible context for interpreting Rogers's fears and apprehensions. Fashanu's apparitional materiality confounds the temporalities of presence and absence, past and present, and the linearity and distinctiveness of firsts. "This," the ghost of Justin Fashanu announces, "could be you."

In US coverage of the narrative, Fashanu "ghosts" quite differently: Fashanu is invisible, rarely making anything but the most transitory appearance. Although Rogers sees and hears Fashanu, when Rogers is re-presented within the context of US sporting cultures, Fashanu is nowhere to be found. However one might explain these differences, whether they be national, temporal, or the result of a general ignorance of the past, Fashanu's abuse from his coaches and football fans along with his eventual suicide are perceptible only to Rogers when they fall out of the narrative. As a result, the nonexistent or weak form of historicizing present in this reporting fails to inform the reader's judgments about the dangers that might accompany one's coming out as a public sports figure. In the US version of the story, Fashanu's absence uncomplicates the narrative, so that Rogers is asked—and eventually asks himself—"What took so long? In an era of gay celebration, why were you so scared?" Absent Fashanu, absent overt homophobia or distasteful displays of disapproval, Rogers's coming-out story slides easily into a larger neoliberal narrative about the cultural acceptance of LGBT Americans, even in the previously impenetrable spaces of professional locker rooms. This tone of acceptance invariably gives way to an anticipatory gesture of additional athletes coming out, and, as such, Rogers—to himself and others—becomes "just Robbie," just a precursor for others to follow. Rather than a narrative about the ways one's actions are part of the fluid of cultural change, the story is a celebration of how far we've come and, in essence, how slow Rogers and others were to recognize this change that has led to a free market of sexuality.

If the first chapter was an attempt to illustrate the way budding neoliberal ideology worked itself into hooligan memories in England, the goal of this chapter (coupled with the first in terms of looking at the sense of self in neoliberal culture) is both more modest and more complex. On the more modest level, this chapter will frame the meaning of Robbie Rogers's coming-out story by illuminating it with different contextual lenses. To note how the presence and absence of Justin Fashanu's own story alters the meaning (and perhaps the motives behind) Rogers's. On a more complex level, however, given that the two contexts are soccer in the US and soccer in England, not only will it be an opportunity to highlight the discrepancy between how one acts in one context and how it is read in another (with a reflection on what this might mean for academic criticism), but this will allow us to also understand, through Rogers's reported descriptions of his own return to play soccer professionally, an understanding of how rhetorics of the autonomy and self-determination of the individual in public have become, at least in some contexts, inclusive of coming-out narratives. Ultimately, Rogers is presented as needing to "man up" and make it in soccer on the merits of the game, as homophobia or other restraints are largely erased. There is nothing stopping him from living his truth, that is, other than himself.

By returning to and revisiting contexts, as opposed to allowing context in the singular to function as a simplified backdrop for the divination of the disposition of the text, we are then able to use Rogers's case study to join the ongoing conversations about paranoid and reparative criticism and its relation to queer world making. That is, the following provides both critical readings of the way contexts alter the meaning of Rogers's act and, through a critical lens, offer a reparative (as opposed to paranoid) reading of the case (and engage in how such a reading shapes queer world making).

Rather than reading the story of Rogers's coming out in such a way that it simply reproduces[8]—in critical narrative form—the same assumptions with which the chapter began, contexts are provided for multiple readings, some paranoid, some reparative. Drawing on Rita Felski's "postcritical" perspective, this chapter attempts to "reframe critique as one form of suspicious reading among others as to break down such dichotomies, to locate it within a diffuse network of discourses and dispositions, to make room for multiple antecedents and acknowledge its entanglement with other words and other worlds."[9] The coterminous possibilities of texts and contexts offer something other than a reproduction of what we already know and feel.

In short, in the case of coming-out narratives, the paranoid frame—criticism that tends to begin with, and reproduce, a dominant ideology thesis—tends to fixate on public personalities and how the mediation of their coming-out narrative is complicit with any number of normativities, especially various forms of respectability politics.[10] While such criticism is valuable and serves the purpose of highlighting the power of ideology and ideological constraints, it is equally important (perhaps more important in this historical context) to read from other frames and contexts, ones that allow openings and reparations. What follows does not insulate Robbie Rogers's public persona from implication in vectors of normativities but instead expands the contexts of these judgments to reread them for their generative possibilities—that is, how to think about context in conjunction with texts to read them both as something otherwise. Hence, this chapter proceeds by providing both paranoid and reparative readings by altering the contexts in which the story may be understood.

Queering Contexts

A growing number of scholars interested in queer studies have made arguments for moving away from paranoid critiques (i.e., those that point toward the reproduction of heteronormative ideology) as the primary moment of judgment associated with queer critique. With an emphasis on the reparative mode of critique, more attention to productive moments of possibilities affords us an opportunity to explore how texts and practices enable or participate in queer world making, while allowing us to also maintain a critical stance toward what we see as problematic discourses. Again, these modes of critique are not necessarily opposites or at cross-purposes with one another—their relationship is more complementary than contrary to one another, as has been rehearsed in multiple forums in recent years.[11]

Following this line of argument, then, the non-necessary nature of texts and contexts requires that we develop "more capacious theories of norms, the normative, and normativities capable of capturing the multiplicities of texts and practices so that we may not render prematurely negative judgments against texts and practices capable of queering cultural formations."[12] Here, I expand and complicate the contexts in which normativities are understood and play a role in behavior and interpretation. While the perspective remains in some ways a rhetoric of suspicion, it also takes a page from the reparative register by multiplying the contexts in which meaning is made. In short, this complicating takes place by understanding the dual role played by the ghost of Fashanu and its haunting of the public meaning of Rogers. In order to expand the "normalizing and normative" negative paranoid critique that is surely to be found in these discourses, the queer critical role of this chapter is one of providing a shift in context (taking suggestions here from Larry Grossberg's explanation of context as another word for culture, in which "culture" refers to local frames of interpretation based on rhetorical and material realities) in order to articulate not only the ways ideology and culture normalize—as surely they do—but also to illuminate narratives of change, the seepages of ideology found in the interplay of contexts.[13] Ultimately, in this specific case, it is in the shadow of the ghost of Fashanu that allows queer world making to emerge. More, translating the focus on context here to other critical cases, I want to emphasize that one role of the queer critic is to highlight the ways that heroic actions are always in part struggles against unseen contexts. In brief, in highlighting those contexts, and highlighting the bravery of what seem to be pedestrian actions through a different contextual (and interpretive) frame, the space for queer world making is enlarged.

Sports may not be the most hospitable of places to think through the queering of cultures and contexts, especially given the dominant conventions and perspectives in academic sports studies. In the most general terms, the scholarship concerned with sports, communication, and culture, as well as the sociology of sport, relies on rather pessimistic renderings of sports, fans and fan cultures, and gender and sexuality.[14] While there certainly are exceptions—William P. Cassidy has provided a lens that illustrates the increasingly hospitable environment for the coming-out stories of lesbian athletes—the general tone of such work remains largely paranoid.[15] Indeed, moving the focus from sports in general to soccer and the culture around it replicates a hermeneutics of suspicion, although a hermeneutics with a focus much more consistently on gender and sexuality.[16] Ultimately, then, there is a landscape that, while offering some hint of transitions,[17] appears largely static.[18] From academic perspectives, then, sports tend to be valuable as a critical enterprise as examples of broader discourses of racism, sexism, heterosexism, and other dominant ideologies that frustrate gender and sexual diversities. Undoubtedly, sports are not immune to the cultures in which they are played and displayed, but they are also not flat fields of representation, experience, and mediation. The relative lack of out male sports personalities[19] stands out as one of the last understandable closets, so what is to be made of the reporting of someone when they choose to leave this closet behind?

Confronted with such a landscape, where do we probe, what politics (of visibility, of action) should be encouraged? How do we make judgments about mediated personalities and personas where intentions and the circulation of one's identity are made available for critique? The question(s) asked are of course ones that have long confronted cultural critics, and while there is no single route to be taken, the conversation about it—as tiresome as it may seem—is ultimately a useful and productive one, helping us maintain a back-and-forth conversation between commitments, writing, and context. In any form of cultural/social politics, then, one finds the recurring argument over whether to assimilate/whether to remain unmarked. Whether different or whether *differend*. And, in the present case, the interimplication of Rogers and Fashanu allows a revisiting of the communicative dimensions of coming-out discourses, especially how judgments are formulated and rendered. Typically, these judgments rely on a narrowing of texts and contexts such that the texts indicate the presence of normativities, and their inducements to normalize is a recurrent theme in these evaluations.

From some of the earliest essays on well-publicized coming-out narratives to more contemporary engagements with this topic, the textual component of the analysis emphasizes the institutional constraints of media outlets and conventions as well as the containment of subjectivities that threaten to undo the supremacy of heterosexual hegemonies.[20] When John Hughson and Marcus Free critique the British press for its sensationalistic coverage of self-identified and suspected gay male athletes, specifically soccer players, they emphasize how tabloid news sources fixate on the male athlete's performance of manhood and nationality, thus acting as a constraining frame of mediation.[21] Andrew Billings et al. remind us of the differences between gay male athletes and lesbian coming-out narratives, as many female sports stars are presumed to be lesbian until proven otherwise. Indeed, as Joah Iannotta and Mary Jo Kane point out, even when some female coaches and athletes are not "out" as lesbian, the mix of assumption and the strategic use of cultural codes allows a reconceptualization of female sports as nonlinear and fluid in terms of sexuality[22] (which may help explain why there are more "out" professional athletes among women than men proportionally). Additionally, gay male coming-out stories are often narrated within a context where the collective homophobia of male sports, particularly the obsession over the locker room, is neutralized by the literal and figurative reliance on level playing fields and the ways the supposed meritocracy of athletic performance acts as a buffer against indicting male sports and hegemonic masculinity.[23] In a similar vein, Marie Hardin et al. demonstrate how reporters act as gatekeepers who focus on individual athletes, who are then transformed into gay men who can transcend the obstacles placed before them (or not), all of which neutralizes critiques of toxic masculinities and collective and institutional homophobia and emphasizes the autonomy and self-reliance required by neoliberalism.[24] In each of these cases, the contexts are determining in the critical judgment such that individuals are confined to their context. I aim to ask, as a supplementary question, what it would mean to read the contexts rhetorically, where the text is not given primacy as a decoder ring to motive or complicity with normativities, but as texts that are coincidental with multiple, overlapping contexts.[25]

This chapter engages with other writers who are making similar moves. Recently, Diana Fisher makes a similar argument regarding gay and lesbian immigrants when she repositions the closet as a productive site of identity work for migrants who desire to maintain cultural and intimate ties to tight-knit communities that are sometimes inhospitable to sexual and gender minorities.[26] Along these same lines, Isaac West and Jeff Bennett's critique of Lee Edelman's *No Future* emphasizes the need to use criticism to enable socialities that foster queer identities and relations. Edelman's concern and ultimate critique of the figure of the child in queer politics (e.g., what we do now, the bravery we enact now, is meant for the safety of future generations) is that it is a politics concerned with the future over the present; it imagines collectivities prefiguring the world now; in short, it ultimately suggests an overconcern with assimilating the present into the conditions for the future, rather than being concerned with our own enjoyment with the here and now. Rather than overturning Edelman's antirelational thesis in total, West and Bennett suggest that we need to imagine unfixed futures (impure politics) that are not based on the figure of the child but recognize that there must necessarily be some shared relations and some shared direction with others.[27] This ties in nicely with the reparative call for a rhetoric or critique of openings rather than of domination, a move from the hermeneutics of suspicion to one of reparation or queer world making. Below, then, by contextualizing and recontextualizing Rogers's actions—despite the fact that, as we shall see, he explicitly invokes the figure of the child and the discourse of normalcy—rather than a chastising of his actions this reading is offered as a re-cognition and re-call of what his actions mean within different contexts. In short—and I do hope to pull this off without ultimately sounding particularly celebratory of "individualism"—I embrace a rhetoric of queer world making, an embrace of an unsure future, an impure politics by not allowing Rogers or his admirers to so easily slip him into the role of the "soccer player who just happens to be gay." By reading this story in a context devoid of Justin Fashanu on the one hand, and with Justin Fashanu on the other, and then in the context of coming-out narratives in a more general sense, I highlight Rogers's queer world making and encourage it in others. I help establish the future conditions for impure politics and sociality that does something more than simply reproduce existing social relations.

The Shared Story

In mid-February 2013 Robbie Rogers announced, via his personal website in a post entitled "The Next Chapter," that he is gay and, as a *result*, retiring from football.[28] Noting the long relationship between his sexuality and his occupation, Rogers wrote, "I always thought I could hide this secret.

Football was my escape, my purpose, my identity. Football hid my secret, gave me more joy than I could have ever imagined." He went on: "I'm a soccer player, I'm Christian, and I'm gay. Those are things that people might say wouldn't go well together." Here, then, Rogers lays out the cultural articulations that reflect what he saw as, in effect, traditional hegemonic masculinity. Football "hid" his secret precisely because of the assumed incompatibility between the two subject positions. If we could have put Simon Critchley in conversation with Rogers at this point, they would have agreed; while the rise in popularity of women's soccer (particularly in the US) marks the potential for change, in other cultures, especially if we go back to 2013, football culture "reinforces a whole series of lamentable gender norms and props up a crumbling sense of masculinity." Among these norms, clearly, is that male football players are by definition heterosexual.[29]

While Rogers understands that the incompatibility is cultural rather than necessary, he is very clear that the incompatibility is real in the sense of having material effects. As the narrative was covered in a wide variety of news outlets, Rogers's comments covered a wide range of ways that he was affected. Indeed, Rogers goes on to observe that he could not both come out and continue to play football because he knew how we would be treated—he had been hearing about it in locker rooms throughout his life.[30] The psychic scars of the casual and pervasive use of "faggot" as a term of derision is palpable across many of these stories, including in his autobiography, where Rogers repeatedly returns to crucial moments punctuated by the searing sting of this word, where it paradoxically pushed him further into the closet while also fomenting his consciousness about the necessity to forgo these external constraints on his person. Moreover, Rogers worried that even if he could find it in himself to play as an openly gay footballer, he would be articulated in public from that moment on as the "gay player." Rogers imagines that if his game were struggling, the press and fans would blame it on his sexuality: "Aw, that gay dude . . . he's struggling because he's gay."[31]

While the argument hinges in part on the differences in discourse communities and logics of the discussion of Rogers's coming out (in overly simple terms, UK vs. US coverage), one of the commonalities in coverage, regardless of the country of origin—and this proves important—is the repeatedly highlighted reporting of the support of other football players (past and present teammates, or players of some stature), coaches, nonsoccer sports figures, and other celebrities. While sometimes expressed in as simple a claim as "There was widespread support Saturday for former US international Robbie Rogers who announced late Friday that he was gay and was retiring from professional football,"[32] there are numerous and repetitious reports of supportive tweets. The *Daily News* (New York) repeats the tweets of Eddie Pope, former US National team player and current director of the MLS Players Union for player relationships, calling Rogers "brave" and asserting that Rogers is helping lead to a day when such announcements are not necessary.[33] The Associated Press (in *Fox News*) reports that those tweeting support include US Soccer teammates, US women's players, MLS commissioner Don Garber, NBA star Steve Nash, and Minnesota Vikings punter Chris Kluwe.[34] London's *Time* highlights that both Rogers and the paper itself were flooded with supportive comments from English football players, including Robert Snodgrass, former Leeds winger, and Ross McCormack, Leeds striker.[35] CNN also provides a lengthy list of supportive tweets, including one from US National team defender Ogushi Onyewu.[36] Major League Soccer itself provided—on its website—a long list of supportive tweets by former and current players and managers.[37] Finally, the *Mail* (London) and a number of other news sources provided other lists of supportive tweets.[38] In brief, in the initial reports about the case, one quickly gets the sense that soccer culture in both the US and the UK is very supportive of Rogers's announcement. The self-congratulatory tone of the public-relations-driven front offices and their recirculation of certain supportive tweets works to present sports as an always already welcoming environment, despite the common sense to the contrary.

The US Context: A Future for Our Children

After these initial discussions of the expressed support of former and current players, there is a *contextual* divide in the "meaning" of Rogers's coming-out narrative and of what it would mean for Rogers to return to the game. It is in this space that criticism can help craft a queer world of the present. In the most general terms, after the announcement of his coming out, retirement, and eventual return to Major League Soccer in the US, the American narrative becomes primarily a story of how mundane the entire event had been, puzzlement that there had ever been any concern of any sort. Indeed, the story becomes one of the neoliberal, always already assimilated, a narrative in which Rogers largely participates by suggesting that he always wanted to be "just a player," "just Robbie," rather than a person or an act situated against a past and toward a queer future. In short, in the US narrative—a narrative in which Justin Fashanu does not figure (or figures as a ghost in hiding)—Rogers helps produce a future for the children in which gayness is acknowledged as a benign difference.

Simultaneous, then, with news of the supportive tweets is an argument—both asserted and implied—that Rogers had no reason to retire, that, in fact, US soccer culture (and the US in general) is beyond homophobia to such a degree that an openly gay player would pose no problem. For example, Orrin Schwarz of the *Chicago Daily Herald* observes, "Twitter was full of American soccer players offering support and assuring Rogers that his announcement alone was no reason to retire"; Schwarz quotes Carlos Bocanegra as tweeting, "Proud of u buddy. Hope u only retired if ur over soccer and want to pursue other interests."[39] The *Montreal Gazette* quotes Clarke Carlisle, the chief of England's Professional Footballers' Association: "I hope retirement is not because of this revelation; you have our respect & support wherever you go."[40] An editorial in the *Huffington Post* expresses puzzlement over Rogers's decision to retire: "Presumably, they will allow him [Rogers] to visit gay bars and join LGBT political organizations after practice is over."[41] Another editorial, two days later, argues that Rogers should play on a team in MLS because the league and its fan base would have no problem with an openly gay player. As evidence the author points to the rainbow flag flying in the end zone of Portland's (then) Jeld-Wen Field, displayed right behind out lesbian capo Sunday White's nest. While acknowledging that Portland is obviously somewhat more liberal than other cities, "a lot of the US soccer community is incredibly understanding of Robbie's situation."[42] Moreover, Bobby Barnes, the deputy chief executive of the Professional Footballers' Association is quoted in a CNN.com essay arguing that Rogers should continue to play because "football has tried hard to create an environment where there is a supportive network around a player should he decide to come out as gay."[43]

One of the stories that is reported multiple times—in news sources on both continents—is that of Rogers's (former) manager at Leeds, Neil Warnock, asserting that Rogers could have played comfortably at Leeds had he simply told the team. Sexuality, Warnock claims, would never have been an issue. Warnock claims that he would have "pulled the lads together" and told them as a group. "The lads would then have just got on with it. There would have been a bit of banter—you expect that in a dressing room, but I don't think it would have been malicious. We're past that now."[44] More directly related to MLS, LA Galaxy coach Bruce Arena noted that the timing is good: "Our league is a progressive league. Our league is a league comprised of all different races, colors, and creeds."[45] Similarly, Sigi Schmid, then-manager of the Seattle Sounders (and a friend of Rogers) claims that he texted Rogers after he came out and urged him not to retire, given that other players and fans would accept him as is. Schmid adds, "It's irrelevant whether you have Jews, gays or Baptists on your team. I think we're becoming more cognizant that it takes all sorts of people to make this world go round."[46]

After he did come out of retirement to play for the LA Galaxy, Rogers himself more or less repeats the "why retire" discourse when musing, "I don't know what I was so afraid of. It's been such a positive experience. The one thing I've learned from all of this is being gay is not that big of a deal to people."[47] In an AP article, Rogers goes further, noting, "It's been normal, just as it should be." Rogers urges others to come out by claiming that if his experience has been so easy, others will find it this way as well. To closeted gay athletes, Rogers says, "You're just going to be treated the same way as any other athlete. It is going to take time, but it's inevitable."[48] After having played for the Galaxy, Rogers notes that his fears were unfounded, and he blames himself for having been a coward: " It's almost like I didn't give people the opportunity to accept me."[49] And he directly refers to himself as "cowardly" for refusing to come out earlier in his career.[50]

This is a good moment to return to West and Bennett's discussion of Edelman's critique of the politics of a future against which the queer is positioned as the embodiment of a relentlessly narcissistic, antisocial, and future-negating drive based on the figure of the child in the present. While wishing to bracket any discussion of assimilation versus difference for the moment, the politics of the child functions in this very case simultaneously with a politics of normality, to seemingly offer sameness over queer worldmaking, as if, in the US context, it is not that "queer difference" needs to be curtailed for the sake of the child but that this has already occurred—a future perfect scenario. That is, Robbie Rogers's own discussion of "the child," coupled with the ultimate understanding of his normalcy, creates an always already muting of the queer.

Indeed, "the child" figures predominantly in Rogers's reported decision-making process. On multiple occasions, Rogers asserts that his decision to return to soccer occurred largely as the result of self-reflection after he spoke to a large group of gay and lesbian youth at a Nike Camp in Portland, Oregon. Rogers notes that after this meeting, he realized that by retiring he was not actually going to be much of a role model for the future.[51] In an interesting turn of phrase, Rogers claimed that the kids at the gay and lesbian camp "very much showed me, 'Hey, you're being a little bit soft. You're not brave enough. . . . You have to man up a little bit'" and return to the game.[52] Rogers repeats this story in the *International Herald Tribune* and says, "It taught me I needed to man up a little bit. It's easy to play a sport that you love and be a role model."[53] If Rogers wants to "man up for the kids," to be a role model, exactly what type of future does he want for them? Evidently, a very normal one.

To provide a little more detail: In an interview with ABC News *Nightline,* Rogers (who is labeled in the transcripts as "Gay Soccer Player" each time he speaks) observes, "Gay athletes are athletes. If I go back to soccer, I want to go back to soccer as, as Robbie, as a soccer player. I don't want to go back as this, this gay athlete."[54] This stress on his being "just Robbie," a "normal" soccer player, runs on a seemingly endless loop. Indeed, after Rogers stepped on the field toward the end of the LA Galaxy victory over the Seattle Sounders to become "the first openly gay male soccer player," Rogers told the *New York Times* that the situation felt "normal:" "I kept saying the word normal, normal, but it was. It was just good to be back."[55] Rogers reported to the Associated Press that the experience in LA was "amazing. It's been normal, just as it should be. I'm a soccer player. I happen to be gay";[56] he went on to tell MLS Soccer News that he felt "just like a regular soccer player."[57] When asked by *CNN* to describe his experience, Rogers again claimed that while he had initially been worried, once he finally got to play a game, "everything was completely normal, as it should be."[58] Or, as another of his oft-repeated claims goes about the experience, "I guess this is a historic thing, but for me it was just another soccer game."[59] When Rogers went on to play in his next game, this time a US Open Cup game in Raleigh, North Carolina, against the Carolina Railhawks, Rogers told *Indy Week,* when asked what he expected the atmosphere to be like outside of his home grounds (indeed, outside of MLS), he expected to be booed, but he wanted to be "booed like any other opposing player is booed."[60] During this same road trip, Rogers reiterated that he is "a soccer player, and I'm Christian and I'm just a human like everyone else."[61] Note the way in which "Christian," which had earlier been a mark of incompatibility, is here marked as a sign of normalcy, very similar to the ways Jason Collins announced his Christian faith in his coming-out statement.[62] Collins's and Rogers's use of Christianity is a marker of being "like everyone else." Finally, as if to emphasize the point of Rogers's normalcy, Kevin Baxter in the *Los Angeles Times* lets the reader know that Rogers is just "one of us": "At the airport, he was just another passenger, wedged uncomfortably into a middle seat for a 4-hour trip across the country."[63]

Indeed, when Rogers published a book-length manuscript about his coming-out story—*Coming Out to Play*[64]—his narrative fit within what Kyle R. King referred to as the third wave of gay male sport coming-out stories.[65]

Here, the person is aware of their visible place in history and sees that space as a rhetorical opportunity for social intervention. And yet even aware—or perhaps precisely because he is—Rogers treats his life as "normal" and positions the promise of "normality" as the political payoff.

The stress on normalcy comes from sources other than Rogers himself. MLS commissioner Don Garber, for example, asserts on the MLS blog that while everyone is different in one way or another, Rogers is "just a soccer player" and should be treated as such.[66] In the weeks after Rogers returned to the field, a number of stories stress that the situation has been so normal that the story about Rogers's sexuality has been conspicuous by the absence of any discussion of it.[67] (One might observe as an aside that being told that it is conspicuous by its absence is, ultimately, of course, another form of presence). LA Galaxy manager Bruce Arena stresses that he would rather not discuss Rogers's sexuality because such a discussion misses the point that the team is "in it to win games," not to pursue social issues.[68] Rogers's teammate Landon Donovan is quoted several times as claiming that one of the reasons he was happy that Rogers played is that "now, hopefully, the hype about it is over and he [Rogers] can get back to being a soccer player."[69] Similarly, teammate Robbie Keane observes that, the initial moment of playing over, Rogers "can concentrate on just being totally part of the team and being a Galaxy player and none of this nonsense that comes along with it [coming out]."[70] The constraints Rogers had thought would hold him back, keep him from playing soccer, in this telling, never existed. The world indeed becomes a neoliberal marketplace where Rogers succeeds or fails on his efforts rather than on any systemic constraints.

If the analysis stopped here, with only the US side of the story, it would be a rather facile tale about the problems with "normal" as a discourse and its alignment with antiqueer politics of the child and other negative forms of normalcy. At the same time, normal is a surprisingly elastic discourse in spite of its typical figuration as a site of containment and constraint. In some cases Rogers's use of "normal" as a term and a perspective indicates a desire to return to the comfortable and affirming rhythms of one's life after the public declaration of one's sexuality—the repeated narrative demands and expectations of coming out wear thin in short order for almost anyone. Among other requests, the resort to discourses of normalcy might be read as a temporal demand to move past the repetitious monotonies where one can feel stuck in place confessing and renarrating oneself to the satisfaction of another. Likewise, requests for normalcy ask for a return to refigured bonds of sociality in the hopes they can withstand the profession of a secret forced upon someone by others in their network of recognition. Finally, normalcy hopes for a future where hope may not be secure or possible, where the past fails to provide possibility models for such relations, and the present is up for grabs. It is at this point, however, that we want to push harder on the context in which Rogers operates and operated, as well as the context in which readers might understand the potentially radical nature of Rogers's story whether or not Rogers wants to mute it, whether or not others understand it. It is here, indeed, that we must understand the ghost of Justin Fashanu not as absence but as presence.

Another Context: The Lesson of Fashanu

In "What's in a Name?" Larry Grossberg notes, "To put it succinctly, for cultural studies context is everything and everything is contextual."[71] More: "Cultural studies is always interested in how power infiltrates, contaminates, limits, and empowers the possibilities that people have to live their lives in dignified and secure ways. For if one wants to change the relations of power, if one wants to move people, even a little bit, one must begin from where people are, from where and how they actually live their lives."[72] Indeed, and Grossberg is compelling on this point, one can say the study and critique of culture—in a case like that here—is an attempt to understand context and to be open to the contingency of social reality and the ways that contingency itself is radically contextual. In the case of Robbie Rogers, we have a case study in which one aspect of context, one way the critical context in which Rogers understands the world and/or is assumed to understand the world by others and/or is understood by others, can be brought into highlight; more, it is ultimately as critics that we can trouble our understanding of the context, of the relation of power, and attempt to understand, just a little bit, how people actually live their lives. By understanding the ghost of Justin Fashanu as a part of Rogers's understanding of the cultural world, we come to understand a way to encourage a queering of the world through a reworking or retelling of Rogers's story, moving the understanding of one context into another.

While it is clearly not the case that Justin Fashanu is exclusively discussed in British and European outlets or completely ignored in US outlets, this is indeed largely the context in which his ghost operates. In US narratives of the Rogers case—in those tellings which expect Rogers's coming-out to be done with ease—Fashanu is a ghost through his absence. In British and European accounts, however, he is an omnipresent apparition. At times his presence is simply noted. For example, the day after Rogers came out, the *Daily Mirror* observes that Rogers "is the first footballer to come out since Justin Fashanu in 1990."[73] More often, however, this observation is accompanied by the reminder of the rest of story: Fashanu "took his own life eight years" after coming out.[74] On most occasions, after the retelling of Fashanu's suicide, Rogers is quoted claiming that he could not imagine how a gay man would be treated in lockers rooms and by crowds even today, given the "pack mentality of players" and the culture of fans.[75] In the *Independent*, Rogers repeats that the banter of locker rooms was so ugly,[76] and the vitriol of grounds so dangerous, that he felt it was impossible to both come out as gay and continue to play.[77]

The connection between Rogers and Fashanu is made explicit, sometimes as if warning bells are being sounded for Rogers. In one of the *Guardian*'s tellings of the story, Donald McRae notes, "Rogers then became only the second gay footballer in Britain to come out in public. Justin Fashanu, his solitary predecessor, hanged himself in 1998 in Shoreditch, just a short walk from where Rogers now lives."[78] Suicide seems almost a necessary outcome of the Fashanu story in these tellings (although the story is far more complicated in time and in motive). David Kent, David McCormack, and Suzannah Hills authored an essay in the *Mail* that highlights the notion that when public figures have come out as gay, it has rarely helped their career. To the point of Fashanu, they note: "Footballer Justin Fashanu was the first and only English player to publicly announce he was homosexual. The Norwich City and Nottingham Forest player committed suicide eight years later."[79] While the *Huffington Post* attempts to disarticulate an easy equation of Fashanu's suicide with his sexuality, they also note that it is easy "to pick out the words 'gay,' 'footballer' and 'suicide' to create a climate of fear that has remained with us, even up until today."[80]

Repeatedly, two sources are brought forth to discuss gay, lesbian, or bisexual players in football in the wake of Rogers's coming-out. First, Ruth Hunt, director of public affairs for UK-based Stonewall, is routinely quoted to say that while understandable, it is a shame that Rogers needed to make the decision to retire.[81] Secondly, Gordon Taylor, chair of the Professional Footballers' Association in the UK, is routinely quoted as observing, "I'm pleased that he's [Rogers] come out for his own sake," and that he hopes it will help others, as a number of players have told him that they are gay but do not feel comfortable coming out.[82] The first time the two are quoted, in the *Mail*, the essay is accompanied by a photo of Justin Fashanu with the caption, "The first—and so far only—top-flight player to publicly admit his homosexuality. He came out in 1990. After admitting he was gay, Fashanu struggled to reignite an already stuttering career and retired in 1997, blaming his downfall on prejudice in the English game. He committed suicide in May 1998."[83] James Masters, telling the story of Rogers's coming out, cites Fashanu again and observes that during his life Fashanu claimed, "Footballers are very narrow minded people. It's the nature of the business." Following Fashanu's death, Masters notes, a small group of fans would sing the following chant whenever up against his former team: "He's gay, he's dead, he's hanging in a shed, Fashanu, Fashanu."[84]

Hence, the importance of context as an interpretive tool for critics and the public, for fans and for Rogers himself. When we look at the multiple claims in the US press that Rogers would find it easy to come out, despite the multiple tweets from friends and coaches in the US, despite Rogers's very own complaints that he now wanted to be "just Robbie," that everything was surprisingly "normal," that it was as if he himself had not given people a chance to accept him, we need to underline, to emphasize, that these claims can be made only in a rhetorical situation, in a culture or context, in which Justin Fashanu is a ghost of absence, rather than a ghost who haunts. If we have Fashanu gay, dead, hanging in a shed, if that is the reality of where a person lives his life, the context and meaning of his actions differ for him and others within that context, a world invisible to so many who are making claims about its meaning. Moreover, it is a world that we—as critics interested in particular types of change—need to highlight in order to make it clear that what Robbie Rogers has done is not normal and can never be a case of "Robbie being Robbie." Indeed, Robbie's actions were queer, and we need to understand his actions as a queer form of bravery.

Rogers describes the importance of Fashanu's memory as part of his decision-making process regarding coming out. In his 2014 autobiography, *Coming Out to Play*, Rogers recounts the toxic masculinities present inside and outside football locker rooms before he came out, including a team lunch where a report about homophobia in football ran in the background, where Fashanu's life and death figured prominently in the segment. The report caught the team's attention, and the outward reactions to the report confirmed Rogers's fears about whether or not he might be accepted if he chose to come out. Although Rogers did not know about Fashanu before this lunch, he went home and searched online for information about Fashanu. What he found saddened him as he read about Fashanu's struggles with racism and homophobia as well as rejection from his family. In Rogers's telling, "Learning about Justin made me so sad and just confirmed for me that if I ever came out, it wouldn't be while I was still playing soccer."[85] Beyond his teammates, the fans also presented a concern for Rogers, as he was aware of the casual prevalence of "faggot" in fan rhetoric, sharing his impression that "football was so far behind where the rest of society had progressed in its views about gay people and homophobia that is was still living in the Stone Age."[86] Thus, the contexts are multiple, rather than singular, when reading what normalcy might mean to someone facing these cultural conditions.

While there was clearly a discourse of "normalcy" around Rogers's return to the pitch, there is also a minor, although important, theme that equates the occasion of Rogers's return to the field as a "Jackie Robinson moment." Indeed, in a *New York Times* essay on the case, Rogers himself notes that the reason he decided to come out included "the release of *'42*, the movie about Jackie Robinson."[87] In a sports blog, *TheOffsideRules*, Shawn Francis notes just before the announcement that Rogers had signed with the Galaxy, "If the reports are true, Robbie Rogers' return to the pitch is a Jackie Robinson moment."[88] More, on the night of his return, LA Galaxy fan Vince Grant is quoted saying prior to the game, "This is a historic night, kind of like Jackie Robinson."[89] Finally, in later coverage in the *New York Times*, John Branch observes that because this is soccer, rather than a more popular sport, it can't quite serve as the "Jackie-Robinson-breaks-the-color-barrier-moment" that everyone desires.[90]

There are any number of reasons that a comparison to Jackie Robinson is problematic (in addition to the popularity of the sports, race and sexuality are not parallels, and the cultural context is very different). Indeed, as Abraham Iqbal Khan points out in his reading of Michael Sam's coming-out story and the subsequent comparisons to Jackie Robinson, the comparisons are made in such a way as to highlight the ways in which Robinson, and now Sam, reflect the norms of white male respectability and erase rather than highlight difference.[91] Nonetheless, there are ways of reading this moment that do demand inspection and illumination. As David Goldblatt has observed, while clubs and the league, especially in England, today claim to be taking direct action against racism, there are still numerous examples of verbal and physical hatred of Black players and referees.[92] When Justin Fashanu was playing and came out as gay, the situation was that much more treacherous. To be direct, it seems reasonable to point to the bravery of the actions taken by either individual as a first step. Rogers's act was an act of queer world making, and the muted public response—including Rogers's own claims that he is "just Robbie," "just a soccer player," that everything "feels normal," and that "he didn't give people the chance to accept him"—misses the point. And that point is that what Rogers has done is not normal.

Indeed, Rogers himself recognizes this once he envisions his actions beyond those of the confines of MLS. As he notes in his critique of FIFA awarding the next two World Cups to Russia and Qatar, yet another reason to not come out lies in the fear of one day playing in countries with "seriously anti-LGBT values and crushing anti-gay laws."[93] Regardless of (or, rather, precisely because of) the way his action is treated as "normal" and ultimately unremarkable, our role—as critics—is to highlight the action as itself heroic, as an act of queer world making.

The Critical Context: Coming Out and Coming-Out Stories; Or, The Importance of Abnormality, the Valor of Bravery

While Justin Fashanu's appearance, or lack thereof, in the above narratives offers two different contexts for understanding Rogers's coming-out story, a third important context is the one in which reflective, academic criticism takes place. That is, part of the job of criticism, of writing a chapter like this, is to illuminate an individual story and to generalize that illumination outward. The Rogers story allows us to think about the "meaning" of coming-out narratives in general.

First, there is the importance of understanding the desire to normalize Rogers and other gay male athletes as having its own neoliberal problematic. In the last decade, a number of sociology-of-sport essays have highlighted, in different ways, the more accepting climate for gay male players within sports culture. Gaston, Magrath, and Anderson compare the disciplinary public reactions to Justin Fashanu's coming out to that of Swedish football player Antonio Hysén (in 2011). They conclude that the more accepting reaction to the latter was a sign of the growth of "inclusive" masculinities rather than solely heterosexual ones.[94] More broadly, Edward Kian monitored "liberal" message-board and mass-mediated framing of the coming-out stories from Jason Collins and Michael Sam and observed that there was somewhat accepting (although contested) attitude toward different forms of masculinity.[95] Similarly, Kian, Anderson, and Shipka observed that sport media framing of the Jason Collins story was far more accepting of homosexuality than expected and, indeed, that many African American commentators equated homophobia with racism.[96] All that said, we need to be careful about implicitly endorsing this level of "acceptance" or Rogers's constant refrain of "normality" without questioning the "normal" itself. To this point, Samantha King, in an insightful critique of queer sports sociology claims that relies on Lisa Duggan's notion of homonormativity, argues that equating "accepted" visibility with cultural change is to solely rely on queer sexuality as the key rather than thinking about the forms or lifestyles permitted under this acceptance. Indeed, King notes, and this analysis concurs, that the "normal" in which gay athletes are accepted is a homonormativity that is fully aligned with the geopolitics and economics of neoliberalism.[97] This is meant not to highlight "acceptance" but to caution critics to think carefully about the larger contexts in which acceptance is endorsed.[98]

Secondly, however, critics cannot turn this into a "normal" moment, a moment in which Robbie is "just Robbie," because it's simply not true. There may have been less outrage than one expected; there may have been less homophobia than expected—although one can certainly see it in the comments sections (never read the comments) where Rogers is accused of trying to get attention by claiming to be gay and of enhancing his star quality[99] and is referred to as a "finger-sniffer," of having a disorder, and of being part of the 3 percent of the world obsessed with being gay[100]—but ultimately what Rogers is doing is most definitely not normal. To call it normal is to ignore the power of homophobia in the sports marketplace; to call it normal is to affirm sports as a neoliberal dream in which homophobia offers no constraints. Again, Rogers was the first out gay male player in any major US professional men's sport. This is not to say that Rogers on his own brings about this queer world; it is to say that he materially substantiates these changes; his reality makes them more normal. Just as the gay folklore cited by George Chauncey altered the psychological living conditions for gay men in New York in the early part of the twentieth century, so does Rogers become one element of a folklore that makes "gay athlete" believable. While we must of course be attentive and cautious about the particular forms that visibility takes, we cannot take visibility seriously as an object of criticism if we are unable to even recognize its existence outside of normalcy. Maybe normalcy sits alongside another host of demands for recognition and legibility.

Thirdly, and more importantly, Rogers's case is not normal and cannot be understood as so if we take context seriously. Again, if as Grossberg argues "cultural studies is always interested in how power infiltrates, contaminates, limits, and empowers the possibilities that people have to live their lives in dignified and secure ways,"[101] then cultural studies must be interested in context at the most local levels, in the ways actions are understood at those levels. While it would be absurd to suggest that we understand Robbie Rogers's fears or hopes, we do know from textual evidence that Rogers was operating when he retired from soccer at Stevenage and Leeds in a context in which the only model of an openly gay player had been hounded by fans, coaches, and teammates; in which he heard the expression, "He's gay, he's dead, he's hanging in a shed"; in which the locker room was a bastion of articulated homophobia. We do not serve ourselves well, nor do we serve the very idea of change or queer world making of any flavor well, if we do not both honor and applaud this attempt to delimit, decontaminate, and empower the possibility of a life lived in dignified and secure ways. Hence, putting aside the face and politics of the child, putting aside Rogers's own politics of the child, putting aside his desire for a fixed future, we—as cultural critics interested in change, interested in queer world making—must mark and highlight this moment, a moment in which an agent took action despite the ghost of Justin Fashanu standing in his sight, if only to encourage others to act similarly when faced with other dangerous contexts. We are reminded here of Chuck Morris's presentation of the rhetoric of Harvey Milk, as Morris routinely asks audiences (especially with young members) to understand Milk through the temporal and social context in which he acted. Regardless of what world we want, then, regardless of its lack of permanence, only with these types of model behavior do we see this change materialized, only with this type of model behavior do we practice an impure politics that alters everyone's context. So, as other gay athletes debut over the course of the next several years,[102] we critics need to highlight and animate local contexts and continue to understand (as do cultural conservatives) that visibility matters and that these first steps are meaningful and deserve both attention and praise, even while the larger context of acceptance—and the ideas that are ultimately acceptable—might deserve to be problematized.

3

Soccer in the Mirror World

> Picking the right team depends on what are you looking for from your Premier League side. So here's a selection of teams that may fit in with some of the most popular answers [based on what you want to see]: "I want to see my team spend big and win trophies."
>
> —Matt Jones, "How to Pick an English Premier League Team," *World Soccer Talk*

During the summer of 2013, NBC announced that it had signed a three-year deal with the Premier League allowing the network to broadcast *every* regular season game on NBC, NBC Sports, one of their affiliated cable channels, and, simultaneously, through NBC apps for cable subscribers.[1] Such coverage was unprecedented and a cause for celebration for existing Premier League fans in the United States; viewers in the UK are not allowed even close to this much coverage, as my British friends lamented at the time.

For numerous sports fans, however, it was also going to be somewhat bizarre. Were they not fans of the Premier League or of soccer in general, it was as if an entirely new league/sport had been created and plopped down in the United States, immediately after a popular World Cup. It would seem newly created for many, despite the fact that these teams have existed, for the most part, for more than a century. The league and individual teams have long, complicated histories, the fans of each having particular "personalities" and ways of supporting their teams. With a large investment, NBC was of course interested in growing the audience. For non-NBC sports writers/outlets, there was also interest in growing the audience, if only to increase the number of clicks by writing about the new circus in town.

As a result, one of the seemingly banal but plentiful side effects of the announcement of the deal was that multiple news organizations and sports/entertainment blogs published what were basically guides on how to choose a Premier League team to support (indeed, many of them used those very words, or similar ones, as the title to the articles). Unlike the normal experience for those in the US who watch leagues based here, most of the new viewers would have no geographic reason to choose a particular Premier League team to support (perhaps some chose based on a family vacation to Liverpool or a study abroad experience, but that's not true in general). Other reasons thus had to motivate the choice of a team, and one easy way to increase traffic to your news site is to offer people just what they need, in this case, a guide to what each team "means." While many of us who are invested in the Premier League will tell you something oddly mystical, like "I didn't choose Chelsea; Chelsea chose me" (and I do have this sense despite being the type of rhetorical critic who would never accept transcendent or mystical statements from others), the guides still seem to fill a pretty significant exigency. Indeed, when friends who wanted to watch the Premier League asked my advice, I routinely told them to search out one of the many available guides.

The number of these guides alone tells us something about how strong the exigence was or just how many fledgling sports sites exist or, likely, both. In all, if one includes guides from all sites, including fan blogs and independent writers, the number easily tops fifty. The number that existed on more conventional news/sports sources or online versions of popular print outlets comes in at just around twenty.

One way to think about these guides is as "translations," not of words from a foreign language into one's own, of course, but a translation of values and meanings into those with which one is already familiar. Indeed, this is precisely how I will read them here, in the first of two chapters concerning the cultural and commercial translation of neoliberalism via soccer. As with any translation, of course, something always gets lost, and the only way to make sense of what is lost is to frame it within the context and values one already knows. When I think of this type of translation, I always hark back to the discussion between the characters Jake Barnes and innkeeper Montoya from Hemingway's *The Sun Also Rises,* about those who are aficionados of bullfighting.[2] Hemingway makes it clear that while the term could stand in for fan or sports lover, there was something more passionate about the aficionado, something that has to be witnessed to really be understood. Until then, you simply have to make do with the terms and experiences that are familiar. Only later, I recall thinking when reading the book at fifteen, will I or the characters come to understand the "real" meaning of "aficionado." Even then, I thought, it's never going to be natural to me but always filtered through my own values and experiences.

Perhaps this is a better way of thinking about it, especially in the context of Premier League soccer guides: in the novel *Pattern Recognition*, William Gibson has one of his (US-based) characters refer to London as the "mirror world," where everything seems very similar, and yet, having developed products and goods in different contexts, everything seems just a little "off" (e.g., electrical outlets, driving on the "wrong" side of the road).[3] In this case, we take a league, a sport, developed in one world and plop its elements down to be made sense of in the "mirror world." In such a case, the values of the mirror world are put into relief as sense is made of the new objects.

George Bernard Shaw is often mistakenly quoted as observing that "England and America are two countries divided by a common language."[4] If we take language in its most expansive sense of not only a system of symbols but also of values and meanings comprehended best through micro contexts, then there is a sense in which this chapter is an attempt to focus on those differences through the investigation of soccer fan culture, as a way of getting at—or understanding—the function of identity and values in a contemporary era, the understanding of culture not only in context but through multiple layers of contexts. Moreover, given that these guides are intended for those unfamiliar with the league, likely not that familiar with the sport, and therefore never having been in the throes of "sensate ecstasy," they are based less on the game itself (or the experience of fandom) and more on familiar values. And while I have suggested that sensate ecstasy itself tends to bring crowds to common sets of value and meaning, here, we see the foundational values of new fans defined not by the game itself but by what is already known. If soccer communities tend toward shared visions and shared worlds, these guides offer invitations that have less to do with those shared values and more to do with values that are important prior to involvement.

Soccer's Appeal: Fans and Postfans

Richard Giulianotti and Roland Roberston observe that if we are serious "about understanding globalization in the twenty-first century, then all of us need to look far more closely at the global cultural form that transfixed and fascinated so many diverse societies, and so many millions of the world's citizens."[5] While the same passion obviously can be found for music, television, and other forms of fandom, music communities come and go, stars live and die, series go out of production. Soccer clubs are, in a sense, forever. More, however, and as I argued in the introduction, the sense of transcendence and "sensate ecstasy" that is experienced by many football fans ties football powerfully to identity and therefore to values.[6] To quote Simon

Critchley once again, "football is a theatre of identity—family, tribe, city, nation. But it is the presentation of identity in its ever-twisting, complicated, collapsing and doubled-over forms. Football is the theatre of the differentiation of identity that plays itself out with the players and fans enacting their drama watch over the forces of fate."[7] But what is the meaning of the family, of the tribe, when you are making a choice based on neither family tradition[8] nor location?

I want to pause on this notion of community for a moment because it is, in my experience, one of the fundamental reasons the members of soccer fan communities have such strong ties with one another. Weekend after weekend in my local soccer pub, I meet neophyte fans who have not yet felt the type of ecstasy discussed here, and yet it is obvious that they are looking for a sense of community. Indeed, "community" (common-ality) is what gets these fans awake at six o'clock on weekend mornings to gather in pubs to watch their favorite teams play. As Wenner observes of soccer fandom, "The phenomenon is of course about belonging. . . . [It is about] announcing one's identity and facilitating the likelihood that others in the fandom community may be found."[9] Indeed, as a slightly humorous illustration of this need for community, a few years back the *Boston Globe* published an article entitled, "The Biggest Threat Facing Middle-Aged Men Isn't Smoking or Obesity. It's Loneliness."[10] I discovered this article when it was reposted or shared by three different men I know—all middle-aged and all men I knew solely through the Middle Tennessee Premier League fan community. When I posted my commentary on how interesting I found it that this article was posted by these particular men, a minidiscussion broke out on the page that kept referring back to the importance of the football community as a site for a sense of belonging (and this claim was coming from men, only men, of a wide range of ages). Over and over, members noted that they shared the essay with spouses and others to explain the time they spent each weekend with their football family, to justify the early mornings they lost with their "real family." It's more than sport, they would say; it's community.

Soccer fandom can be important, historically *has* been important, then, from the perspective of transcendence and community, but its potential at this moment in the United States, arguably, could not be more profound. Laurent Dubois remarks that soccer's play on "the margins of mainstream sports [in the US] is part of what has made it a vector for different ways of thinking about what this country is and can be."[11] In a somewhat similar manner, Franklin Foer notes that part of what makes the uptake in soccer in the US so potentially interesting is that because the US is not exceptional with the sport, there is more room for a rethinking of who and what "we" are; it provides an opportunity to reflect.[12] As Richard Giulianotti observes in *Football: A Sociology of the Global Game*, nomadic football supporters are well aware of the complexity of values and norms that must be taken on as they learn the social structure and moral values of their team.[13]

Yet, after all I've said about the importance of football fandom in numerous ways, after the large body of literature that points out its value in the lives of fans and the strong sense of meaning it provides, turning to the appeal of these guides seems to, at least initially, undermine that thesis. Or perhaps it takes us to a different stage in the process. Let me explain. In an interesting twist on the concept of tourism, mobility scholars John Urry and Jonas Larsen coined the term "post-tourist:" they describe the post-tourist as one who approaches tourism with experience, reflexivity and irony, the type of tourist who knows they are getting a constructed experience but works with it anyway.[14] Richard Giulianotti, reflecting on the term, has argued that a similar phenomenon occurs in modern soccer, with some soccer fans as "postfans," the type of fan who is also reflexive, ironic, and participatory. This fan is cognizant of the constructed nature of fan reputation and the vagaries of mass-media outlets in exaggerating or inventing such identities, while simultaneously willing to take on this identity.[15] He goes on to note that fans are somewhat less attached, less emotional than ever before (in line with all types of commentary about contemporary commitments).[16] Simultaneously, however, as he argued with Roland Robertson, fans do wish to have an identity that has unique, universal qualities that transcend civilization differences.[17]

While my experience with soccer fandom and supporter groups lies heavily in the "fan(atic)" camp, the notion of the "postfan" is useful here, I believe, in that it helps explain the style and tone of the "How to Choose Your Team" guides. Indeed, my assumption is that fans often come to sports, including soccer, with something of a distanced attitude but grow firm in their commitments to a particular team. While they may have to struggle with their team's history or current values (e.g., as I have to struggle with Chelsea's history of racism amongst the hooligan Chelsea Headhunters of the past), their commitment to the team and the community is firm and finalized prior to understanding the full dynamics of that community. Hence, these "guides" have a distanced and light attitude, giving off a sense of postfandom, despite the fact that some of the adherents will go far beyond such a distanced attitude.

Ultimately, however, because the guides are designed for novice fans of the league and hence have something of a "postfan" attitude, they necessarily provide easy and familiar values with which to begin one's position. Unmoored from geographic boundaries as a result of digital globalism, these guides provide a sense of the values and meanings that are highlighted not by the teams, their supporters, or their history but by the recipients, the potential US fans. As Giulianotti and Robertson observe, due to changes in mediation there has been something of a deterritorialization of identity on local levels and a reterritorialization of identity on a global level.[18] As almost every follower of the media ecology tradition would note, this creates a fragmented global village in which "even transient or migrant groups inscribe geographical marks upon their identities."[19]

The case of NBC's acquisition of Premier League broadcast rights, then, gives us an opportunity to see what are "values" and ideological logics to potential US fans. While there is a great deal of evidence that fans of various clubs have shared but different values based on their geographic home (e.g., Twitter searches illustrate that US fans of Premier League clubs and UK fans of the same clubs have a gap in terms of what they value both in their fandom and in the club itself),[20] there is also a route to draw out and discuss the values a fan is asked to take on, or how they are to interpellate, when "called" to fandom. As David Rowe and Callum Gilmour observe, the translation of a sport or league from one culture to the next is never one of a simple logic of adoption and imitation; it almost always implies the reflection of the host culture's values.[21] What I want to highlight here is that the discourse in the guides under analysis in this chapter presents readers with the idea that fandom operates like all other free markets (i.e., one is able to choose the values and items one wants, without restraint). Fandom is simply a free market of values.

Mirrored Objects: Sports and Entertainment

The thing with mirrors is that while you never get a perfect reflection, you always get a sense, no matter how bad the reflection, no matter what type of funhouse you've entered, of most of the features. So, when writers familiar with US sports and popular culture (and most of these are US-based writers) attempt to explain what something from the mirror world is like, they give the best approximation from our own, "real" world. Hence, Premier League clubs might be translated for "new soccer fans picking a club"[22] by a comparison to NFL teams or MLB teams or rap stars (but surprisingly—or perhaps not—only in one case to the US's Major League Soccer teams). Because I am interested in the most common and consistent signifiers of commonality across teams (i.e., I am more interested, for example, when MLB teams are lined up one by one with Premiere League teams than when one item, such as a film or book, is connected to only one team), I will ignore some of the common signifiers that arise. Hence, I am not going to discuss such articulations as Arsenal with Nick Hornby's *Fever Pitch*[23] or West Ham's connection to the film *Green Street Hooligans*,[24] except to point out the ways that popular mediated texts are a sign of a particular type of value of spectacle.

A very common line of comparison is to other US sports leagues and specific teams. For example, Ty Duffy mixes sports when he claims that Manchester City of the past was "the Mets to [Manchester] United's Yankees"; after being purchased by an Abu Dhabi royal family, Man City has become something of a second version of the "Yankees or Dallas Cowboys" and are a "universal brand."[25] Ellen Peacock also calls United "the Yankees of English football" (because, in her understanding, they have won a lot of titles and are the team to hate), while Chelsea is more like the 49ers, in the sense of a fairly new but ongoing legacy.[26] Rather than offer a few NFL or MLB comparisons, Ben Barros writes a column directly entitled "What NFL Team Is like Your Premier League Side."[27] Amongst his suggestions are that Everton is like the Green Bay Packers in that they have close, local, blue-collar-family roots, while Hull City is more akin to the (then) Washington Redskins, in that they have a name-change controversy[28] and an owner who courts arguments. Somewhat understandably, he equates Manchester United with the New England Patriots to the degree that they "always win" and get "favorable decisions from match officials."[29] Jared Leeper suggests in *The Tailgate Society* that United is most like Duke basketball, Alabama football, or the New England Patriots ("Choosing them as your favorite is easy and boring"), while Spurs is like the Chicago Cubs ("sometimes delusional fanbase") and West Ham United is the Oakland Raiders ("tough, hard-nosed, working class").[30] Nick Schwartz of *USA Today* suggests that you support Manchester United "if you're a Duke fan or if you hate Piers Morgan."[31]

In *Gaming the World*, Markovits and Rensman argue that given its global popularity and the ways players move from team to team around the world, soccer has great potential to reshape worldwide politics and culture simply by advancing a sense of "cosmopolitanism" in different markets.[32] Their analysis, however, focuses largely on the way that the influx of foreign players and movement has led often to "counter cosmopolitanism" in which the "foreign" or alien is critiqued and the domestic or familiar is reaffirmed.[33] In this first category of comparisons, then, we see an affirmation of their thesis in that the Premier League is articulated not as alien, not as cosmopolitan, indeed, not as different but as same. In doing so, we look at the mirror and see ourselves. While some of the "dirt," in Lawrence Wenner's sense,[34] of some of these comparisons might make for some uneasy articulations (e.g., for some, the implied racial content of a Duke basketball comparison), and while I do not mean to belabor the point, the implied argument here is one that reinforces one's preexisting cultural meanings. The strange is being made familiar.

While a majority of these guides refer, then, to the traditionally most popular US sports, two of the guides work in more marginal fashion, offering a different means of comparison. First, Julius Lasin provides "Choosing a Premier League Team Based on Your Favorite Rapper." This approach is decidedly "postfan" in orientation. Lasin begins by noting the growing popularity of the English Premier League in America but recognizes that since Americans do not have ties to teams, they may need advice on how to make a choice. "Don't worry," Lasin writes, "we have you covered. Choosing a Premier League team to root for is as simple as choosing your favorite rapper."[35] The articulations he makes between teams and rappers identify what he/we value about each. For example, Arsenal is like J. Cole because they err on the side of conservatism and are frugal, just as Cole is with his music. Chelsea is to be supported by Kanye West fans because they are both at the top of their game and full of hubris. Aston Villa should be supported by fans of Troy Ave because they are both bottom feeders who continue to stay in the game despite having very little success.[36] He goes through each team in this fashion, aligning teams whose characteristics have changed many times over the course of over a hundred years with rappers whose personalities and success rates will change and diverge as well. That said, what makes this guide interesting is that it takes an alien but globally popular sport and aligns it clearly with an artistic form that is primarily associated with, and primarily practiced by, African American artists. Moreover, it is a comparison most likely understood by a younger audience (i.e., "this ain't your father's sport"). While this type of comparison is made by only one author and hence cannot be said to be dominant, it does tell us something about an emergent way of positioning soccer.

The other minor discourse concerns the rare but noticeable (at least to MLS fans) lack of comparisons to the US's own professional soccer league. This lack is telling as well of what is, and is not, valued culturally and should be concerning to those interested in growing the domestic league in the US. While cosmopolitan only in a minor sense, this comparison does provide value to US soccer by a comparison to the Premier League, which is held up as the world's strongest league. One of the most striking "reveals" of David Goldblatt's *The Age of Football* concerns the effect of the popularity of the (English) Premier League on domestic leagues worldwide. While Goldblatt makes mention of this phenomenon in many parts of the globe, it is most striking in his discussion of domestic leagues throughout Africa. As he travels, he notices far more jerseys from Premier League teams than domestic teams, far stronger fan bases for Premier League teams, and disastrously falling attendance for African domestic leagues since the advent of cable and satellite TV brought the Premier League to television monitors throughout Africa.[37] Taking Goldblatt's observations and turning to the discussion of the popularity of soccer in the United States found in *Soccernomics,* the reason for concern becomes clear. After illustrating the growth of the popularity of soccer in the US (and the way it outstrips the specific growth in the popularity of MLS-brand soccer), Kuper and Szymanski observe, in something of a depressingly visual metaphor: "It was therefore wrong to imagine [David] Beckham could save American soccer by playing for the [Los Angeles] Galaxy. American soccer is alive and well and lying on the sofa watching Manchester United on NBC."[38] While soccer in the US already faces what Markovits and Rensman refer to as counter-cosmopolitanism in the sense of soccer players being framed as both soft and somehow anti-American[39] (perhaps the most famous case of such a claim was by pundit Ann Coulter),[40] those most interested in soccer prefer what they see as the best and "most authentic" football. The relative absence of MLS as a value in these comparisons seems only to confirm that. If one is to watch soccer at all, the guides seem to imply, one should watch a league that is as strong as US dominance in football, basketball, or rap.

Moreover, the single essay that does advise the reader on which Premier League team to support based on your support of an MLS team does so in a fashion that only serves to reify the dominance of the Premier League. Sky Sports' James Kilpatrick makes his recommendation of which team to support based on where different Premier Players have come to play for MLS teams toward the end of their careers.[41] For example, Arsenal is like the New York Red Bulls, because Thierry Henry played for both clubs,[42] and both are looking for a title. Chelsea is aligned with Montreal, because Didier Drogba played for both teams. Chelsea legend Frank Lampard's short stint with Manchester City becomes the connection for City fans to support NYCFC. When a team does not have a former PL player, he compares the style of an MLS player with the style of a player in the Premier League (e.g., Leicester City's Jamie Vardy and Riyad Mahrez are mirrored by Kei Kamara, then of

Sporting Kansas City and Ethan Finlay, then of the Columbus Crew). In short, then, in the single instance of an author comparing like sport to like sport, the emphasis implies the value of the Premier League over the domestic MLS league.

Nationalism through the Looking Glass

Franklin Foer argues that one reason soccer in general never became popular in the United States is that it works against the idea of American exceptionalism and seems to highlight Europeans as better than "us."[43] With the exception of the United States Women's National Team, which I discuss in chapter 6, this is fundamentally true. If the comparisons to US sports leagues, teams, and stars provide a route by which to reaffirm existing "American" values and symbols, this second category offers a route to take literal and metaphoric ownership of the objects in the mirror, not simply placing common values on them (although that is assumed) but also taking ownership of them literally or through having players stand in for the nation. In short, suggestions of which team to support are made on the basis of just how "American" they are, highlighting those elements of the game in which there may yet still be something exceptional about "us." At the very least, this appeal offers a route for a partial redemption of American exceptionalism.

For example, Ty Duffy recommends that fans might choose to support Liverpool, because they are owned by John Henry and Company, the owners of the Boston Red Sox, or they might want to choose Manchester United, owned by the American Glazer family, who also own the Tampa Bay Buccaneers.[44] Moving from owners to players, Duffy also suggests that one might choose to support Everton, then home of US Men's Team goalie Tim Howard or Stoke City, where USMNT players Geoff Cameron and Brek Shea were on the roster.[45] Similarly, Jonathan Segura of *Rolling Stone* magazine refers to Everton as the "American team" and notes, stressing the nationalism, that "any Bud-swilling nonhipster" should be able to support them.[46] Everton is similarly referred to as a good "American" choice by Ellen Peacock, although she also recommends Tottenham Spurs, because they had signed US player DeAndre Yedlin and also were the former team of (then) US men's coach Jurgen Klinsman;[47] Sam's Army also references Yedlin, although this time in support of choosing Sunderland, where he was then playing on loan.[48]

Examples of such articulations are plentiful. In *World Soccer Talk,* Matt Jones claims that one of the better ways to pick a team is by choosing one with American players or American connections and points to Liverpool as having American owners and Everton having a history with American players, including Landon Donovan and Tim Howard.[49] David Fleenor of *Soccer365* recommends Everton for the same reasons and also notes that Aston Villa now has American owners.[50] Finally, Roger Bennett recommends Fulham, as it historically had housed several American players (e.g., Clint Dempsey) and makes the common reference to the team as Fulhamerica (Bennett also recommends Sunderland, who had just signed US striker Jozy Altidore).[51]

Laurent Dubois notes that soccer teams may be the most powerful contemporary form of global collective representation and that part of what is so much fun about events like the World Cup "is that many people who might rarely make a show of nationalism can, in the festival atmosphere, deck themselves out in flags and national symbols in a way that feels joyful and playful and creates connections across social and class barriers."[52] In short, Dubois sees soccer, especially international soccer, as a nontraditional form of nationalism that allows identification with one's nation without a sense of jingoism or closed borders, something akin, I would think, to a "postnationalism." While I will return to a discussion of how soccer works in terms of US exceptionalism later in this chapter and again in chapter 4, for now I want to highlight that these guides are fundamentally different than the nationalism discussed by Dubois. Indeed, rather than emphasizing crossing social and class barriers, these guides place the emphasis on supporting Americans in the context of "foreign" teams in a "foreign" league. If we are going to support something alien, in this logic, the best way to do so is to take ownership of it, making it, as much as possible, part of the nation.

One of the interesting elements of this strategy is that it takes as permanent what is clearly temporary. Owners sell teams, players are routinely traded. Indeed, even as I write this, not a single player mentioned in the examples is with the same team recommended by the guides. While no better or worse a strategy than any other, it, like the metaphoric identification of soccer teams with NFL teams, makes the strange familiar and, as a result, leaves one's current values and preferences unquestioned. Indeed, if we take a football fan like Nick Hornby to be a "modernist fan" as opposed to the post-fan, who has a more casual, sometimes ironic, relationship with the team, we can see the difference stressed. As Hornby reminds us, players, managers, and owners come and go, but the fans remain for a lifetime: "The only difference between me and them [the players] is that I have put in more hours, more years, more decades than them."[53] "I am a part of the club," Hornby writes. "Just as they are part of me, and I say this fully aware that the club exploits me, disregards my views and treats me shoddily on occasions, so my feeling of organic connection is not built on a muddle-headed and sentimental misunderstanding."[54] Hornby understands his relationship to the team as one that is permanent and yet not necessarily a reflection of his values and desires. He is intimately a part of the team and arrived there somewhat organically. He knows that he will have to struggle with his fandom over time as both values and players change. Hornby will need to put in the work to smooth out those differences, as the sense of the ecstatic communal public demands. Not so the consumer of these guides. Not having experienced communion, not having experienced the public ecstasy of the game, she or he chooses a team based on preexisting values, rather than negotiates his or her values along with the community.

Roy's Keen: A Constellation of Stars

In 1997 pop singer Morrissey released the single "Roy's Keen" off the album *Maladjusted*. While not a particularly successful song in the marketplace, it had the benefit for some of referring, in part, to Manchester United midfielder Roy Keane. I cannot possibly recall the number of times that a Manchester United fan has explained this little fact to me. To be fair, it's not as if fans of other teams aren't also guilty of reeling off the names of celebrities who support (or supposedly support, or once held up their club's jersey at a photo op) their favorite team. The number of websites dedicated to or including this information, is testimony to the popularity of such information.[55]

It is thus not particularly surprising that this is a third major way that potential fans are asked to think about which team to support. What this strategy shares with the first two is that it offers a way of making a decision based on already-familiar values, although ones that have little to do with the history or core "meaning" of the club. For example, Nick Schwartz of *USA Today* recommends Arsenal if you like Piers Morgan, or Fulham if you are a Michael Jackson fan.[56] David Fleenor highlights celebrity fans as one of his five major categories for team choice, providing such couplings as Leicester City and Dr. Phil, Stoke City and Sugar Ray Leonard, West Bromwich Albion and Ron Wood and Eric Clapton, and, finally, Watford and Elton John (former owner and fan).[57] In what is often referred to as the "classic" of this guide genre, Bill Simmons of ESPN.com makes the case that one should both choose a club because of its celebrity fans and consider crossing clubs off the list because of the negative values associated with some of their more infamous fans: "Pay careful attention to the list of celebrity fans attached to each team. For instance, one of the EPL teams . . . counts John Gotti and Osama bin Laden among its fans. I'm not a celebrity, but just in case somebody mistook me for one, that's not a list I'd want to be on."[58] (As a snarky aside, I'm not at all opposed to noting that the team is Arsenal). While there is little value here of my recitation of each team and its celebrity following, it is striking just how often celebrity followers are utilized as a tool or mechanism for choice. While the lists of celebrity fans often (and obviously) include numerous individuals whose values and politics might contradict one another, the use of this mechanism for choice allows the "post-fan" or early fan the opportunity to imagine the values of their choice of club aligning neatly with their preexisting values.

The Value of the Bandwagon

While, given the existence of a promotion-relegation system in English (and most all) soccer leagues, victory is clearly more important than it is for American sports franchises (in terms of finance and visibility), making a choice on a successful win-loss record would be anathema to most British fans. That is, one of the key points of pride for many fans is loyalty, or imagined loyalty, in the face of a team that is consistently failing. Not only can you find discussions of standing by a team through thick and thin in both academic and popular writing on soccer (see, for instance, the hooli-lit discussed in the first chapter), but it is also a common trope with which any hardcore fan is familiar. Indeed, I have friends who appear at times to have a secret wish that Chelsea would go on a long-term losing streak, just so that they can prove their loyalty to the team. Derision is often laid upon "new" fans who come to a team during a period of glory, despite the fact that this is often when a team grabs someone's attention for the first time.[59] What I want to stress here is that while everyone loves to win, of course, there is a powerful romance around the idea of having supported a team through its most difficult periods. This is not to claim that fans do not love recounting their history of glory and victories—they definitely do—it is instead that these victories are seen as the spoils for sticking around during periods of loss.

As a result, while the stress on victory as a choice for choosing a team would be off-putting for many fans, it is an astute way to appeal to post-fans. Hence, numerous of the guides are broken into categories of winning. Ty Duffy breaks his suggestions into "Teams That Can Win the League," "Fourth Place Teases," "Mid-table," "Embrace the Relegation Battle," and "Just Promoted," warning new fans to stay away from anything below mid-table teams.[60] Ellen Peacock solely recommends teams that can win the league and/or will remain viable.[61] Nick Schwartz of *USA Today* suggests the need for a competitive team and warns about Sunderland: "This team exists in a relegation battle. The season hasn't even started yet, and they're in a relegation battle."[62] Again, while I do not mean to state that winning or a winning tradition is not part of the bragging rights and discussions that take place around teams in supporter group sections, I do mean to suggest that the topic of avoiding or leaving a team based on the win-loss record would never come up in a supporter fan base. Again, when one chooses—rather than feels chosen—one makes decisions on a basis that reflects one's values rather than aligning values with a community's.[63]

Working-Class Heroes, Oligarchs, and Sheikhs

It is common in many conversations about English football to bemoan the way the working-class fan base or the "common man" has been priced out of the game. Indeed, as I note in the chapter on hooli-lit, and as Tim Crabbe and Adam Brown have illustrated convincingly, both the discourse about/marketing of soccer in England and much higher-priced ticketing have worked to exclude or limit the number of working-class fans that can attend the games.[64] The global phrase "Against Modern Football" serves as a blanket critique of the ways high finance has altered the game in multiple fashions, including games being played throughout the week, television access through premium channels, multiple jersey deals, luxury box seats, and a general tendency to make the grounds safer by attracting higher-class fans who can afford higher-priced tickets. For fans who have been around for many decades, these changes work directly against the historic notion that football is the sport of the working-class and that ownership of a team is a mission of love rather than a way to make profits. In the guides, however, class is played in a much looser, almost flippant form, as if choosing the class of the club were simply one more playful signifier. For example, teams like Chelsea and Manchester City are routinely pointed to as "rich" teams, with Chelsea being owned by wealthy Russian oligarch Roman Abramovich,[65] and City owed by Sheikh Mansour.[66] Roger Bennett goes as far as to note that while American Chelsea fans are out of touch in terms of understanding what "true" English soccer supporters are like, the choice of Chelsea as a team makes sense to Bennett, because they are, with money and success, "living the American dream."[67] It's a fascinating turn to take the wealth of a British team and a Russian owner, and refer to it as part of the American dream.

When supposedly "blue-collar" teams are suggested, it is on the basis of commonplace signifiers; this is not an appeal to working-class sentiments in any political sense but in the sense of surfaces. Hence, we are offered to identify with the blue-collar supporters of teams like Newcastle ("they are often shirtless") and Sunderland ("Sometimes they beat rival Newcastle and get tattoos to celebrate").[68] Burnley, we are told, is a "blue collar, working class, no nonsense team for a blue collar, working class no nonsense place."[69] Bill Simmons points out that Newcastle's "blue-collar" fans are one of the most charming aspects of them as a choice,[70] and Nick Schwartz argues that West Bromwich Albion is so blue-collar and rough that "if your idea of how to fix a chipped tooth is to punch your dentist in the face, support West Bromwich."[71] What I want to point in the direction of is that while discussions of class are only a minor signifier in this discourse, the way class is presented is far different than in discussions amongst long-term fans of these clubs. As I illustrate in the chapter on hooligan memoirs, that discourse posits the large working class in England as the backbone of football support in general, and the breeding ground for most of the old hooligan groups. When those memoirs discuss a club's relationship to class now, it is often to bemoan the ways clubs have turned to new "moneyed" fans and turned their backs on the working class. In these guides, however, "working" class becomes, like all other signifiers, just one of many contingent values that might be chosen by the new fan. One chooses the "class" of the team, in short, as a matter of style. Class is a signifier rather than having a material basis.

What the Mirror Doesn't Show

When one thinks of the hooligan era of the seventies through the nineties, even if one knows little about English soccer in general, one thinks of violence, riots, and racism. Indeed, Simon Kuper, in noticing the counter-cosmopolitan reactions found in fan groups, suggested in 2010, "Soccer grounds have become perhaps the last bastion in Europe in which the worst kind of racist, sexist, anti-Semitic, xenophobic . . . language and behavior have not only been tolerated but actually extolled."[72] While I explore how these topics are re-membered in hooligan memoirs, and in chapter 5 analyze how race and racism are discussed now in the midst of the Black Lives Matter movement, these issues are largely ignored in the discourses of these guides. That said, it is certainly not the case that racism, racist chants, and regressive politics and behaviors have been eradicated from fan bases (if one follows the Premier League, or any number of European leagues, one will see several instances of racism and nationalism from fans each season, directed either at other fans or at players), and these points are largely ignored. Again I stress that overarching racism should not—cannot—operate in a neoliberal world in which people are expected to compete with one another without such constraints getting in their way.

For example, at the time most of the guides were being published, the manager of Sunderland was Paul DiCanio, who was widely criticized for being openly fascist (he claimed to be fascist but not a Nazi). What we find in the guides are only brief mentions of veiled allusions to his beliefs. For example, Jonathan Segura suggests that readers "may want to Google Sunderland manager fascist for a bit of context on last season's rocky start,"[73] and Aaron Gordon mentions that Sunderland's manager has a tendency to valorize Mussolini.[74] While these brief mentions would indeed be damning for many readers, it is remarkable that the references are so rare and that they are presented in a rather flippant manner.

In addition any current fan of the Premier League would be surprised at the absence of a great deal of discussion of the "meaning" of Tottenham Hotspurs to Premier League fans. One of the most remarkable aspects of their fan base is its identification with Judaism, regardless of the ethnicity or beliefs of the particular fans. Because Spurs played in an area of London with a large Jewish population, they traditionally had a large Jewish fan base. Overtime, anti-Semitic fans of other teams, or simply fans of other teams who needed a route by which to deride Spurs fans and players, not only would refer to the players as Yids but would also sing anti-Semitic chants and, almost unbelievably, make hissing sounds to simulate the gas chambers of the Holocaust. As a result, and still to this day, Spurs fans have inverted the use of the term "Yid" from a point of derision to a marker of pride; they refer to themselves as the Yid Army and are known to shout "Yiddo" at favored players (regardless of whether the fans or players are themselves Jewish). While the league has at times tried to put an end to this behavior, it has never been fully successful, especially in terms of the fans' recuperation of the term "Yiddo." While for many fans, this is a fascinating use of signifiers in football fan culture, this sense of identity and pride is only briefly mentioned in two of the guides.[75] Whether an explanation of the "Yid" phenomenon is simply too difficult to explain in a short space or if it has the potential to be too explosive, I do not know, but its appearance is rare. As a result, the exclusion of this information in favor of more surface-level, slightly humorous signifiers to match the preexisting values of the fan base, appeals more to Giulianotti's postfan than not. Again, the choices are offered on the basis of surface-level signifiers, rather than on identity.[76]

Postfans and Contingent Connections

While recognizing that fandom is ultimately far more complicated than an initial appeal of a guide found through a Google search, for a particular type of fan, such guides do set the context for an approach into a new discourse community. Given this context, these "how to choose" guides offer an ironic and reflexive type of fandom, based largely on the values one already brings to the table, largely ignoring the complexities involved in the long histories of these clubs and their point of origin. While I am optimistic that, as Verner Møller and Jakob Genz argue, the spectacle of the sport itself allows for a drive toward a discussion and reevaluation of cultural values, I also think this entry point gives us plenty of cause for caution, or, at least, thought.[77]

The first point I want to stress, and this is not simply about soccer but about the cultural discussion of values in general, the presentation of these guides places the league and the individual teams within the value system already existing for the reader. This is not a profound claim; in fact, it is simply a truism about popular culture discourses. In order to be "popular," mass-mediated messages must necessarily appeal to the understandings and values of the audience.[78] We rarely watch shows or events we don't like, don't understand, or find offensive. While we might not mind some challenging material in our entertainment choices, we rarely want to watch entertainment that solely extols virtues or values to which we are opposed. This does not mean that there is not a good entry point later for discussions of articulations around football, but it does mean that the first translation is into our own terms, language, and values. Importantly, however, these values, in the hands of the postfan, are ones that can be chosen as if in an open market.

Secondly, being introduced to teams and the Premier League in such a way provides a model for fandom that one receives rather than creates. That is, the possibilities of fandom can be creative and spur imagination in multiple different directions. It is in fandom, as James Montague notes in his global study of fan culture, that people are creative both ideologically and aesthetically, and these spaces can lead to multiple changes on political and social levels. For example, after the ultra culture in Turkish football led the way to bringing down former President Mubarak, one of the "top" supporters observed in conversation with Montague that while the ultra groups would not take full responsibility for the fall of Mubarak, he saw the job of ultra culture as making people dream, of seeing the world differently through building solidarity.[79] While I am not claiming anything as absurd as "All fan cultures develop into political movements" or that entering fan culture through fan guides leads to moribund fandom, I am suggesting that the "guide" approach to the Premier League call for a passive rather than an active fan base. Laurent Dubois notes that US soccer's existence largely on the margins of mainstream sports culture has allowed it to be "a vector for different ways of thinking about what this country is and can be, and what role sports will play in that."[80] To be introduced to soccer in a way that shapes it as the "same old song" is to discourage this other-worlding that soccer has been able to encourage elsewhere. While I illustrate in the introduction and the first chapter the ways the communal nature of sensate ecstasy encourage a dampening of difference amongst fan groups, here I illustrate the way that "guides" necessarily and naturally (at least within a market-driven economic system) encourage values that reflect ones with which we are already comfortable.

Taking this a step further, if we see fandom as received rather than created, and if we see fandom as a matter of choosing signifiers as we choose style, this portion of the fan base is less likely to be open to its political dimensions. Or, rather, as I show in the chapters concerning gender equality, sexual freedom, and the Black Lives Matter movement, it encourages a flattening of the politics toward the center and toward preexisting cultural logics. To keep pushing this point, neoliberalism relies on some sense of equality and cannot recognize systemic constraints like racism, sexism, and homophobia. Such a rhetoric of open choice is one that undermines active politics.

Third, and in the most practical terms of the development of soccer in the United States through the growth in popularity of the national teams as well as MLS and the USL, I turn back to David Goldblatt's discussion of the "effect" of Premier League popularity on domestic leagues around the world. If the Premier League is being shaped rhetorically to reflect the NFL, MLB, and various celebrities, and if the sole valuation of MLS in this discourse is as a home for former Premier League stars, the discourse is undermining the value or potential value of the domestic league. That is, by highlighting the parallels between the Premier League and the most popular sports in the US, one equates the Premier League with those leagues, hence valuing it over the United States' own domestic league.

On the upside, however, those who have looked at the ways US discourse has configured soccer in the past as foreign and therefore soft (i.e., not masculine) would have to see this discourse in an optimistic light. To the degree that football is being configured here not as other, not as foreign, but as American as NFL-style football, the status of soccer itself becomes noticeably American. And for soccer as a global game that encourages globalism and multiethnic teams to become popular in the United States, it needs to be seen as part of the United States ideologically.

Finally, to end on a more positive and speculative note, David Goldblatt observes that his discussions with USMNT and USWNT supporters provided evidence that moments of soccer support gave these individuals a chance to be patriotic without having to think that their (i.e., US) ideology is better than others (fandom is simply love of the game and team). He then quotes a blogger discussing one of the most intriguing aspects of being a fan of US soccer: "For a generation who have watched over-confidence in American power lead to disaster, cheering for the US in a context that we know we wouldn't win offers a similar existential thrill. Soccer fandom in America is speculative fiction: What if the US was just a country among countries?"[81] To "sell" the Premier League to Americans as the best in the world, to decenter the United States as exceptional, is a powerful idea.

What if, indeed, it were just a country among countries?

4

Liga MX, MLS, and the Neoliberal Corporate Politics of "Othering"

> The BBVA MX League (Liga MX) is suffering a lot with the growth of MLS, to such an extent that even owners like Alejandro Irarragorri bet on the creation of a binational competition for Mexican clubs to adopt the business model and the benefits of the USA league, which grows in leaps and bounds. The little that Mexican football can boast compared to its awkward neighbor is its dominance on the pitch, where there is still a marked difference—at least this is indicated by the clashes between the teams at the international level.
>
> —Joani Cruz, "Five Hateful Comparisons between Liga MX and MLS," *CE Noticias Financieras*

One of the anomalies of being a soccer fan in the United States who is not of Mexican ancestry or origin is that,[1] outside of the US Women's National Team and the US Men's National Team, one is very likely most familiar with the (English) Premier League and (US) Major League Soccer.[2] While there are a variety of other European clubs for which one often sees jerseys and fans (e.g., FC Barcelona, Real Madrid, Borussia Dortmund, Juventus, Paris Saint-Germain), the two major leagues that own the attention of these particular fans are MLS and the Premier League, especially given that these two leagues continue to have the greatest amount of English-language television and traditional sports coverage.[3] And yet, in terms of numbers of television viewers in the United States, the Premier League and Major League Soccer are not the leaders. In fact, they do not even come close to receiving the highest ratings. This fact almost always comes as a surprise to fans whose primary allegiance is to either of these leagues or to some other European team. Indeed, articles that mention this fact to MLS or Premier League fans do so understanding that it will come as a surprise.

For example, in December 2020 reporter Connor Fleming noted that the twelve most-popular Premier League and Major League Soccer games during Thanksgiving week had television audiences of between 203,000 and 744,000 viewers. While not great numbers for one of the "major" sports in the United States, for soccer over the last several decades, these numbers are not bad at all, especially given the upward trajectory of the Premier League ratings over time.[4] After making this note, Fleming drops the real bomb of the article: the number of viewers for the Premier League and Major League Soccer, as impressive as they might have been, were completely eclipsed by the most popular soccer league (by television viewers) in the United States: Liga MX, Mexico's professional soccer league. As Fleming observed, "Univision's TUDN—the self-proclaimed 'home of soccer in the U.S.'—lived up to its billing while drawing a total audience of 2.5 million for Saturday's decisive second leg in El Súper Clásico between Chivas and América. That total is the highest-rated soccer match on any American network in 2020, regardless of language."[5] This figure more than doubles the number of viewers for the 2021 MLS final.[6]

Again, one of the telling aspects of the reports concerning the dominance of Liga MX games in US television ratings (and this is a very routine observation on blogs and news sites) is that, almost every time, the report makes it clear that she or he assumes that the article's readers are surprised by this fact. Indeed, a quick Google search for "Most Popular Soccer on US television" retrieves an article that begins, "It's a very interesting question. Which football league is the most popular in terms of TV viewership in the United States? The *Bundesliga*? No. Major League Soccer? No. English Premier League? No. The answer is the top tier of Mexican football, Liga MX."[7] Similarly, Dan Adu-Gyamfi of *World Soccer Talk* begins an article about the ways one can find Liga MX broadcast in English (the default is in Spanish, although you can find the broadcast in English on some supplemental channels) by saying, "Believe it or not, the most popular soccer league in the U.S. based on television ratings is Liga MX."[8] Note the options the first writer assumes his or her audience will run through and the expectation of surprise in the second. Of course, it is an enigma only if one somehow ignores the large Mexican American audience (which is, evidently, easy for MLS and Premier League fans and reporters to do), but the fact that it is a surprise is telling of just how little English-language sports reporting in the United States discusses Liga MX at all. When reporters ask, "If most soccer fans can't name a single team in Liga MX, how is it the most popular league?" they are of course positing "U.S. soccer fan" by somehow, paradoxically (and not ironically), not including fans of the most-watched league as soccer fans.

Many MLS fans find it further baffling that the gap in television ratings between Liga MX and MLS hasn't narrowed much at all, even as MLS continues to grow in size (number of teams, overall number of attendees at games) and visibility (in terms of showing up in sports reports online and elsewhere). Indeed, reporter Christopher Harris observed in *World Soccer Talk* that MLS, despite its steady growth in the number of fans in live attendance at games (obviously, pre-Covid), MLS was getting no closer whatsoever to closing the gap between its viewers of either the Premier League or Liga MX.[9] While it is true that Liga MX's television ratings are not rising a lot, neither are those of MLS. While geographically much closer to the United States than, say, the Premier League, the fact that its broadcasts are mostly in Spanish and because many MLS soccer fans identify their ancestry in Europe rather than Mexico, positions Liga MX as so foreign as to be invisible in the daily life of fandom.

In addition to being a somewhat interesting tidbit of information for reporters, the situation is also one fraught with economic concerns for both leagues. MLS needs to have its ratings grow in order to demand television contracts that would bring in enough revenue to make the teams profitable. As Graham Ruthven of *The Guardian* notes of MLS's prospects in the future: "2022 and the new TV deal negotiated to start then will reveal a lot about where MLS stands. If there is no real progress by then, either in the growth of TV audiences or in the money pulled in through rights, MLS may have to consider taking a different route [than the traditional sports route of relying on television revenue to make up for losses]."[10] Similarly, because Liga MX is facing dropping attendance at its home grounds, its television ratings need to rise, and, as Mark Goodman Asher observes, it very specifically needs the revenue that comes from the audience that lives in the United States.[11] Theoretically, of course, it is possible for both leagues to increase the size of their audiences (in both the US and Mexico, as well as other countries). That is, this is not necessarily a zero sum game.

More specifically, it should of course be possible for both leagues to find ways to increase their viewership in the United States. As Laurent Dubois observes of soccer in an age of digital access to soccer leagues from around the world, "fandom no longer had to be local. You could read or hear or watch any team play, and fall in love."[12] The effects of satellite and digital "broadcasting" of soccer, however, are contradictory and mixed. Because digital access and outreach can allow fans to "feel" as if a geographically distant team is local (after all, if I can constantly engage in a team's outreach and games, it is as local as a team that is in physical proximity), that can help a team to build a global audience. However, this in effect multiplies the number of teams one can follow, and, because no one has infinite time, it provides competition for teams that are actually geographically local.

As a result, the influence of global access has cut in a number of different ways. For instance, as Franklin Foer once noted, in writing about globalization and soccer, "I kept noticing the way that globalization has failed to diminish the game's local cultures, local blood feuds, and even local corruption."[13] At the time of his writing, what Foer said was relatively true, and it remains so in a number of nations. However, the situation is also changing in places as media access to the global game continues to improve. As David Goldblatt has illustrated in his look at global football, globalization has absolutely damaged some local cultures' games. For example, African soccer leagues have been "marginalized culturally and reduced to penury" with the arrival of satellite television, as there has been a "mass export of fans' affections and custom to European football in general, and the English Premier League in particular."[14] The fan base of many African leagues has been decimated as fan attention has turned to Europe. Hence, while globalism in many ways has loosened the necessary bounds one has to supporting the geographically local and opened up opportunities for leagues to spread their fan base outwards, this does not happen for every league or every team. While theoretically the African league teams could have been building their global fan base, the behemoth of the Premier League has in many ways supplanted the support of those local teams, broadening the popularity of the Premier League while shrinking the popularity of the geographically local leagues.

The relative popularity of different leagues and the shifts in fandom are based on a number of metrics or beliefs, of course. If one league is seen as superior in skill and "stardom," that certainly provides reason for attention to be drawn toward it. Anyone who has been around soccer fans long enough will hear fans say, in a matter-of-fact way, "Well, the Premier League [or other league] is clearly the best league in the world." You will also hear the inverse of this equation at times (e.g., "The reason I don't watch Major League Soccer is that it's not as good as the Premier League"). However, given that these are often the same types of people who can enjoy fandom at a variety of levels in other sports (e.g., both NBA and NCAA basketball), we know that ideology, of course, is also raising its head in this equation. Hence, when we turn to the popularity of soccer in the United States in this particular moment, we have something of a puzzle.

First, in terms of the quality of play of these three leagues, most everyone would agree that the Premier League would be at the pinnacle in terms of quality (the value of their contracts and the visibility of their players on national teams would confirm this), but almost everyone, until relatively recently perhaps, would have placed Liga MX's quality above that of MLS. While some of this would simply be based on observation, some of it is based on game-day experience. To the point, the best teams from each of those leagues (as well as other clubs from Central America and the Caribbean) also compete head to head each year in Concacaf Champions League. Since the current structure of the Champions League began in 2008, it has been won every time by a Mexican team.[15] While MLS teams are making it further into the tournament now than a decade ago, it remains something of a point of pride for Liga MX fans (and the league's front office) that it has been a given that one of their teams would succeed. If based on quality alone, then, one would expect the general attention to be on the Premier League first, Liga MX second and MLS third. And yet Liga MX has he highest television ratings in the US, albeit ratings that are held up almost exclusively by Mexican immigrants to the United States. The games are primarily broadcast in Spanish, and if one searches for news about Liga MX in the US, one will rarely find much that isn't related to MLS in English-speaking news outlets. Liga MX is a quality league, then, but one that is almost invisible in terms of non-Mexican-immigrant audiences.

Secondly, while Liga MX clearly outperforms MLS in terms of US television ratings, MLS is both continuing to grow and expand. By 2023 there will be thirty different teams in MLS, while Liga MX will be limited to twenty. Franchise fees in MLS are skyrocketing, with the fee for the club to be housed in Charlotte costing $325 million dollars, dwarfing the cost of franchise fees in Liga MX. More, Erik Siemers of the *St. Louis Business Journal* notes that the $200 million fee St. Louis paid for a team was 500 percent higher than franchise fees only a decade prior.[16] The attendance figures in both leagues are relatively the same per game, with Liga MX having a slightly higher number (although MLS has a larger number of attendees as a whole, given the larger number of clubs).[17] Nonetheless, while Liga MX has been in great shape compared to MLS in certain metrics, financial bets seem to be being placed on MLS, with Liga MX, through various spokespersons, expressing a great deal of fear about MLS becoming dominant as it continues to grow.

The stakes right now are high, then, for both leagues. It is in the discussion of the strengths and weaknesses of Liga MX, and the competition between Liga MX and MLS for larger market shares, that I argue we are witnessing what can best be seen as a *neoliberal logic at the level of the corporation* (rather than the individual) that ignores the way both concentration of capital and Eurocentric biases operate to undercut "fair" or free market competition for a fan base. In looking at the "translation" of values, rather than looking at how the Premier League is translated in normalized US hegemonic values, I am interested in how the values of the free market (rather than, say, the ideology of American exceptionalism, nativism, or racism) are used to explain the assumed eventual success of MLS. That is, the discourse here largely ignores the ways MLS is positioned financially and rhetorically in ways that favor its growth over Liga MX, and only by ignoring this discourse is the understanding of a free and fair global market sustained. In what follows I turn first to the ways Liga MX (or those who speak for/about it) is situated (as a league as well as in terms of individual Mexican players) as superior to MLS. Second, I turn to the ways Liga MX discusses its stagnation, the growth of MLS, and the blueprint for the future, making note of the ways these discussions highlight the "superior business model" and visibility of MLS without making note of some of the ideological and material reasons for these differences. It is in and through these arguments that I illustrate the "corporate neoliberal" logic that ignores the conditions (based on race, based on wealth) that hinder Liga MX and provide support for MLS.

Ratings and Skill: Liga MX's Argument for Dominance

Liga MX is shown in the United States on television through the cable/satellite channel (Spanish-language) Univision's TUDN. While it can be watched broadcast in English through supplementary online streams, the games are largely broadcast in Spanish. In multiple news reports about Liga MX, especially those quoting representatives of the league, the focus on ratings dominance for Liga MX over other leagues within the United States is held up as a sign of superiority of the league. Hence, for example, in a news release regarding Univision TUDN's decision in late 2020 to telecast the final game of one-half of the soccer season (Liga MX breaks the season in half, with a winner for the Apertura half and a winner for the Clausura half), readers learn that "Univision's TUDN, the Home of Soccer in the U.S., will bring *fanaticos* all the action" and that "so far, with the semifinal and final rounds still to play, the Liga MX playoffs on Univision's networks have delivered three of the four top-rated matches of 2020 on any network and in any language, showcasing why it remains the most-watched soccer league in the US."[18] Similarly, in an article about the possibility of playing Liga MX games outside of Mexico, reporter Perry Kostidakis observes, "It can also enable Liga MX to further explore opportunities in an American market that already prefers watching the Mexican League, according to some television ratings."[19] Similarly, in a report on the financial incentives of broadcasting games to the US, readers are informed, "There is a population of 57 million Latinos in the United States, more than 63% of Mexican origin,"[20] and that Liga MX is extraordinarily popular with this audience.

Mainstream English-language US publications (and websites) also note this disparity in television ratings. Again, such articles are almost always written in a way that highlights the discrepancy while acknowledging that it is not what most readers would expect, given that their coverage focuses on MLS and the Premier League. For example, John Marthaler of the Minneapolis *Star Tribune* observes the contradiction between the leagues that garner a lot of mainstream press attention and actual television ratings: "MLS is the American Soccer league, and the English Premier League might get the most American media coverage, but the viewership statistics don't lie. More American soccer fans watch Liga MX, the Mexican top division, than any other soccer league."[21] Similarly, Kevin Baxter of the *LA Times*, in an article specifically about the TV ratings for soccer in the US, observes, "The English Premier League is the most-watched sports league in the world. But in the US, it isn't even the most-viewed soccer league. . . . Liga MX averaged 1.1 million viewers each week, while NBC averages 19% less each weekend with the Premier League."[22] Like Marthaler of the *Star Tribune*, Baxter writes the article because the idea that Liga MX has higher ratings comes as a surprise to most readers, many of whom are only vaguely aware of Liga MX. Baxter notes that the unfamiliarity is likely because the games are all broadcast in Spanish on Univision and are watched mostly by people who immigrated from Mexico and see the league as a "postcard from home."[23] When the reports are written for a Spanish-speaking audience, the ratings are simply pointed to as a matter of pride and superiority. On the other hand, when the essays are written for a mainstream US audience and in English (e.g., the Minneapolis *Star Tribune*), the author will acknowledge that Liga MX has higher ratings than either MLS or the Premier League, but the logic of the articles also in a larger sense marginalizes those ratings by underlining that the viewers are "other," alien within the United States (e.g., Mexican Americans who are looking for "postcards from home"). It is not a matter of the legal status of the Mexicans living in the United States (i.e., they could all be US citizens); instead, it is a matter of positing them as other. They speak a different language and are still fascinated by sports from a different country, which is referred to as their "home." In this logic Americans watch MLS and the Premier League, while visitors, away from home, watch Liga MX.

In addition to higher ratings, those who speak of the superiority of Liga MX often do so by pointing to the superiority of Mexican players at the level of skill. While this ultimately proves to be a problematic argument when more Mexican players sign on to play for MLS sides, the superiority of players and Liga MX teams is often pointed to (as in the epigraph of the chapter) as an explanation of the superiority of the league as a whole. For example, Joani Cruz of *CE Noticias Financieras* suggests that one advantage that Liga MX has over MLS is its "marked difference" on the pitch, as evidenced by the ways the MLS teams lost to Mexican clubs during Concacaf Champions League matches.[24] Similarly, in an article titled, "MLS Grew, But Still Doesn't Reach Liga MX," focusing on the growth of MLS as a league, Mexican players observed that while MLS may be improving, Liga MX teams still maintained "hegemony in this (Champions League) tournament."[25]

When reporters place their focus on the way MLS has recently improved in quality compared to Liga MX, players and commissioners from Liga MX routinely observe that a great deal of this improvement has been due to former Liga MX players moving to MLS teams. For example, in an article titled, "Carlos Vela, the Mexican Looking to Dethrone the Liga MX in Concacaf," the reader is first reminded that Liga MX teams have dominated Concacaf Champions League, winning it all fourteen years of its existence. The streak is threatened, however, primarily because former Liga MX star Carlos Vela has moved to MLS's Los Angeles Football Club (LAFC) and has been "a sensation since his arrival in the United States," immediately taking his team to the finals of Champions League.[26] Both the article and its title make LAFC's potential victory more a *product* of Vela, the Mexican player, than of either MLS as an improving league or of LAFC as a quality team. In a different investigation of the increasing competition between the leagues, Julia Poe notes in the *Orlando Sentinel* that Mexican star Javier "Chicharito" Hernández decided to go from the Premier League to MLS rather than return to Liga MX, and that nine other Mexican players moved to MLS from Liga MX during the off-season. In effect, the article preserves the superiority of Mexican players, allowing that to account for the difference in quality of MLS sides.[27] Similarly, Francisco González argues that MLS teams have reached a quality never seen before by signing multiple Mexican players. If Mexican players continue to move to MLS, he notes, there is concern that it will topple Liga MX.[28] Marthaler argues that it is clear that MLS is closing the gap between itself and Liga MX, and that one primary reason is by making it an attractive location for Mexican stars to turn toward.[29] Finally, Oswaldo Alanis, a Mexican defender for the San Jose Earthquakes, suggests in a recent interview that in addition to better business practices and stronger infrastructure, one of the reasons MLS is improving is the "arrival of Mexican footballers"; he notes that a lot of changes have improved the league, but the main factor is "all the players of the MX League who are coming here, players like us, who are Mexicans, who are also taking this option."[30]

Hence, over the past decade (at least), those who discuss Liga MX (primarily from the perspective of Liga MX) in the context of MLS have felt comfortable highlighting its higher popularity (via television ratings), the superiority of the teams in head-to-head competition, and the superiority of the skills of those who play in Liga MX. As MLS continues to grow, however, in terms of attendance, number of teams, and overall quality, the discourse around MLS is placed into a strange set of puzzles and contradictions. On the one hand, as illustrated above, explanations for the improvement of the league skill-wise can be accounted for by the immigration of Mexican players, hence preserving some of the prestige of Liga MX. That said, the growth of MLS is clearly a threat to how Liga MX has positioned itself in the past, and there is evident concern about what the continued growth of MLS might mean for Liga MX financially and in terms of future growth. Consequently, as I illustrate below, as the two leagues begin a process of discussing multiple partnerships, those who speak for Liga MX will articulate more thoroughly the ways that MLS has managed its growth and why, in fact, MLS threatens to overtake Liga MX in both quality and popularity. That is, while attempting to maintain an argument about the superiority of Liga MX, the growth of MLS forces representatives of Liga MX to provide an explanation for the growing popularity of a "lesser" league. It is, in an odd sense, a translation of the meaning of Liga MX within US culture at large. These arguments fit snugly within a logic of neoliberalism, while ignoring structural and ideological factors that benefit the US league over the Mexican.

Liga MX-MLS Partnership

In May 2019 Major League Soccer and Liga MX announced a partnership that would include an annual competition called the Leagues Cup, in which four teams from Liga MX and four MLS teams, assumedly the best teams in each league, would be invited to compete against one another. In addition MLS announced that its annual All-Star game would put MLS All-Stars up against Liga MX All-Stars, rather than against one of the European clubs who were on their summer tours.[31] The partnership, both the tournament and the All-Star game, is intended to be mutually beneficial for the two leagues. The tournament would allow MLS to market itself (or at least make itself more familiar) to Mexicans and Mexican Americans who earlier had paid it little attention, while allowing Liga MX teams to play in front of its sizable US audience live and perhaps draw the attention of new US fans who follow MLS and/or the Premier League.

While the announcement was exciting for fans of either league, it was also an event that led to the production of a good deal of discourse centered on the motivations for the partnership. There are certainly numerous arguments to be made about how the merger would benefit both leagues, and yet the arguments posited that while Liga MX was suffering financially or stalling, MLS was growing. Regardless of the actual motivations, the discourse drew up a situation in which Liga MX—despite its much higher television ratings—was stumbling and threatening to fail in the pathway of MLS growth. While, as I point out above, Liga MX and its supporters were consistently making note of their strong television ratings and better talent on the pitch, it simultaneously found itself in a position in which individual teams were not prospering economically and were losing players to MLS while watching MLS grow new franchises at higher fees, hire more international players, and attract a growing live audience.

In the section below, I work through the public discussion of the differences between the leagues and the motivation for the tournament. I wish to stress that, rather than acknowledging what would seem to be rather obvious problems in the sense that viewers in the US and Europe position Liga MX as "other" and MLS as "familial," those who speak for Liga MX more readily attest to the "business savvy" of MLS and the need for Liga MX to learn to better compete in the open market. Thus, while those speaking for Liga MX focus on multiple ways they should improve their production and compete with MLS, they do so without acknowledging the types of ideological and material factors that work against them and in favor of MLS.

Visibility, Infrastructure, Business Savvy: Liga MX's Case for MLS

Press coverage of Liga MX over the past decade has increasingly pointed to the financial difficulties faced by both the league as a whole and by individual teams within the league. For example, in December 2020, reporter Fred Figuero wrote that Mike Andoni Arriola Peñalosa had been hired by Liga MX to help turn about the financial failings of the league and help it "generate growth conditions, maximize assets."[32] Joani Cruz reported that attendance was starting to dwindle at Liga MX games for multiple reasons (e.g., there had a been a lot of geographic dislocation of people who were also soccer fans; the atmosphere at games was less "family friendly" than in the past) and that this drop in attendance was of course leading to an overall drop in revenue.[33] One issue repeatedly pointed out is that the league allowed individual teams to sort out individual television contracts, rather than have the league as a whole negotiate, meaning that teams were receiving uneven amounts of revenue, unlike in many other leagues, including MLS.[34] Moreover, a report titled "The Crisis of Owners in the Liga MX" points out that Liga MX and its owners have never learned to craft a sustainable business model for the league, as illustrated by the convolution of television contracts.[35]

The discourse around Liga MX's financial problems simultaneously, and persistently, refers to the financial strength of MLS as a league as well as that of individual teams. While many who observe MLS wonder how financially sound the league is, often referring to it as a pyramid or Ponzi scheme[36] (in short, even with fairly strong attendance, the television rights can be bought for very low fees compared to other major US sports, and each team has several very highly paid players, but rapidly growing franchise fees keep the league afloat), the discourse derived from the discussion of Liga MX vs. MLS illustrates a belief in the financial soundness and financial savvy of MLS. Joani Cruz reports that Liga MX teams are looking at the sound financial business model of MLS and hoping to learn new business practices from working with it.[37] Erendira Hernández reports that representatives from Liga MX suggested that the league thought it needed to copy aspects of the US league if it hopes to grow and survive. Moreover, the owners expressed concern that the growth in quality of MLS, based on its better business model, threatens to further undermine the strength of Liga MX.

According to this set of arguments, two of the routes by which MLS has shown more fundamental business sense than Liga MX is, first, by having multiple entrepreneurs and owners in the league and, second, by stronger development of academies throughout all the league to generate revenue through the sale of players.[38] Julie Poe reports that in attempting to understand Mexican soccer players' shift in attitude toward MLS (i.e., they have in general become much more impressed with it as a league and potential destination for their own careers), notes that the US league was simply "steps beyond" Liga MX in terms of understanding the importance of strong infrastructure in growing the league.[39] In an editorial Elihũ Hernández argues that while there is no shortage of patriotic "analysts" in Mexico who attempt to act as if Liga MX is among the best soccer leagues in the world, the truth is that the United States is leaving Liga MX behind because they had enough business savvy to market and brand the league as a whole rather than as individual teams.[40] Marthaler argues that one reason Liga MX is beginning to falter is that they have not worked hard enough to make inroads into non-Mexican audiences in the United States.[41] In short, then, over the most recent couple of years, reports indicate that Liga MX sees itself losing its luster compared to MLS (despite the continued gap in television ratings, despite the lack of a sizable national audience for MLS). The supposed business savvy of the US league is said to be one reason they have been able to outdo Liga MX.

Liga MX looks at the success of MLS also through the way the latter has made itself more acceptable to European viewers. When Javier "Chicharito" Hernández joined the Los Angeles Galaxy in 2020, he told reporters that he had no qualms about joining MLS rather than Liga MX, because MLS had made itself more visible and more watched globally, especially in Europe.[42] Liga MX club Monterrey manager Javier Aguirre observes that one reason Liga MX is starting to suffer compared to MLS is that, on a global level, it is simply not as visible. "The Mexican (League) is not seen," he notes. "You don't see the Concacaf, you don't see the Gold Cup."[43] An article focusing on attempts to internationalize Liga MX observed that while the league is a "good product," it is really watched only within Mexico and the US, leaving itself invisible to Europe, Asia, and most of the Americas. What is seen is MLS, and the Mexican League needs to learn this lesson. Recently, prior to the Concacaf Champions League matchup between Los Angeles Football Club and León, LAFC's Dutch goalkeeper Kenneth Vermeer asserted that one reason he chose to sign with an MLS club is that "in Europe the football seen is from the United States Professional League (MLS) not the Liga MX."[44] Vermeer observed that he felt very comfortable with MLS because he had been watching it on television in Europe for several years and had become a "great connoisseur of MLS," while knowing little about Liga MX's existence.[45] Finally, in a side-by-side comparison of the two leagues, including the star power of the leagues, Joani Cruz observes that the paucity of stars in Liga MX "has to do with the low international profile of the league, which is difficult to see in continents such as Europe. Mexican football is also affected by the proximity to MLS, which eventually attracts the eyes of the world by lifestyle, wages, and projection."[46]

While Liga MX has partnerships to help provide global marketing and streaming,[47] the reports above repeat a theme that posits Liga MX as relatively invisible outside of Mexico itself (save the Mexican market inside the United States border). Indeed, part of the issue is reportedly that even when Liga MX signs foreign players to teams, they find it difficult to pick up viewers from the home countries of those players.[48] One need only look at the number of Christian Pulisic jerseys from Chelsea FC that are now worn by numerous people in the United States to know that this is a route by which teams/leagues often draw "foreign" viewers and sales.

Liga MX and the Perils of Corporate Neoliberalism

While some have argued that the globalization of the game never fully undermines the local (as Simon Kuper observes, while globalization may begin to melt borders, there is always a countercosmopolitan kickback that reestablishes those ideological borders),[49] the effects of globalism are certainly not even. In the case here, we find a situation in which, while Liga MX has for years been the highest-rated televised soccer league in the United States, it has never been very visible in the English-speaking press or among the large number of US fans not of Mexican ancestry. Moreover, while it has also been clearly the superior league in terms of head-to-head matchups of soccer teams, this, too, has received little attention in the English-language press. Hence, representatives for Liga MX and reporters writing about the league have persistently made claims that it was superior because its players were better.

As MLS has continued to grow in size, visibility, and franchise fees, and as Liga MX has experienced financial difficulties, Liga MX has felt an increased need not only to partner with MLS in order to find routes for financial stabilization but also to explain why MLS has continued to improve. Ultimately, because Mexican players are still positioned as "superior" in skill, one route for explaining the growth of MLS is that the "better" Mexican players have moved to MLS, raising its level of competition while lowering that of Liga MX. That said, however, those players have often moved to MLS because of better pay, better infrastructure and better visibility in Europe (where the players might ultimately wish to move in their careers).

Therefore, Liga MX officials and those reporting on the league are placed in a position of making sense of the reasons why MLS is better financially established and how they have made themselves more visible globally. What is most remarkable about this discourse is what is not said: there is little exploration of the ways that the very large MLS franchise fees allow a constant influx of cash based on financial potential rather than "real" income. That is, the league is continuing to grow, in part from the finances of the teams' owners, while not necessarily producing overall profits based on the promise of future income (i.e., until the league's television viewership rises, television contracts still do not have enough value to spread amongst the teams).

Secondly, there is little discussion that the visibility of the Premier League to the US audience and the visibility of MLS to the European audience are based on mutual recognition of a reflection of European heritage (not that the US league is all white, any more than the Premier League is—it's more that the broadcast, language, and ownership reflect). Let's not forget that David Goldblatt observes that despite overt and open efforts in English football to fight racism, news reports of racist incidents at games occur routinely (as illustrated herein, in chapter 5).[50] Hence, with no or little concern with the way Europeans and white Americans reflect each other and are more comfortable watching each other, the ghettoization of Liga MX and its falling power in the marketplace are posited as simply the fair effects of competition, ignoring the effects and influence of racism and economic inequality.

Ultimately, the logic of La Liga's turn to partner with MLS and to explain the ways they are stalling in comparison to MLS is a form of what could best be described as "corporate neoliberalism." In a way, to discuss neoliberalism as "corporate neoliberalism" is something of a contradiction, as neoliberalism in large part places focus on the behavior of the individual in the community, not corporations but the ability of individuals to move freely in the economy, succeeding through their own wits. Indeed, this is how the story of the fall and rise of the leagues is translated through news outlet narratives.

Multiple people in critical studies have discussed neoliberalism, its history and its effect. In doing so the focus is generally placed on its influence on the ideology and actions of individuals. Recall that in *The Burnout Society*, Byung-Chul Han suggests that we have moved ideologically to a space beyond Foucault's disciplinary society,[51] to a "society of achievement," with a fixation on the individual as an "entrepreneur of self."[52] The idea of the entrepreneur of self fits snugly within any thesis concerning the neoliberal marketplace (e.g., labor, social, political). Indeed, the current public conversation situates all social actors as working within markets, whether or not money is at stake.[53] Because the focus is placed on the individual working "on oneself constantly to survive competition," neoliberal logic denies the ways racism, sexism, classism, etc. work against individual actors.[54] By "flattening difference and discounting inequality, a neoliberal public assumes that everyone can adopt the position of *homo oeconomicus*."[55] In each chapter of this book, to varying degrees, I have pointed out the ways that this neoliberal logic influences the ways actions and arguments are shaped. It appears here, then, if in an amended sense.

While focusing on leagues rather than individuals, there remains something of the logic of neoliberalism at work in the arguments regarding the relative success and failure of MLS and Liga MX in an international market. Rather than individuals competing in the marketplace and encouraged to compete as individuals against each other (without acknowledging issues like systemic racism, sexism, or unequal starting positions in terms of wealth), this is a case of Liga MX and its representatives positioning the league as in global competition with other leagues. As a result, rather than underscoring some of the differences in the current successes of the leagues as reflecting implicit racism (otherism) and differences in capital, Liga MX is more simply positioned as not having the same business savvy to succeed or grow as well as MLS. Like an individual who positions himself or herself as needing to become more flexible and skilled in order to succeed in the market despite the many systemic strikes against him or her, Liga MX is positioned as needing to develop better business acumen and savvy from MLS clubs. While there are no rules, of course, to account for individual consumers' preferences for one league over another, or for the holding of capital with which to bet on the future, the ability to articulate these differences, to point out the ways no market is fully free, leads to a more useful public dialogue.

5

What Is American Exceptionalism *Doing* in a Place like This?

"The numbers speak for themselves," [Hope] Solo said. "We are the best in the world, have three world cup championships, four Olympic championships, and the USMNT get paid more to just show up than we get paid to win major champions."

—Amanda Gonzalez, "US Women's National Team Stars Fighting for Equal Pay on Soccer Field," *Hilltop Views*

There is no compromising on equal pay. Equal is equal.

—Rachel Bachman, "U.S. Soccer Offers Women Equal Pay in Some Matches—and They Reply, Do Better," *Wall Street Journal*

The core fact is not in dispute: The players on the World Cup–winning United States women's national soccer team earn less money than their counterparts on the men's national team. After that truth, things are muddier. How much less? How can that be fair? And most important: What is being done about it? . . . What we found suggests a complicated battlefield.

—Andrew Das, "Pay Disparity in U.S. Soccer? It's Complicated," *New York Times*

For those who watched, it's difficult to forget the moments after the US Women's National Team (USWNT) won the 2019 World Cup against the Netherlands. While the sold-out crowd in Lyon began by cheering the team, they quickly changed their tune and began chanting "Equal pay!" as the team were awarded their medals. The next week, when the team took the stage for a celebration ceremony at New York City Hall, once again the crowd began to chant "Pay them!" and "Equal pay!" The cheers were notably directed at (then) US Soccer Federation (USSF)[1] president Carlos Cordeiro.

The timing for this public fight for equal pay was in some ways perfect for the players. Not only had they just won another World Cup (and with record television ratings), but this victory came on the heels of the US Men's National Team (USMNT) not even qualifying for their most recent World Cup. How extraordinary that moment of their victory felt. The USWNT was not only World Cup champion but seemed larger than life, heroic in an almost transcendent fashion. Indeed, its success has been so impressive that Andrei Markovits and Steven Hellerman that not only were the best players in the world coming from the United States but the women "represent the best chance in this country to traverse the vast divide between [soccer as] activity and [as] culture."[2] To top it off, Megan Rapinoe, their captain, stood, walked, and talked as if she represented a progressive version of the entire nation.

When their argument for equal pay—an argument between the USSF and USWNT that had a long history—became an integral part of any discussion about them, many people were hearing about it for the first time, and many of those were sympathetic to it. With comparison charts appearing on social media that simplified the level of pay on a game-to-game basis, it seemed outrageous to have national heroes treated so shabbily. And while numbers can never "speak for themselves," as much as Hope Solo may want them to, arguments that made the numbers appear transparent rather than the "complicated battleground" the *New York Times*'s Andrew Das describes in the third epigraph, were the most highly effective ones, traded back and forth over Twitter and Facebook. The optics of the moment clearly favored the women's overall position.[3]

The history of the relationship between the USSF and the USWNT has always been somewhat fraught. While the USSF has been fairly supportive of the USWNT (e.g., they put themselves at financial risk in staging the 1999 Women's World Cup), especially when compared to how other national women's teams have been supported historically, they have also consistently negotiated different collective bargaining agreements (CBA) for the men's and women's teams that have provided the men with better compensation as well as better work and travel conditions. While the current crisis can be said to have roots in the very beginning of the relationship, it is more illuminating to begin to look at the arguments since the 2015 Women's World Cup, because it is at that moment, with the team more popular than ever, that the team (via five of the players) requested a right-to-sue decision from the Equal Employment Opportunity Commission and a renegotiated CBA.[4] While moving forward with the pursuit of a legal case, the USWNT signed a new contract that would run through 2021. The new CBA gave the women raises in their base pay, bonuses, and better provisions for travel and accommodations. Of this contract forward Alex Morgan noted, "It felt very empowering. Because there is a whole issue going on in the country as far as equal pay and the fight for the gender pay gap. And I felt really happy with the agreement that we reached and the fact that we can now do what we came for and play soccer."[5]

Regardless of Morgan's satisfaction with the contract at the time, the CBA still offered very different compensation than the one held by the USMNT. In short, the USWNT guarantees the players an annual salary with bonuses for winning games, while the men's CBA provides them with no salary but larger bonuses for simply playing the game, win or lose. Because most (all) of the men have higher-paying salaries with club teams than the women, the preference for a guaranteed salary by the women seems reasonable. The specifics, however, did not work out in the women's financial interests.[6] Simply put, in the first year of the contract (the pay rose nominally each year), each USWNT player received $72,000 from the USSF to play at least twenty friendlies. In addition the players would receive a bonus of $1,350 for each win but no additional compensation for a loss or draw. Ultimately, if the team lost or drew all twenty games, each woman would receive $72,000, and if they won, $99,000. For the men, there was no base pay, and the men were paid only for those games for which they were chosen to play. However, the compensation ran about $7,000 per game, regardless of the outcome. If a player was chosen to appear in twenty different games and lost them all, he would earn $100,000. If he won them all, he would receive $263,320 that year. In addition, there were some marginal differences in the per diems the men and women received ($75 vs. $60), as well as different working conditions (e.g., the women were not guaranteed to play on grass and did not travel on chartered flights, as did the men).[7] On the one hand, "the numbers speak for themselves" in the sense that the women clearly are not being paid at the same rate as the men. On the other, the USWNT players had a guaranteed base, while there was no individual US male player who was guaranteed to ever be chosen to play for the team. More, this is all bound up in the fact that the USWNT and the USMNT both had expressed satisfaction with their CBAs at the time they were signed.

When the five USWNT players (Carli Lloyd, Alex Morgan, Megan Rapinoe, Becky Sauerbrunn, and Hope Solo) received the right-to-sue letter from the EEOC in early 2019, they moved forward with the suit, despite having signed the CBA only a few years earlier. As it turned out, with many victories in hand and a growing status as "American heroes," they had a full stage to continue to build their case for equal pay in the public eye. Indeed, the case seemed like such a no-brainer that it was something of a shock when, on May 1, 2020, federal judge R. Gary Klausner ruled in favor of the USSF's motion for summary judgment with regard to the Equal Pay Act, stating that the players "have not demonstrated a triable issue that WNT players are paid less than MNT players."[8] Klausner noted that the women had actually received higher compensation annually than the men (this, however, because the women played far more games and went further in tournaments than the men) and, significantly, that the differences in payment structure were the result of choices made by the women's players in their CBA and by the men in their separate agreement. As a result, the differences for Klausner were differences in negotiation, not differences based on discrimination.

In December 2020, the USSF and the USWNT announced that they had reached an agreement that made all work and travel conditions equal between the USMNT and USWNT, but it did not address equal pay or back pay.[9] While the women are continuing to appeal the decision legally, much of the public discourse around the meaning of equal pay and of the *justifications* for it, have settled. In the give-and-take in public arguments between various of the USWNT players (most notably Megan Rapinoe), statements by the USSF (including the rather boneheaded legal arguments that the women did not perform work of equal skill, effort, or responsibility), and, perhaps most importantly, editorial claims made by a number of writers, we find a very particular argument and justification for equal pay.[10] It is this public argument, rather than the specific legal argument, that engages me as someone interested in the meanings circulating in popular culture and the ways these meanings affect and influence our overall ideology.

Here, in the first of two chapters looking at the intersections of neoliberalism, social movements, and soccer, rather than investigate the legal claims for equal pay (for which I very much sympathize with the USWNT), I am interested in, and quite frankly troubled by, some of the justifications put forth for equal, and sometimes unequal, pay. Because the arguments for equal pay are made at the intersection of changing norms of gender/sport with the circumstance of the women's team playing the role of the purveyors of American exceptionalism and the USMNT seen as not only lesser, but as failures, the arguments for equal pay are ofttimes an inversion, rather than a displacement, of historical arguments in favor of higher pay for the USMNT. As a result, while the arguments for equal pay could (I say *should*) have been made on the grounds of the *principle* of equality itself,[11] the global success of the USWNT allows a reestablishment of elements of the ideology of American exceptionalism and neoliberalism—including individuality, personal responsibility, and winner-take-all economics—that the women and fans have inadvertently helped to restake. Again, much in the way that Abraham Khan is less interested in what baseball player Curt Flood "really meant" with his arguments than in how those arguments were covered in news media,[12] I am not suggesting that the USWNT or its representatives made these arguments, especially in court; instead, I argue, as I have throughout this book, that the public arguments made by the fan community (especially by those lost in the oneness of the fan community) tend back to the middle, back to familiar ideological arguments, in this case, back to a logic of neoliberalism.

In what follows I begin with an overview of the problematic history of women's soccer both as an idea and as practiced, and suggest the ways attempts to discipline or contain the sport continue to shape the arguments that are made in its favor. I then follow with an overview of the public (US arguments) made about the USWNT and equal pay, highlighting potential problematics. The arguments that seem to have the most resonance publicly are also arguments that potentially rebind us to problematic ideological logics. And that is precisely what American exceptionalism *does* in public argument.

When Women Play

In a poignant passage of *The Language of the Game*, Laurent Dubois describes his attendance at the 2015 Women's World Cup game in Montreal pitting the USWNT against the German women's team. Rather than focus on the game itself, Dubois provides a description of the "sound" of the fans that, in large part, was simultaneously the sound of change, of progress. Dubois tells us: "It was the sound of voices of many different ages, of children and elders, but most of all of both men and women, boys and girls. Many young women had come with their teams, wearing their own club jerseys, looking on with a mix of admiration and ambition."[13]

Clearly, football is a game that can be played and enjoyed by both men and women. So, the fact that even the sound and look of this crowd is so different as to signify change and progress begs a look into the history of women's football, where it began and why it did or didn't thrive. This understanding is important as well, of course, in understanding the (discursive, cultural, legal, contractual) situation in which the current USWNT finds itself. Fortunately, while there need to be many more thorough histories of women's soccer written globally, both Dubois[14] and Markovits and Rensman[15] have drawn added attention to Gail Newsham's fascinating *In a League of Their Own! The Dick, Kerr Ladies 1917–1965,*[16] to provide not only a brief history of women's soccer but also (and interconnectedly) a brief history of how and why women's soccer was disciplined and marginalized. The story Newsham tells is one of those narratives that is so to the point, such an extreme case of gender discipline, that it is somehow difficult to fathom. I should also add that without Newsham's recovery of the stories given by the women of *The Dick, Kerr Ladies* team, it is a narrative that may well have been forgotten.[17]

In the briefest terms, women's soccer has existed as long as soccer has existed. Moreover, women's organized soccer has also existed almost simultaneously with the men's game. Indeed, there were enough organized women's teams[18] in England in the 1880s to hold international competitions. While there were the expected concerns for that era that the physical activity might be dangerous for women's health or that it was immodest for men to watch women running around the pitch, numerous teams were formed, and the games drew rather large crowds. The most successful and most famous of these teams was The Dick, Kerr Ladies, and its story helps capture why Dubois hears the sound of change, even at this date so removed from its existence. Like a number of men's teams at the time, The Dick, Kerr Ladies football club was a factory team, organized by women who worked at the Dick, Kerr company in Preston, Lancashire. The company was mainly a locomotive and electrical equipment manufacturer, but during the first World War, it (like a lot of companies) turned to the manufacture of munitions and hired a great number of women to work the factory floor, as many of Preston's men had gone off to war. While Newsham's account provides a number of fascinating narratives of individual players and games that would be worth anyone's time to read,[19] what I want to stress here is that the team was extraordinarily successful in most ways that would matter for any soccer club. For example, when The Dick, Kerr Ladies invited a team representing France to play them for a series of matches to benefit war veterans, over twenty-five thousand people watched the first match; the two teams then went on a tour that took them to such grounds at Chelsea's Stamford Bridge. Later Dick, Kerr Ladies returned the favor by attending a number of games against the same team, this time in France. While playing upward of three times a week (while still working their factory jobs), the team raised a massive amount of money to benefit families affected by the war. In 1920 Dick, Kerr Ladies played a game at Everton's Goodison Park in Liverpool to a crowd of fifty-three thousand spectators (with a reported fifteen thousand more wishing to get in), at the time the second-largest soccer game ever played, for men or women. Had everyone who wanted to been able to get in, it would have been the largest game ever. The team played all over England, against around 150 other organized women's teams. In 1921 their record was sixty-seven wins, no draws, and no losses, with 448 goals for and 22 goals against. Their opponents were teams such as St. Helens, Scotland, Hull, Stoke, and Swansea, as well as teams composed of the all-stars of England as a whole (e.g., Dick, Kerr Ladies vs. The Best of the Rest of England). Moreover, it was not uncommon for there to be more than twenty thousand fans at their games, and newspaper coverage of the team was extensive. While some of the initial popularity may have been based on the curiosity of watching women play, by the end of 1921, it could be said that theirs was the most popular soccer team in England.

A few decades later, women's football barely existed and had largely disappeared (at least in organized form) from most nations around the globe. While Dick, Kerr Ladies continued on in different forms, they no longer played at professional football grounds and no longer could be said to be drawing crowds of the same noticeable size. So, what happened?

As Newsham and Dubois relate,[20] the popularity of the women's game made the leadership of the English Football Association nervous and take note, especially as some of the men's teams in the association struggled to draw crowds. The worry was twofold but, of course, interconnected: one, that competition from the women's game would draw fans away from the men's teams (indeed, it likely already was doing so), and two, that the game itself would come to be known as a "women's game" rather than as a men's game. The English Football Association Council passed a unanimous resolution (sixty in favor, none opposed) in 1921 declaring football unsuitable for women, and it followed this resolution with actions that were, on the surface, supposed to protect women. In short, it established a number of rules that made it very difficult for women to continue playing in any organized or large-scale manner: first, clubs belonging to the English Football Association were told to forbid female teams from playing matches at their grounds; second, credentialed referees were *not* allowed to work women's matches. Because these rules made it difficult for Dick, Kerr Ladies to play games in England, the women worked to organize a tour, a trip abroad. At this point, the English Football Association had enough global power to convince most other nations to ban the women from traveling or playing in their countries (significantly, however, given the different level of popularity here, Dick, Kerr Ladies did have a successful tour of the United States, often playing men's teams). Moreover, given the power of the English Football Association as a rule maker for the game, the English ban on women's football on professional grounds became a ban on women's football in most European and Latin American countries.

To stress, the women's game was disciplined both in terms of law (rules, regulations) and in terms of discourse. The relationship between rules (as material) and discourse is one in which each affects the other. As Hortense Spillers notes in a different context, "material values engender symbolic and discursive ones (and vice-versa) in perfect synecdochic harmony."[21] Hence, in both progressive and regressive or constraining ways, changes in one can shape changes in the other. This is important for how women's soccer was muted, how it arises in the United States, and how "equality" comes to be understood. In this case rules and regulations made it difficult, if not impossible, for women to play organized games, and they were coupled with discourse that underlined the sport as masculine and dangerous to women's health. This articulation was reified to such a degree that, as Markovits and Rensman note, in many places in the world, the phrase "women's football" seems incongruous. In the same way that Robbie Rogers understood "gay" to be incompatible as a category with "football player," such discourse has historically created an incompatibility between women and football. Recall Nick Hornby's description of his first experience at a game: "I remember the overwhelming maleness of it all—cigar and pipe smoke, foul language."[22] In chapter after chapter of David Goldblatt's *The Age of Football,* we see that this is largely a global issue. In South America, he notes, "It was easier for a woman to become the president of the country than the president of the national football federation."[23] In China "the fact of the women's teams and their tournament is a distantly second-rank concern."[24] Even where things seem to be changing, they are not: in 2018, "at a dinner celebrating FC Basel's 125th anniversary, the men's team ate and mingled with fans and dignitaries, while the women's team sold raffle tickets and ate sandwiches in a side room."[25] The Iranian film *Offside*[26] provides the narrative of women who simply wanted to watch the 2006 World Cup qualifying match between Iran's and Bahrain's men's teams and were not allowed into the stadium. Recall that as late as 1988, secretary of the English Football Association Ted Croker said of female players: "Football is a game of hard, physical contact, a form of combat. It is, and must remain, a man's game. Women have no place in it except to cheer on their men, wash and iron their kits and prepare and serve refreshments."[27] From an academic perspective, Lindsey Meận illustrates how male referees speak to male players as if they understand the rules of the game, while they speak to female players as if they do not.[28] Indeed, to differing degrees, this articulation is solid and nearly everywhere we look.

This combination of policies and attitudes, rules and discourse, then, has a long history, and while a change in articulations is taking place, not only do such changes not take place overnight, but the historic articulations continue to shape arguments in the present, something we need to understand as we look at the USWNT's fight for equal pay. The pressures of the past shape the arguments of the present. The weight of rules and perceptions is so heavy, in fact, as David Goldblatt notes, "after more than a century of almost unchallenged male domination of the game, on and off the pitch, and the saturation of its collective imagery and sense of self with masculinity, every women's game, every woman in the men's game, is an act of resistance, a reminder that another world is possible and necessary."[29] The success of the USWNT on and off the pitch is part of this changing world. Yet change, as I continue to stress, is always pulled back toward the center, especially in a sport relying so much on the kinship and community of fans.

Women's Soccer, Women's Football: A Different Kind of Exceptionalism

The dominance of the US Women's National Team in international soccer is undeniable.[30] While the skill and hard work of each generation of players keep the team dominant, clearly numerous factors go into this level of superiority. Just as we can look to the ways both discourse and regulations shut down "women's football clubs" in Europe, globally we can also look at policy and culture as factors for the success of women's soccer in the United States. As Brian Bunk illustrates in his recent history of soccer in the United States, it is not as if the nation covered itself in glory in terms of women's soccer in the US. While advocates for the game abounded, he finds a familiar history of women's soccer being a curiosity, a space for men to gaze upon women, and an overall marginalized event.[31] Similarly, Eileen Narcotta-Welp argues that to the degree that women's soccer was noticed, it violated the gendered space of sport and hence "distinctly aligned the game with the corruptive influences of modernization."[32]

Just after the USWNT's victory in the 2019 Women's World Cup, numerous articles appeared in publications pointing out the benefits of Title IX. My favorite of these, due both to the "factoids" it includes and the bluntness of its title: "USA's Formidable Women's Soccer Team Is No Accident. It's a Product of Public Policy."[33] Moira Donegan, the author, points out that Title IX created both more opportunity for women to play sports and, importantly, because its implications meant more athletic scholarships were available for women's sports, more incentive for women to continue to pursue athletics. As she notes, when Title IX was first passed in 1972, only seven hundred girls played soccer at the high school level in the entire United States. By 1991, the year of the first Women's World Cup, there were 121,722 high school girl players—a 17,289 percent increase. And the number has far more than doubled since then.[34] Those are astounding figures from any perspective. While the 1970s growth of the family-friendly North American Soccer League may have opened the door to a lot of recreational youth soccer that involved girls and young women, as Markovits and Hellerman observe,[35] it was Title IX that really altered the landscape. While Title IX sometimes seems like old news, it is important to underline how public policy such as this can be very, very effective in the long run and can help reshape popular discourse. Just as policy put the brakes on women's soccer in England and elsewhere, Title IX works as policy to encourage women's sports, including soccer. And while Title IX relies on tenets of liberal feminism rather than postfeminism, as Rachel Allison observes,[36] it nonetheless changed the horizon of possibilities. Material or rule changes, in this case, work to encourage a change in discourse and ideology.

Policy, I should add, was also working hand in hand in the United States with a very different cultural setting with very different public articulations for soccer as a sport. As Markovits and Rensman note, while the term "women's soccer" rolls off the tongue quite easily in the United States, the term "women's football" does not.[37] Importantly, however, for the longest time (but referring to a different sport), the term "women's football" also did not roll off the tongue well in Europe (as Gail Newsham's history of The Dick, Kerr Ladies illustrates). Ultimately, they argue, in the United States women were able to take up a sport that was not masculinized and became trailblazers. Meanwhile, in Europe, women were pushed away from the game precisely because it was so masculinized, and there was fear that feminization of the game would lead to lost popularity.

Indeed, while there are some other countries in which policy and feminist politics have produced strong women's soccer teams (e.g., Scandinavia), David Goldblatt's global survey of women's soccer still sees the support in the United States as fairly unique. For example, across Central America, there are female leagues, but Goldblatt notes, "Describing these leagues as professional, however, requires some imagination. Many clubs with women's teams, even wealthy ones like River Plate, offer no medical insurance . . . the players have to pay for this themselves from earnings of around $40 a week, which is around 1/200th of the average wage in the men's team."[38] While England, Germany, and France have begun taking the women's professional leagues more seriously (as a way to strengthen their national teams), most of the women in those leagues barely eke out a living.[39]

In short, women's soccer in the US is exceptional, in the sense that policy and culture have worked together to produce a space that is inviting and encouraging of success. While we could point to a number of other intersections that continue to be alive and perhaps fraught for the sport (e.g., the hyper-heterosexualization of some of the players on the one hand and the articulations between some players and lesbianism on the other), ultimately the exceptional combination of policy and discourse has crafted a space for women to be successful on the pitch. It has also put the women's team in a somewhat unique position that works into the arguments for equal pay. While, as Goldblatt pointed out elsewhere, following and cheering for the USMNT is in fact a practice of learning, at least for a moment, to forget the politics of American exceptionalism, cheering for the USWNT allows the firmest possible belief in American exceptionalism. As I hope to illustrate below, while arguments for equal pay born out of exceptionalism may in fact be fairly successful in altering pay scales, they also are unintentionally effective at rearticulating and reinforcing a modified form of neoliberalism. That is, rather than equal pay on the basis of principle, we begin to see arguments for equal (or better) pay on the basis of economic and athletic success. As I illustrate in each chapter herein, the public arguments that work are often the public arguments with which we collectively are most familiar. We thus pursue material change while reinforcing the rhetoric of "winner takes all."

Winnings, Revenue, and Popularity: The Problematics of Equal Pay

To understand the public logics through which equal pay is understood and justified regarding the USWNT, I gathered together two hundred news articles dealing with the issue.[40] The articles fall into a wide array of categories, from news items to editorials to open letters from politicians. What I illustrate below is that a strong case is made in public argument that articulates the specific pay situation of the USWNT to the historic and contemporary struggle for all women in the US to receive pay equal to their male counterparts.' More, by aligning the USWNT's struggle with the long-term struggle of women for equal pay, the arguments also tie the struggle to women of the future. Finally, this argument was being made in a rhetorical situation extraordinarily well situated for its success. Not only had the women performed well on the world stage, not only were they being touted as "American heroes," not only did they set record ratings for their World Cup final, but arguments made by the USSF suggesting that the women's game required less skill than the men's game were widely panned and criticized by corporate sponsors and public commentators. This was clearly a crystallizing moment allowing for rapid change, new articulations. When the articulations were fleshed out, however, they also tended to reify many existing cultural values.

The abundant success of the USWNT, on the pitch and on television, also allowed for (perhaps encouraged) arguments that evacuated the idea of equal pay as principle to (equal) pay based on athletic and economic performance—the very same metrics that had traditionally been used against the USWNT and many other female sports. Because the women's team is so successful, arguments that are easy to draw upon, although not necessarily directly tied to the mission of USSF, ultimately are ones that illustrate the American exceptionalism of the USWNT, often in direct comparison to the failure of the USMNT. Rachel Allison has illustrated that women's professional soccer historically argued over whether it was a cause or should be judged solely on the logic of return on investment.[41] The dominant cultural arguments over the USWNT settle this question in the direction of seeing success in the logic of a business's ROI, rather than as a right. In short, there is an underlying implication that the women's team is fulfilling the destiny of the US in global competitions and hence should be given equal *or better* pay because of their athletic success and their robust economic performance. In short, the arguments for equal pay are ultimately brought out on the grounds of successful effort and popularity, rather than on the grounds of principle. By drawing upon the "exceptionalism" of the team, those arguing the case for equal pay often unwittingly justify the case on the grounds of American exceptionalism and a logic of neoliberalism. This occurs so seamlessly in public discourse precisely because these justifications are ones that already freely and habitually circulate. As always, that's what American exceptionalism *does* in a place like this.

Public argument, of course, is cumulative in its influence. That is, it is not as if a person sits down, has one conversation or thought about the USWNT, and then has a complete understanding in mind. Rather, to varying degrees, we all participate in conversations with friends, reading news, watching public events, and so forth to gain an understanding of the meaning of "equal pay," the way the USSF has dealt with compensating the women, and the justifications calling for change. We gain these through picking up fragments from the larger mosaic of argument. In my reading of a large dossier of documents, as critic, I receive more of a repetition of themes than I do individual arguments. As a result, the picture I paint here comes from arguments whose themes emerge and are repeated in reporting on the case.

The USWNT as Working Women

One of the most progressive and interesting aspects of the argument concerns the way that the USWNT's position is articulated to the position of all women. That is, the argument that they are not receiving equal pay is not simply about soccer or about athletes more generally but is seen as the condition of all working women, and women of all races/ethnicities. Moreover, their position is tied to women in the past and to women in the future. Indeed, the argument being made is that their fight (both their public fight and their fight through the legal parameters of the EEOC) is in full or in part to protect the women who come after them.

For example, when US senator Dianne Feinstein comments on the case, she notes, "What's happening to the women's soccer team isn't an isolated event.... Women are paid just 79 cents for every dollar earned by men. This means that every woman who works full time is paid $10,700 less—every year.... And, the wage gap is even bigger for African American and Latino women. African American women are paid just 60 cents. Hispanic women are paid just 55 cents."[42] Kevin Baxter of the *Los Angeles Times,* who does a deep dive into the complexity of the argument, begins by asking, "Who's opposed to equal pay—other than the US Senate, which has failed to pass the Paycheck Fairness Act, and the majority of American businesses that continue to pay women 21% less than men?"[43] The *Wall Street Journal*'s Rachel Bachman, who writes numerous articles about the case, observes that, given the popularity of the team, the implications have gone beyond the USWNT, indeed, beyond women in the United States: "The case took on a global profile as the team dominated the World Cup in France, winning it in July. After the final against the Netherlands, fans chanted 'Equal pay!' and have continued chanting it at subsequent games."[44]

The editorial board of the *Los Angeles Times* clarifies that this high moment for the equal pay argument is not solely about the soccer team, that it must go across the board to all types of female workers: "We're glad it [the USWNT argument for equal pay] is happening and hope it is translated into substantive action that benefits women in every profession . . .

female athletes should be paid a fair and equal wage for doing substantially the same job that male athletes do, but *so should factory workers, food servers and accountants*" (emphasis mine).[45] Finally, along the same grounds, Nancy Armour of *USA Today* literally articulates all women in the lawsuit brought forth by the USWNT, making the issue much broader than soccer: "It's the U.S. women's names who are on the lawsuit, but it might as well include every woman in America. Each one of us knows what it's like to be marginalized and dismissed, for no other reason than our gender. It's infuriating and exhausting, and with greater frequency and louder voices, we're saying we're no longer going to accept it."[46] This moment, these arguments, then, affect all women.

Women: Past and Future

The argument is made to be elastic not only across all working women but also temporally elastic, tied to women in the past and future. That is, in addition, the public argument makes it clear that the work being done by the USWNT is in the service of women and girls who have yet to even begin to work and on the shoulders of working women of the past. For example, Barry Svrluga of the *Washington Post* notes that the pay gap needs to get fixed because of the message we are sending to the next generation: We're telling our daughters—in soccer, yes, but in the workforce as well—that their work isn't as valued as that of their boy classmates."[47] In an editorial Jesse Jackson Sr. observes that the USWNT is fighting "for their country, for themselves, but also for all those who will come after them" and quotes USWNT star Alex Morgan saying, "Even if I don't reap the benefits, my hope is that the next generation's sole focus is what it's meant to be: and that is to play football."[48] Finally (I say, although the examples are almost limitless), Rep. Joseph Morelle (D-New York) released a statement in which he stressed that he saw the lawsuit and the movement as about future generations more than anything else: "I want my granddaughters to grow up knowing they are just as talented, capable, and valued as their male counterparts—and that starts at the top by ensuring their roles models are treated with the respect and equality they deserve."[49] In each example we find the desire to stretch the fundamental right of equal pay from the USWNT to all female workers, especially those most harmed by such inequities, as well as the women still to come.

Moreover, numerous commentators make it clear that this is a long history, especially in the sports world in a broad sense, in which women have struggled for equal treatment. The clearest example of this emerges from a Western Michigan University press release called "A Long Road." After an explanation of the USWNT lawsuit, the author notes, "For centuries, women have displayed a desire to participate and an ability to excel in sports in America. There were women's baseball leagues (in America) in the late 19th century, but once professional baseball took off and rules were codified, it was promoted as a manly, outdoor game and the women's leagues were slowly phased out."[50] The author goes on to focus on women competing in a number of sports, including swimming and diving teams, and highlights the competitive disposition of these women. For example, "athletes like Gertrude Ederle, who in 1926 became the first woman to swim the English Channel, besting the previous record held by a male by two hours, continued to emphasize the physicality of female athletes."[51] Moreover, her arguments recount the power of Title IX in altering the landscape and notes the well-known battles waged over equal pay in sports like tennis. While the article highlights the progress that has been made over time, it simultaneously underscores the way men's sports have been actively and passively resistant to such change. To get equal pay now is to honor those who have fought for it in the past and protect those to come later. The public argument for equal pay effectively draws all women together now; it flattens time. While a potentially progressive move, it simultaneously also runs the danger of placing all women's "equality"—in the past, in the future, in soccer, and in all other occupations—under the aegis of neoliberal logic.

Simplifying the Concept

While complicating and broadening who is affected by the court case, most of those arguing about equal pay simultaneously simplify its meaning. An argument with less nuance is often one that is easier with which to agree. As I noted earlier in describing the case, because of the very different CBAs signed by the men and women's teams, it is somewhat difficult to clarify how the men and women are being compensated. Indeed, many of the articles leave out multiple factors (e.g., per diem, medical insurance, guaranteed annual salary) that sometimes benefit the men and sometimes benefit the women. It makes for a much cleaner argument to make the comparison apple for apple. Hence, Kevin Baxter of the *Los Angeles Times* notes that while "equal pay" is a nice, unambiguous phrase from which to work in public, "deciding what constitutes equal pay and how to achieve it, [. . .] can't be summarized in a slogan."[52] I would argue that he is wrong. The public argument for equal pay was so attractive not only because it affects all women but also because most representations of it simplify it by only comparing what men and women were paid per game. While the women are paid less no matter how you slice it, and while their benefits by no means make up for the difference in pay, simplifying the argument makes the contrast stand out much more sharply.

The USSF and Regressive Arguments

For their part, the USSF helped make the USWNT's argument even more attractive publicly by painting itself as the voice of regression rather than progress. With the USWNT and others who support their position arguing that equal pay should be granted on the basis of equal work, the USSF filed documents in legal cases that served only to make the women's position more attractive in the public eye. To wit, in March 2020, the *Wall Street Journal*'s Rachel Bachman reported that USSF president Carlo Cordeiro had been forced to resign because the legal brief bearing his name argued that even if it could be shown that the pay scales were uneven, that would be justified because the men's game required a "higher level of skill" than the women's and that the men had "more responsibility" in representing the nation.[53] In response, Molly Levinson, spokeswoman for the USWNT, asserted that Cordeiro's argument "belongs in the Paleolithic Era. It sounds as if it has been made by a caveman. Literally everyone in the world understands that an argument that male players 'have more responsibility' is just plain simple sexism and illustrates the very gender discrimination that caused us to file this lawsuit to begin with."[54] The backlash was immediate, as sponsor after sponsor, including Coca-Cola, Nike, Secret, Visa, and Deloitte published statements expressing a high level of disappointment with Cordeiro.[55] Further, the makers of Luna Bar paid each woman on the team the wage gap of $31,250 as a route of taking a stand against the USSF.[56] With attention on discrimination—long-running discrimination—on their side, and an almost overtly sexist statement as evidence of the problem, the USWNT was in an interesting position to make a successful argument on the very principle of receiving equal pay for equal or equivalent work. Indeed, both discursive forces and economic forces were working on the equal pay side of the argument.

Equal Pay as Principle

Ideally, the notion of equal pay for equal work is not only a legal one but based on principle rather than on separate metrics of success. Hence, because USSF's mission is to help grow soccer, the notion of paying men and women equally should be based on nothing but the principle itself. Indeed, for years the USWNT (and women in other sports) had to fight against the notion that equal pay should be based on revenue, on-pitch success, television ratings, or other factors. Representing the nation in global competition was itself the grounds upon which equal pay arguments could be staked. In my mind these are the safest arguments to make, because they assure equal pay regardless of external factors, and they reinforce this notion across all careers, sporting or otherwise. While rare, the argument based on principle is at times made. For example, Barry Svrluga of the *Washington Post* comments, "Instead of saying, 'Here's the revenue each group brings in separately,' it could think of the operation—and the sport—more holistically. That is what's good for American soccer going forward. Not here's how we value men's and women's soccer. Here's how we value our sport—period."[57] After noting that the revenue streams for both the USMNT and USWNT were beginning to equalize, Ben Gartland claims that it is an irrelevant argument anyway: "It shouldn't have to take revenue projections to show that, however. The USSF is the governing body of soccer in the United States. Their mission statement declares, 'Clear and simple: to make soccer, in all its forms, a preeminent sport in the United States.'"[58] At times women on the USWNT make this same argument. For example, Hope Solo noted that there should not be a discussion about revenue or about success, because equal pay is a principle: "The women do not need to win the World Cup for us to get equal pay."[59] Finally, Carli Lloyd, in an editorial she wrote for the *New York Times*, also argues that equal pay is based on principle rather than on other metrics: "It has everything to do with what's right and what's fair and with upholding a fundamental American concept: equal pay for equal play."[60]

In short, there are clearly some very progressive arguments being made. By tying their cause to all women, across race and class, across occupation, and across time, the arguments for equal pay transcend the success of the USWNT at the moment, while allowing a large platform. Moreover, with the missteps made by the USSF, those making public arguments seemed to be open and sympathetic concerning equal pay. And finally, the attempts to base it on principle was yet another step toward establishing this as a fundamental right, not open to ancillary arguments. However, given that the mostly successful arguments of the past had been based on such issues as revenue, skill level, and success in favor of men in soccer and in most occupations, it was all too easy for those same arguments, which work against seeing equal pay as an principle, to get picked up here by those supporting the women's team. While some discourse cuts across the center, the center largely holds.

Ideological Clawback: American Exceptionalism, Success, Profit, and the Neoliberal Market

Hence, one of the dominant arguments made overtly or implicitly is that the women deserve equal or better pay because they are far more successful in their global game than are the men. Indeed, in these two hundred news stories, it is nearly impossible to find a mention of the women's success (in terms of on-field success and in terms of television ratings) without a comparison to the men's lack thereof. This comparison is made in an offhand way in the middle of some news articles (as opposed to opinion pieces). For example, the *Wall Street Journal*'s Rachel Bachman, in reporting on one of the legal decisions, observes, "The US women have won four World Cups, including the past two. The men haven't won a world Cup and failed to qualify for the 2018 tournament."[61] Elsewhere, Bachman observes, "The women's team won the 2015 and 2019 Women's World Cups while the men's team didn't qualify for the 2018 World Cup."[62] Janet Adamy quotes US presidential candidate Hillary Clinton saying that while the women's team had won World Cup championships and Olympic Gold medals, "we noticed that our men's team hasn't done that."[63] Andrew Das of the *New York Times* provides the following "soccer history" that took place since the lawsuit began: "Since February 2015, the agreed-upon start of the class-action period in the case, the women's team has claimed two World Cup titles. . . . The United States men's team, on the other hand, has plumbed new lows, with even its failures serving to cripple the women's case."[64] At risk of overkill in making this point, I want to point to one more article that highlights that success is evidence in support of equal pay: "To win the battle, however, some comparisons can be used as evidence in their favor. Having now won four out of eight World Cup finals since the women's competition originated in 1991, and four of the six Olympic gold medals awarded since 1996, the US women's team stands as one of the best soccer teams in history."[65] By comparison, the article notes, "the men's national team has never won a World Cup and failed even to qualify for the 2018 tournament. The last Olympic medal won by the men's national team was in 1904."[66]

In each of these examples, relying heavily on American exceptionalism, the relative success or failure of the teams in their competition becomes evidence for the equal pay argument. Indeed, if one of the charms, as David Goldblatt notes,[67] of watching the USMNT play, is the undermining of American exceptionalism, here—in part because it is an argument that meets rhetorical expectations for "success" in the United States—American exceptionalism is put forth as being rescued by the USWNT and hence provides an argument for equal (or better) pay. When, as the *New York Times* reported, moments after the US women won the World Cup (2019), Nike released a bracing commercial celebrating the championship as a triumph of female empowerment. What is telling here is that it seems empowerment through centering the US women rather than females in general. A victory by any other team would not have been regarded as "female empowerment," but a victory by the US women, exceptional as they are, can be.[68]

That said, the argument does not stop with the USWNT's success as evidence for equal pay. For many, it is the beginning of an argument that leads to the women receiving more pay than the men. By making success a justification for equal pay rather than equal pay being a given, the argument already gives in to both a logic of American exceptionalism and a rhetoric of neoliberalism. Kevin Baxter, while underlining the complicated nature of the pay structures between the men's and women's teams, observes, "When the women returned this past week with their second consecutive world championship and fourth overall, it seemed like they were selling themselves short by simply asking to be treated the same. The men have never made it past the quarterfinals of their World Cup and didn't even qualify for the last one, so maybe the bumper sticker should read, 'Pay Them More!'"[69] The editorial board of the *Medicine Hat News* argues, "It is difficult to understand the argument that the United States women's national soccer team should get paid just as much as the men's national soccer team. The women are much more successful. They should earn more."[70] To add one other example, Maddy Birch argues, "It is now time to pay woman what they are worth—and in this case, more than the men."[71] As Wendy Brown notes, part of the neoliberal logic is to turn away from discussions of equality and toward discussions driven by metrics and economics (i.e., you get what you deserve based on merits).[72]

In a similar vein, one of the arguments that has traditionally been used against equal pay in numerous sports (the tennis Majors are an obvious example) is that the men bring in far more of the revenue. In fact, as reported repeatedly by the *Wall Street Journal*'s Rachel Bachman, a source from the USSF had defended the higher pay for the men by arguing that "market realities are such that the women do not deserve to be paid equally to the men."[73] The USSF had also informed the *Wall Street Journal* earlier that the USWNT's complaint against them "is especially unfair . . . because the men's game is more lucrative."[74] More, in a lengthy article about the equal pay "debate" in the *Washington Post*, Adam Kilgore notes the similarity between the argument in soccer and across many other sports. He first references tennis, where every major tennis tournament has distributed equal purses since 2007 (Wimbledon being the last aboard). He then notes, "Even in tennis, though, the notion of equal pay is met with resistance."[75] Kilgore quotes Raymond Moore, chief executive of a prominent annual professional tennis tournament in Indian Wells, California, who recently was forced to resign when he claimed that female tennis players "ride the coattails of men. If I [Moore] was a lady player, I'd go down every night on my knees and thank God that Roger Federer and Rafa Nadal were born, because they have carried this sport."[76] Further, while male tennis star Novak Djokovic was asked about the equal pay argument, he applauded the women for fighting for equal pay in all tournaments and sports but added that men "should fight for more because the stats are showing that we have much more spectators on the men's tennis matches. I think that's one of the reasons why maybe we should be awarded more."[77] The article—in favor of equal pay—quite rightly rejects the notion of revenue or popularity as the basis for equal pay. Again, however, just as in the argument for success and exceptionalism, this argumentative frame is many times called upon in defense of the USWNT argument for equal pay.

In a *Washington Post* editorial entitled, "The U.S. Women's Soccer Team Has More than Earned Equal Pay," the editorial board is explicit that the USWNT has out-earned the USMNT in terms of revenue production: "If it were just about the numbers, maybe the women's team would be facing fewer hurdles. Sportswear giant Nike reported that the US women's team home jersey has become the No. 1 soccer jersey—male or female—ever sold on the company's website in one season. . . . the national women's team's games have generated more revenue than the men's since their World Cup victory in 2015."[78] Moreover, the women are now responsible for bringing in more income in terms of television viewing: "This year, US viewers watched the women's team victory in record numbers."[79]

Similarly, the Wilkes-Barre *Citizens' Voice* argues, "Another key disparity is revenue. During this fiscal year, the women's team has generated $18 million in revenue and $5 million in profit; the men's team has generated $9 million in revenue and a $1 million loss. So it appears that the women are paid less while subsidizing the higher-paid men's team."[80] And, again, similarly, they move to a discussion of television ratings: "And last year the women's World Cup final, which the United States won, drew the largest-ever U.S. television audience for a soccer match."[81] This same evidence is reported elsewhere in different terms: "The women seem to have a strong case. Last year, the women say, they generated nearly $20 million more in revenue for US Soccer than the men did."[82] Earlier, in 2016, Ben Gartland emphasized that unequal pay does not make financial sense: "This makes little sense considering how the projected revenue for the 2016 and 2017 years are expected to shake out.... In 2017, when neither team has a World Cup or Olympics, the women are projected to bring in more than $8 million more in revenue than the men."[83]

While the matter of equal pay is both a legal issue and a moral principle, it historically has been argued against on the basis of the popularity and earning power of men—in tennis, and elsewhere. Faced with attempts to argue toward equal pay, the USWNT found itself in an enviable position for public argument—they were popular, successful, and seemingly in line with public sentiment, while the US Soccer Federation was making arguments that undercut its position. Ultimately, however, rather than the successful argument for equal pay being made on simple principle, which would have been a discursive change, the rhetorics of American exceptionalism and neoliberalism—being discourses that resonate—were the discourses that were brought forth repeatedly in public argument to defend the women's position. Moreover, given that earlier arguments also made the USWNT case a stand-in for all female labor, past and future, it applies the arguments of the neoliberal market universally. I want to be clear that it was not the USWNT as a team or its legal counsel that brought this forth; instead, it was those arguing in the general public who brought this frame to the discussion. In short, ideology is a frame that constrains, that draws arguments back into its own logics as a whole. Regardless of how the pieces are moved (hopefully, toward equal pay), in this case American exceptionalism and neoliberalism maintain their grasp, despite the change in players.

Conclusion: The Seductive Qualities of Familiarity

I am not only an unabashed fan of the USWNT (I am part of the ecstatic public); I am also an unabashed fan of fairness, including equal pay.[84] Regardless of how the CBAs were hammered out and agreed upon, the USWNT and USMNT should both be satisfied that they are receiving equal pay for the same workload (including training, matches, appearances). Simultaneously, then, I am both supportive of, and troubled by, the overall public argument concerning equal pay in the case of the USWNT. Regardless of how it is handled legally or by the USWNT's spokesperson, the public discourse of this case is problematic to the degree that it relies on arguments and tropes that are problematic in general and, more specifically, have been used as an argument against equal pay for women (and others) in the past. Indeed, these same arguments, assuming a free and open marketplace, are consistently utilized against ethnic minorities and others who face systemic disadvantages.

Cheryl Cooky and Dunja Antounovic point out that while intersectional feminism does a better job of identifying the embedded relations of power and structural inequality faced by women in sports, neoliberal feminism often wins the day publicly by relying on "the central tenets of neoliberalism (individualism, entrepreneurship, free-market solutions to social problems[,] the shift of power from the State to multinational corporations)."[85] By tying equal (or better) pay to the on-pitch success of the USWNT, and by tying equal pay to the popularity and revenue streams created by that popularity, the public arguments in effect handcuff, or reaffirm, the articulation between equal pay, success, and revenue. While in this particular case, it might reverse the positions of the men's and women's teams, it ultimately works against the principle of equal pay and resharpens a tool that has been utilized against women and people of color in other situations.

Again, I want to stress that it is not that I think those arguments would be successful in a court of law. Rather, I am concerned about the reification of such arguments in the public domain, where they continue to place value, or at least monetary value, solely on popularity and familiarity. And while the USWNT has been extraordinarily successful in rearticulating a number of values and ideas (e.g., women with a variety of sexual preferences and identities enjoy soccer; out lesbians can be heroes to all types of people; women's bodies can be athletic, skillful, and powerful), on this one particular ground—through no fault of its own—a regressive or conservative argument concerning labor value is rearticulated. In the end, we learn a familiar lesson: the norms and tropes of public argument are strong, especially when "community" encourages them, and sometimes we need to fight against those tropes even when, for the moment, they work in "our" favor.

6

"Black Lives Matter" Matters

Soccer, Slogans, and Spectacle

> When the [Premier League] season ended July 26, there were just [BLM] patches, well, a patch? "OK. That's cute," says Jordan Jarrett Bryan, a reporter for Britain's Channel 4 and a radio host for talkSPORT, of his initial response to the patches. "But when people are being murdered because they're Black, I'm not interested in feeling good. I'm interested in actual reform."
>
> —Amos Barshad, "Premier League Embraces Optics of Anti-Racism; but Many in Soccer Say Much More Must Be Done," *National Post*

> Let's hope the Premier League and other equally silly organizations learn from this mess. Do your research. Don't fall foul of social-media peer pressure to back a political campaign, especially one that's quite openly calling for capitalism to be smashed. Black Lives Matter defiles British values and should be ignored and disregarded as the opportunistic and extremist Marxist organization it is.
>
> —Calvin Robinson, "The Premier League Should Have thought Twice before Getting into Bed with Black Lives Matter," *The Telegraph*

Like a number of professional sports leagues, when teams started playing again after the pandemic-induced hiatus, the (English) Premier League turned its attention to the Black Lives Matter movement to varying types of audience response, as indicated in the statements above. Also similar to many other leagues, soccer—including Major League Soccer and the National Women's Soccer League in the US—found itself in the midst of a puzzle of signifiers. What did it mean to have players and staff wear BLM patches and T-shirts? What did it mean for the players to begin games with a moment of silence while bending one knee? And to whom does it have these meanings? And what will it mean for their market? Without a doubt there is something unprecedented about having leagues replace the names of players with the slogan of a political movement. Clearly, there is something interesting about the fact that entire leagues—not individual players—inside *and* outside of the United States aligned themselves with a slogan, a movement, that originated by African American women as a response to police brutality against African Americans.

As both a soccer fan and someone influenced by/sympathetic to/allied with Black Lives Matter, I found myself heartened by the spectacle and by what players, commentators, and coaching staffs had to say about the movement. As a critic (and a critical fan), I was, however, also skeptical, and maybe a little suspicious. How does a league, like the Premier League, in which fandom has often been articulated with racism, simply clean the slate? Or, to put it in the more updated tone of Anoop Mirpuri, how does a league that now claims to operate beyond racism work to understand how its (especially) Black players are understood publicly?[1] In a league in which Black players still relatively often encounter racist abuse by fans, in a league with very few coaching positions occupied by men or women of African descent, how do Black lives matter? In the US-based leagues, does the slogan, the taking of a knee, help change culture? Given the controversy that ensued prepandemic whenever a player "took a knee," why were the leagues now suddenly embracing it? The situation felt both full of possibility and very puzzling. And while I illustrate in the previous chapters many of the ways that certain soccer cultures have centered ideologically toward neoliberal market logics that tend to act as if racism and other barriers are trivial or have become so, this seemed to be a moment that significantly highlighted the ways this was not true.

As I hope I have made clear throughout this book, in general I hope to unfold the ways mainstream mediation often tames or tempers attempts to change dominant meanings. In this chapter, then, I will provide a drawing of the ways BLM "mattered" within the culture of soccer fandom, the ways it was gendered and disciplined. Ultimately I will argue that while Black Lives Matter as a slogan was put into play in soccer in some fairly innocuous ways by the leagues, the articulation of the meaning of the phrase by some players, reporters, and columnists opened up routes by which radical transition could take place. Just as clearly, however, the articulation of the meaning of the phrase by other players, reporters, and columnists worked to constrain or claw back such transition. This was a moment rife with progressive possibilities, and those possibilities were met by logics that to some degree required a reemphasis of the fantasy of the neoliberal political sphere.

I begin by setting up the dynamics of how Black Lives Matter has "represented itself" and the dynamics seen for it/in it by communication and cultural scholars. Next, I want to briefly discuss the racial context of soccer, especially in the leagues I will focus on in this chapter, as well as soccer/soccer fans' history of operating within realpolitik. Finally, I will turn to a discussion of how Black Lives Matter has played out in the discourse surrounding its "use" in the Premier League, Major League Soccer, and the National Women's Soccer League. While I will illustrate progressive articulations and possibilities within this moment and social movement, I am, as always, especially interested in the ways radical and minor change gets disciplined or curtailed.

Communicating Black Lives Matter

The common reference for the origins and meaning of Black Lives Matter is the "Herstory" section of the Black Lives Matter web page. Here we are told, "In 2013, three radical Black organizers—Alicia Garza, Patrisse Cullors and Opal Tometi—created a Black-centered political-will-and-movement building project called #BlackLivesMatter. It was in response to the acquittal of Trayvon Martin's murderer, George Zimmerman."[2] There are multiple items worthy of note in this self-description. First, while the movement is not solely about state-sanctioned violence, the website mentions numerous cases of the death of Black men and women at the hands of police officers. While it stresses that the movement is working to eradicate white supremacy and create space "for Black imagination and innovation, and centering Black joy,"[3] the description specifically notes, "We affirm the lives of Black queer and trans folks, disabled folks, undocumented folks, folks with records, women, and all Black lives along the gender spectrum. Our network centers those who have been marginalized within Black liberation movements."[4] More, they acknowledge that Black liberation movements of the past have often created room and leadership "mostly for Black heterosexual, cisgender men—leaving women, queer and transgender people, and others either out of the movement or in the background to move the work forward with little or no recognition"; as a result, the authors note, they hope to center the leadership of women and queer and trans people in the Black Lives Matter movement.[5] Hence, while the movement has an origin point in reactions to a case involving the death of a young Black man (Trayvon Martin), it is a movement that hopes to center a full spectrum of Black individuals and to create a global network that works on these principles rather than on specific laws or programs.

A number of scholars interested in communication and rhetoric have staked multiple claims on the ways BLM attempts to alter the discourse or ideology of dominant culture. Allissa Richardson, for example, observes that the radical intersectional analysis of the movement demands that actors work against the "politics of respectability" not only by challenging state-sanctioned violence but also by centering Black women, queers, and trans members.[6] In short, the movement cannot simply recenter Black males, nor can it expect to meet with success by trying to meet the standards of respectability established by dominant culture. As Armond R. Towns observes in his groundbreaking essay combining media ecology and Black feminist materialism, "Black 'Matter' Lives," we exist in a present in which Black humans are treated as matter, as extensions or vehicles to carry out the desires and wants of others. As a result, the BLM movement is demanding that we see the multiple ways all intersections of difference have been treated as tools to maintain the dominance of whiteness in general and white masculinity in specific.

Such a reaction against the politics of respectability always already works up against the demands of capital and popularity in mainstream media. Hence, Jade Petermon and Leland Spencer note the difficulty of telling the "black queer herstory" of the movement itself in popular television dramas. Carrying out case studies of storylines on *Scandal, Orange Is the New Black,* and *Queen Sugar,* they argue that the first two shows—streaming on platforms designed to get the largest possible audience—-erase the queer and gendered backstory of BLM itself and provide narratives of violence against Black people as cases of one white inflicting violence on Black characters, rather than acts being based in structural and systemic racism. *Queen Sugar,* on the other hand, showing on Oprah Winfrey's network and not in need of the same large, general audience, places its focus on systemic racism and the queer founding of BLM. Hence, they argue that while BLM may attempt to work against respectability politics and against a focus on straight Black men and women, mainstream shows reinforce violence as the acts of individuals while ignoring the queer and gendered founding of the movement, allowing viewers to work, rather than challenge, their own assumptions. Carolyn Eldering reaffirms this analysis with her materialist feminist account. Eldering illustrates how digital capitalism incentivizes and exploits differences of gender, sexuality, and race, and hence paints BLM into a box where it can be charged with "reverse racism" rather than with highlighting the systematic dangers of being Black and of existing in the intersectional margins of gender and sexuality.[7]

In what I think is a very optimistic reading of the possibilities for BLM in the public sphere, Catherine Langford and Montené Speight, while understanding the ideological challenges BLM faces (often under the guise of "All Lives Matter" or "Blue Lives Matter"), see a number of possibilities for epistemic and ideological success for the movement. To that point, they argue that BLM 1) provides Black men, women, and nonbinary individuals with a positive presence (not invisible and not a stereotype), 2) highlights violence against the Black body as news, 3) unmasks white privilege by calling attention to the violence and marginalization of Black people, and 4) counters the rhetoric of colorblindness by making it clear that we do not currently live in a postracial society.[8]

What these scholars have in common is both a desire to see the intersectional analysis offered by Black Lives Matter be successful and a suspicion of how powerful mainstream discourse can shut down change or difference. In some small way, the investigation I carry out here of how Black Lives Matter worked within the world of soccer (in the US and elsewhere) is a case study of how well the intersectional analysis and the dismantling of respectability politics works within a particular sphere. Ultimately (previewing what follows), while it is clear that some powerful changes have taken place in terms of the willingness to grapple with systemic racism are occurring, dominant ideology remains powerful enough to blunt a great deal of the more radical changes.

Race and the Global Game

Given the history of football as "the English game" and the intertwinement of sports with popular culture (and therefore with the history of patriarchy and white supremacy), it is no surprise that both masculinity and whiteness have been somewhat protected in how soccer has played out in numerous countries. That is, even as there have been transitions and change in the roles and status of women and people of color in many Western nations, the vestiges of patriarchal, white supremacy still emerge. As shown in the chapter concerning equal pay arguments for the USWNT, the history of soccer is also the history of marginalization of women's soccer in general. Even recently, when Danielle Sarver Coombs and Anne C. Osbourne provided an ethnographic study of an English men's soccer club, they had to learn how to use the bias against female alignment with the sport as a strategy.[9] A similar story can be found regarding almost any type of "difference," and the literature concerning football illustrates this time and time again.

Laurent Dubois offers the story of a referee in Quebec in 2007 who refused to allow an eleven-year-old Muslim girl to play soccer while wearing her headscarf, or hijab, citing concerns about safety (supposedly, concerns that she might get wrapped up in the scarf and choke herself).[10] The case first became a matter of regional concern, with politicians and sporting agencies weighing in, and then became an international matter as representatives from FIFA and other soccer organizations got involved and were joined by politicians and pundits from numerous countries. Ultimately, it took seven years before an athletic-style hajib was allowed to be worn during a game by female soccer players. While change comes, then, it does not come rapidly.

Often, and as I illustrate in the chapter on hooligan memoirs, we tend to tell ourselves a story that such overt racist discourse and behavior is a thing of the past. That said, the literature of soccer's past is filled with racist discourse, although many of the authors themselves claim to be appalled by it. In *Fever Pitch,* Nick Hornby relates how strange it is to watch soccer and be grateful for the times one player calls another a "cunt but not a black cunt" because the reference to race is all too common.[11] Indeed, in *Among the Thugs,* Bill Buford not only highlights the numerous leaders of the National Front who were trying to infiltrate football fandom but also tells the story of a time when he was at a game with a friend and the crowd started making gorilla noises every time a Black player had the ball. His friend asked him about the sounds, and Buford observes to the reader, "I couldn't explain it. I was embarrassed to be living in this country."[12] Franklin Foer points out that for years, Black Brazilians were not allowed to play soccer at all. While over time it has become one route that impoverished Black Brazilians see out of poverty, the vestiges of racism still hold power.[13] Even in places as unexpected as Holland, scholars have pointed out the way sport media professionals and policy makers, even with the most sincere purposes of inclusion, still work to exclude and discipline around the areas of race/ethnicity.[14]

However, there is a sense in which we, like the former hooligans themselves, posit racism as something not only of the past but also as something not to be taken seriously anyway. Multiple recent examples would tell a far different story. Indeed, a look at the period just before the pandemic shut down league play (hence, before the Black Lives Matter project within the Premier League) illustrates that racist incidents in leagues under the (English) Football Association were on the rise, with more than 150 football-related racist incidents reported to police during the 2018–19 season.[15] The rise in incidents during that season was the third in a row, according to Home Office minister Susan Williams.[16] *The Independent* provided a long list of specific racial incidents that had occurred during football matches that year,[17] including such incidents as "January 27—Racist chanting mars Millwall's FA Cup win over Everton," "April 7—Derby, Wigan and Northampton all reported abuse of their players," "April 11—A video of Chelsea fans singing a racist song at a Europa League game in Prague is condemned by the club," "August 19—Manchester United condemn racist abuse aimed at Paul Pogba after he misses a penalty. Teammate Marcus Rashford says, 'If you attack him, you attack us all' but is later abused himself," and "October 7—Aston Villa condemn social media footage of fans chanting a racist song which references their own players."[18] The list is long, so long, in fact, that no team appears spared, and one leaves reading the list wondering how any Black or Asian player is able to tolerate being on the pitch. The abuse doesn't stop with race, of course; as an exhaustive CNN article notes, harking back to my discussion of Robbie Rogers, there are also multiple examples of homophobic issues, such as Everton "investigating claims of alleged homophobic chanting in its home win against Chelsea," with the same weekend including Brighton throwing out two Wolves fans for "homophobic abuse."[19] The situation was/is bad enough that Danny Rose, playing defender for the England national team, noted after England's Black players had racist chants directed at them from Montenegro fans, "At the minute how I programme myself I just think to myself: 'I've got five or six more years left in football and I just can't wait to see the back of it."[20] Finally, in yet another exhaustive look at racism and xenophobia, *The Guardian*'s Jacob Stein notes that there was a great deal of concern that the Kick It Out campaign, funded by the Football Association, Premier League, English Football League and the Professional Footballers' Association, would lose its funding after its own report showed that racism was on the rise.[21]

Lest I leave the impression that racist abuse has been confined to English football, *The Athletic* published a rather lengthy piece in which Major League Soccer (US) players explained their experiences with racism in America and on the soccer pitch in America.[22] Incidents range from FC Cincinnati's Joe Gyau recalling how parents referred to him and his friends as "over-aged Africans" during youth football to DC United's Julian Gressel discussing his fears while training on his own to Atlanta United's Mo Adams's memories of hearing monkey chants from the sidelines.[23] Finally, coverage of the National Women's Soccer League (US) provides evidence yet again of the racism faced by Black players. Indeed, in an article in *The Equalizer*, OL Reign forward Jasmyne Spencer makes the point that "the problem is not only in a far-off stadium on another continent: it is front and center at home, even in the relatively progressive world of women's soccer."[24] In a specific incident from 2019, Utah Royals FC began an investigation of racist chants being directed toward Portland Thorns FC goalkeeper Adrianna Franch.[25] In short, racism and xenophobia are intertwined with soccer/football to some degree both in England and in the US. While the discourse concerning hooliganism's rise and fall may push racism to the past and to "others," there remains a problem. And while outsiders may look at the young, urban audiences who largely make up the MLS fan base and think that the fans are "enlightened," the context is one in which racism continues to haunt the league to varying degrees.[26]

Soccer and Political Activity

While not always the case, soccer fans (specifically, ultra fans) have had a long history of involvement with real, or material, politics. Many of the recent scholarly studies of soccer and fan culture have noted the many ways ultra groups have been involved in political struggle. For instance, many of the ultra groups of some of Cairo's oldest teams were leaders of revolution in Egypt during the Arab Spring.[27] Patrick Potter puts it this way: football fans were the groups that became the revolutionary street fighting and propaganda-producing force, marching, as well as creating songs and street art that defined the spirit of revolution.[28] As a further example, during the Turkish version of the Arab Spring, "Ultras brought and shared their experiences of fighting the police to the other protesting groups."[29]

Regardless of expectations, soccer fans range across the political spectrum. As Foer notes, it was the fans of Serbian team Red Star Belgrade who served as Milosevic's original shock troops.[30] Indeed, in his *Ultras: A Way of Life*, Patrick Potter observes that a football game is often pointed to as the origin of the war. In a game between Dynamo Zagreb and Red Star Belgrade at Maksimir Stadium, a riot broke out: "It was part of a chain of events that led up to war and people at the time coined the phrase, 'the war started at Maksimir.' Similar to later events in the Ukraine, football ultras transformed into the militia groups that would fight the war."[31] As David Goldblatt observes, progressive ideologies "have no monopoly on dissent. The new football has also driven the steady drift of Italian ultras toward fascism, the vast outbreak of neo-Nazi, white supremacist and ultra-nationalist football firms in Eastern Europe, and the mutation of Latin America's *barras bravas* into organized criminal operations."[32]

What I want to stress here is not that the politics of fan groups lean left or right; they decidedly do not. Nor am I wanting to leave the impression that all supporters groups are directly political. Indeed, to the degree that clubs or leagues have control over such groups, there is something of a tendency to close down direct political dissent or movements. For example, when in late 2019 United States soccer fans (especially in the Pacific Northwest) began utilizing the Iron Front symbol (a logo that was used in the 1930s as part of a movement against Nazism), MLS at first banned the symbol from stadiums on the grounds that it was "political." After much protest by the fans, the league finally relented, giving in to the (dubious) logic that these were symbols of human rights, and not political symbols.[33] The point is, rather, and as I have stressed throughout this book, there is something about the gathering and passion of football fans in groups that contains the right environmental factors for united action (sometimes, united *political* action) to occur. However, because politics can sometimes divide audiences, those who are in charge of leagues are often in the position of needing to muzzle or centralize political signifiers for the obvious reason of maintaining the largest possible audiences. Hooligans are one way of scaring away upwardly mobile fans, and political affiliations are another (not that hooligans didn't arrive with their own politics). Hence, leagues like MLS, the National Women's Soccer League (NWSL), or the Premier League have to be very careful when they delve into any project that may be deemed political. There is money at stake, and economic discipline can be powerful indeed.

Hence, in this context, one in which racism and racist abuse continues to exist, and one in which political activity is eschewed, how does Black Lives Matter make its way in? How do players and the league align themselves with a movement that not only emphasizes the value of Black lives but also is supposed to be supportive of the wide variety of Black life and people, including those who are queer and trans? How do leagues present their alignment without making it a political line in the sand? In effect, what does Black Lives Matter mean in this environment, and what are the factors shaping that meaning?

The Meaning of BLM in Soccer

I focus here on the steps taken by the two US major soccer leagues (NWSL and MLS) and England's Premier League, because they received the most "mainstream" US coverage of their responses to BLM.[34] Prior to a discussion of the discourse about the use of BLM in soccer itself, I want to highlight the material steps these leagues took as a response to the movement. Beginning with the Premier League, when games relaunched in mid-June after the pandemic pause to complete the 2019–20 season, all of the players' names were replaced on their jerseys with the slogan "Black Lives Matter" for the first twelve matches of the restart. In addition, a Black Lives Matter patch was included on all uniforms for the remainder of the season. Finally, games began with ten seconds of silence with players taking a knee.[35] During the first game of the restart, featuring Aston Villa and Sheffield United, both teams tweeted photos of the players taking a knee, with the caption "Black Lives Matter." In addition, the teams released a joint statement indicating, "Both clubs hope that the act of 'taking a knee' will send a strong message of unity and amplify the many messages of support from Premier League players and the wider football family."[36] When the 2020–21 season began fairly quickly thereafter,[37] players continued to take a knee with ten seconds of silence, but they had replaced the "Black Lives Matter" patch with one that read "No Room for Racism," the name of a campaign run by the Premier League with the support of other English football bodies, with the goal of eliminating racial discrimination from the sport in stadiums and online.[38]

When the National Women's Soccer League returned to play (as the first major American professional sports league to return since the pandemic), players from the North Carolina Courage and the Portland Thorns FC all wore pregame Black Lives Matter shirts and many, although not all, players knelt during the national anthem. Players from the two teams released a joint statement: "We took a knee today to protest racial injustice, police brutality and systemic racism against Black people and people of color in America. We love our country and we have taken this opportunity to hold it to a higher standard."[39] Buttressing the players' stance, Megan Rapinoe, who had advocated for Black Lives Matter long before this period, spoke out in support of the term being used at games, stating that it was obvious that "as a country," we can do better.[40]

Major League Soccer returned on July 8, 2020, in Orlando at the "MLS Is Back" tournament. At the beginning of the first game, between Orlando City and Inter Miami, while players and officials stood outside the center circle, a large group of Black players walked out, all in a line, wearing black gloves, masks, and T-shirts. Their shirts had different slogans, like "Silence Is Violence," "Black and Proud," and "Black All the Time." These players, members of MLS's "Black Players for Change," raised their right fists in the air (as a nod to 1968 Olympians Tommie Smith and John Carlos), while the other players knelt in the center of the pitch. With no noise or discussion, the kneeling continued for eight minutes and forty-six seconds, a tribute to George Floyd, who was killed when Minneapolis police officer Derek Chauvin knelt on his neck for that period of time.[41] In each game thereafter in the tournament, the players took a knee for a brief moment, while managers and other off-field staff wore Black Lives Matters shirts throughout the game. When audience members were allowed to return to some games and the national anthem was once again played, players were allowed to kneel during it.

The Black Lives Matter slogan (and movement) was reflected in other European leagues as well, although the Bundesliga, La Liga, and Serie A left it to clubs and individuals to communicate their commitments, rather than having blanket league policies.[42] Hence, for example, Borussia Dortmand midfielder Jadon Sancho took off his jersey in the celebration of his second of what would be three goals, to reveal an undershirt with the words "Justice for George Floyd" written on it. While he was initially given a yellow card for this display, it was later overturned by the league.[43] Similarly, then Schalke (Bundesliga) midfielder (and USMNT midfielder) Weston McKennie wore an armband with "Justice for George Floyd" written on it.[44] In Mexico, prior to the start of a game between Cruz Azul and Toluca, referee Adalid Maganda, an Afro-descended Mexican, knelt briefly in solidarity with Black Lives Matter and to protest discrimination he has suffered throughout his career.[45]

While soccer, then, like a number of professional leagues in the US and abroad, has found some way to incorporate Black Lives Matter into the spectacle of the game, the uptake by fans, managers, and columnists, has of course been all over the map. As noted earlier, Black Lives Matter is, or can be, many things: a very complex aphorism, a statement on the meaningfulness of each Black life, an acknowledgment of the history of treating Black lives as matter, an organization, a movement. If you told me a year prior to this moment that soccer leagues in Europe would be incorporating the phrase into their games, I would never have believed you. Indeed, I would never have believed it would be embraced by soccer leagues (and other professional sports leagues) in the United States, despite their rather limited audiences. In this section, I want to query the meaning of that phrase in practice. That is, while it appears on T-shirts and jerseys, while it appears unspoken in those moments of kneeling solidarity, it does not speak on its own. It is discussed and made sense of within the rhetoric of popular culture, including its articulation in news accounts and editorial columns. It is crafted on social media and then reflected back outward onto digital forms and editorials.

Below, I answer the question of what "Black Lives Matter" means by drawing upon almost two hundred different news articles and editorials concerning the intersection of BLM and soccer.[46] Here, I hope to illustrate that while BLM as a discourse is wildly successful in becoming centered in soccer leagues, and while it does have some progressive elements to its framing, it is, as are all words in mainstream discourse, also ideologically constrained. While the need for Black Lives Matter as a movement and a discourse is of course based on a situation that none of us would endorse, this moment of its visibility offers a great space for transition and change, one of those moments when a war of positions can lead to material change that should not be wasted.

The Progressive Readings

Although a vague, wildly divergent public sense had already been developed of what it meant to "take a knee" at the start of the game, given the controversy over Colin Kaepernick (and those who followed), and doing so during the national anthem, having soccer players and other sports figures do so now, largely en masse, provided a new nodal point around which the meaning could be articulated. Indeed, repeated throughout the beginnings of the move to take a knee at the restart of soccer is the notion that the act should be seen as a stand against "police brutality" and "systemic racism." That is, the act was taken not to be a simple stand against racism or racist acts by individuals but a stand against a system of racism that led to, indeed encouraged, police brutality.

This label emerges in discussions with players and managers, as well as in the simple descriptions offered by reporters. For example, Marc Stein writes in the *New York Times*, "Athletes from the N.B.A., W.N.B.A., Major League Baseball and Major League Soccer took their boldest stand yet against systemic racism and police brutality."[47] The Associated Press's Anne Peterson notes, "Now that Major League Soccer has restarted, a group of Black Major League Soccer players is using the moment to call attention to systemic racism across sports and society."[48] Describing a matchup between the North Carolina Courage and Portland Thorns of the NWSL, reporter Andy Clayton observes that with all the players in the starting line up taking a knee while wearing Black Lives Matter T-shirts, it was "a scene never before seen in U.S. team sports." Its meaning was articulated in the statement quoted above: "We took a knee today to protest racial injustice, police brutality, and systemic racism against Black people and people of color in America. . . . We love our country and we have taken this opportunity to hold it to a higher standard."[49] *The Guardian*'s Jonathan Liew, in a fairly specific description of systemic racism, suggests, "One of the greatest achievements of the Black

Lives Matter movement has been to expose how racism operates in its totality: how an economy built on white exploitation and a self-image built on white supremacy generates white boardrooms and white administrations, how racism sustains itself through the nudge and the wink as much as the assault and the insult."[50] While he recognizes that it's a small step, Liew acknowledges that there is something to be said when a league that has been so "allergically hostile to the discourse of politics, ethics and human rights that it allowed clubs to be purchased by nation states now feels obliged to align itself publicly against systemic racism, a phenomenon some people will still try to tell you doesn't exist."[51]

One of the most widely reported acts when the game was restarted was performed by (then) Montreal Impact manager Thierry Henry. At the start of a match against the New England Revolution, after all of the players and officials knelt in silence before the game and had stood again, Henry stayed on his knee for eight minutes, forty-six seconds, well into the first quarter of play, while wearing a Black Lives Matter T-shirt. This was pointed out as the same amount of time that Minneapolis police officer Derek Chauvin kept his knee on the neck of George Floyd prior to his death.[52] In a CNN article on the lengthy kneel, Henry says, "I sat down for 8 minutes and 46 seconds, I guess you guys know why." The reporter, Calum Trenaman, clarifies that this was the length of time "prosecutors initially reported Minneapolis police officer Derek Chauvin knelt on Floyd's neck."[53] Floyd, signifying Black men killed by police, shows up routinely in articles about Black Lives Matter and soccer. In a *South China Morning Post* article, reporter Fiona Sun observes, "The Black Lives Matter anti-racism protests gained momentum globally after African American George Floyd died on May 25 when a white police officer knelt on his neck while trying to arrest him in Minneapolis."[54] A report in *La Prensa Latina* concerning the return of the Premier League says, "In solidarity with the protests in the United States following the police killing of George Floyd, all of the players had 'Black Lives Matter' instead of their names on the backs of their shirts and both teams kneeled on the pitch before the opening whistle."[55] Liverpool players were said to show their solidarity with BLM "following the death of George Floyd in the United States by taking a knee around the centre circle at Anfield."[56] Even United Soccer League 1 (USL) team Forward Madison released a statement: "Last Sunday, we watched the appalling video of a Black man in Wisconsin, Jacob Blake, shot seven times in the back by a police officer. We have said that Black Lives Matter. . . . When there is still no change, we must do more."[57] Of his own fears, Los Angeles FC's Mark-Anthony Kaye tweeted, "I can't sleep some of these nights! My mind just races and goes on and on at the amount of possible scenarios in where I lose my life or I'm harmed by a police officer who took an oath to protect us. The police force has lost its credibility."[58]

These are not isolated quotations. Part of what is so fascinating about the articles is that Black Lives Matter is highlighted repeatedly as a recognition of the value of Black lives in the face of not only systemic racism but police brutality. While George Floyd is mentioned repeatedly, the movement and discourse imply that the brutality of police against Black (male) bodies is systemic, routine, and frightening. This is an issue of human rights in general, rather than a protest about individual actions.

Another way BLM was configured in soccer culture progressively was the degree to which a global coalition of sports figures was said to be in favor of it. That is, rather than isolated, individual protests, the idea becomes one of uniting across difference as a way of challenging systemic issues. Unlike a neoliberal approach to change, much of the discussion focused on coalition building, altering the understanding of the issue. Anne Peterson of AP News notes that in order to fight systemic racism across "sports and society," the group Black Players for Change joined "forces with the Players Coalition, the NFL players group founded by Anquan Boldin and Malcolm Jenkins."[59] She goes on to quote Toronto FC's Justin Morrow: "We're standing with all of our brothers and sisters across the world—definitely across the North American sports landscape, but we see what's happening over in Europe as well, how soccer players are fighting against racism there. We're standing with all of our brothers and sisters to fight this fight."[60] Elsewhere, Morrow notes how important the links and coalitions are between players in the NFL, the NHL, and the NWSL.[61]

Similarly, at the relaunch of the Premier League, the players made a statement: "We, the players, stand together with the sole goal of eradicating racial prejudice wherever it exists, to bring about a global society of inclusion, respect, and equal opportunities for All, regardless of their colour or creed.... This symbol [BLM] is a sign of unity from all Players, all Staff, all Clubs, all Match Officials and the Premier League."[62] Later, the English Professional Footballers' Association made it clear that their actions were meant to be in concert with what was happening in the United States: "We want America to know that the world is watching."[63] Crystal Palace defender Patrick van Aanholt observed of the need to build a coalition to support Black Lives Matter: "They've done it in Germany and [Premier League] teams have done it in training. We have a platform and as a global sport, we have to come together. Everyone has [been talking about it], not just the players. The manager has . . . the whole club. The white players are asking: 'How can we help?'"[64] Former England captain and current owner of MLS's Inter Miami David Beckham posted on Instagram that he was standing "in solidarity with the Black community and millions of others across the world who are outraged by these events."[65] Again, then, this portion of the articulation of Black Lives Matter makes it clear that rather than individual struggles against racism, this is a global coalition across sports, across countries, that is meant as a rethinking, a rearticulation, of rights and lives. It is a recognition that Black lives matter as a principle, as a given, and not as something to be struggled for individually or in particular circumstances or places.

Importantly as well, however, and as indicated by the epigraphs to this chapter, those arguing for Black Lives Matter as a movement and ideological change understand that such change needs to be followed up by material changes. The primary, although not only, one of these material changes is an enhancement of opportunities in management and other front office positions for Black players. Some of the initial calls for change ask for material or tangible acts and yet remain vague as to what this means. For example, in a CNN article about play stoppage in most US sports after the Jacob Blake shooting, Martin, Asmelash, and Close quote an MLS statement: "The entire Major League Soccer family unequivocally condemns racism and has always stood for equality, but we need to do more to take tangible steps to impact change."[66] Former Celtic Rangers star Rod Wallace noted in the *Sunday Post* that Scottish football needs to show that Black lives matter through real change: "The words and the intentions are very encouraging—but they need to be put into action, and new rules and guidelines set in stone."[67] Poet and journalist Musa Okwonga argues that when the Premier League returned, each team was acting as a de facto ambassador for Black Lives Matter, and therefore every journalist should ask the clubs what material changes they are making to provide safety and greater social and economic justice for Black people.[68]

In one of the strongest, most specific, and most widely reported arguments for material changes in terms of management positions within football organizations, former Nigerian forward Segun Odegbami asks in his reflections on Black Lives Matter, "Why are Black players considered good enough to play the game, but never good enough to manage it?"[69] He offers the following revealing evidence: "At the World Cup, France '98, when the number of participating African teams was increased from three to five, no Black African coach led any of the five African teams. All the coaches were White. In 2010, when an African country, South Africa, hosted the

World Cup for the first time in history, there was not a single African coach at the party."[70] Providing such vivid illustrations, Odegbami suggests that Black lives really matter only when we make the material changes to make them matter. This call is reflected globally. For instance, the MLS coalition Black Players for Change called "on the league to increase diversity hiring in coaching, front office and executive positions, appoint a chief diversity officer, implement implicit bias training and expand cultural education."[71] Former Celtic star Rod Wallace points out that one clear material change would be to hire Black managers, as "Black players will tell you that they feel it's a waste of time taking their coaching badges as they feel there will be next to no opportunities given to them."[72]

The idea that trying to become a manager as a Black player is a wasteful pursuit is reflected by Crystal Palace defender Patrick van Aanholt's observation that while he was interested in managing, he was put off by how few Black coaches there are in football.[73] In the *Washington Post*, Musa Okwonga cites Manchester City's Raheem Sterling noting that Black footballers find it nearly impossible to find coaching jobs after retirement and that this is an important change to be made.[74] A news service editorial ties the lack of management positions to systemic racism: "The lack of black football coaches stems in part from a lack of black chief executives and sporting directors and owners. This stems in part from a systematic and racist assumption that black people cannot be trusted with positions of executive or financial power."[75] The article adds, as if to underscore how important such changes are, and how easily overlooked: "Try and stitch that to the back of a football shirt."[76] Jason Lee, education executive of the Professional Footballers' Association notes that teams must force themselves to consider hiring more Black people in executive and managerial positions, and he pushes for a version of the NFL's Rooney Rule to be established in English football.[77] One entire editorial in *The Independent* is dedicated to arguing that football as a whole must illustrate that Black lives matter by diversifying all Football Association and team boards.[78] Finally, in an editorial entitled, "Allowing Logos Has to Be More than Just a Sop to Players," Oliver Holt argues that Black Lives Matter cannot simply be a slogan, but that the change must be made in football itself: "They are protesting about the lack of black coaches in the English game. They are protesting about the lack of black managers in the English game. They are protesting about the lack of black executives in the English game."[79]

While the examples are plentiful, the point to be made here is that in this crisis moment, some of the articulations that came with Black Lives Matter were progressive and visible. Not only did the discourse largely point out that the need to claim Black lives matter could be found in systemic racism and physical brutality toward Black men by police, not only does the meaning of Black Lives Matter operate globally rather than locally or situationally, but it was also the case that the change needed to take place in material ways, not only in discourse. Chelsea defender Antonio Rüdiger made a similar argument in an article entitled, "This Article Will Not Solve Racism in Football." Here, reflecting on the materiality of his own life experience, he argues that change must be systemic rather than simply the addition of a slogan or campaign.[80] Manchester United's Marcus Rashford expressed vocal support for the movement and, in noting the material changes needed to support the poor, he not only provided material goods to the homeless but criticized the Boris Johnson administration publicly, in effect forcing it to make a U-turn on a food program for children who otherwise would have gone without.[81] By altering rules, by hiring Black managers, executives and board members, by adopting strategies like the Rooney Rule, soccer would be going beyond slogans, beyond patches; BLM demanded material changes. It is in these moments that the activism around the movement seemed to aim at specific material change. All that said, there remain ways that the ideology of the present reshapes the meaning of Black lives matter—especially in the world of football—that reiterate preexisting values.

Regression and Erasures

In a very insightful essay regarding the #SayHerName hashtag, Jennifer L. Borda and Bailey Marshall investigate the ways the hashtag both challenged the fact that brutalized women had been erased from #BlackLivesMatter discourse and encouraged activists to center the stories of those Black women killed in interactions with police.[82] Indeed, the original #SayHerName report published by Kimberlé Crenshaw et al. is a painful read, just in terms of how such brutality disappears in public discourse, even in the midst of a movement as vocal as Black Lives Matter.[83] This absence is striking, especially given a movement that, as noted earlier, was founded by Black women and dedicated to being supportive of the wide variety of Black life, including women, queer, and trans individuals. Striking, I say, but perhaps all too predictable.

Here, in the midst of a very visible movement in soccer, we are once again faced largely with the erasure of Black women as victims of police brutality. In the entirety of the archive looked at here, there is only a single mention of a Black women brutalized by police. When the Premier League,

Major League Soccer, and the National Women's Soccer League returned after the pandemic pause, the discourse of Black Lives Matter centered almost exclusively on George Floyd. When the teams later followed the NBA by stopping games from being played, the focus was on the murder of Jacob Blake. It is not that every article mentions either one of these two, but rather that they are the only ones mentioned. In this way the discourse frames the movement as focused on how Black men are brutalized; Black women, as victims, are largely erased.

Indeed, if we look at the restart of the National Women's Soccer League and the coverage of the moment, we find that even there the focus is not on Black women. When the Chicago Red Stars and Washington Spirit kicked off the relaunch of professional sports in North America on June 27 at the 2020 NWSL Challenge Cup, defender Julie Ertz reportedly consoled teammate Casey Short while they were taking a knee. Short, an African American, found the moment very moving and cried on the field. While many columnists noted her emotional state, they were also distracted when teammate Rachel Hill remained standing, placing a hand on Short in order to comfort her. Facing criticism for not taking a knee, Hill later released a statement in which she noted that she chose to stand because of what the flag means to her family members who are also in the military and also claimed, "I support the Black Lives Matter movement wholeheartedly. I also support and will do my part in fighting against the current inequality."[84] *New York Times* reporter John Branch, writing about why standing (rather than taking a knee) is now controversial quotes Charles Ross, history professor and director of African American Studies at the University of Mississippi: "You cannot sit around now in this post–George Floyd period we're in and say, 'We're going to continue to take this safe position.'"[85] And, of course, it is a post–George Floyd era. But it is also a post–Breonna Taylor era. And a post–Natasha McKenna era. And a post–Michelle Cusseaux era. As Alisha Gupta points out in the *New York Times*, since 2015, forty-eight Black women were killed by police, with only two officers being charged.[86] The value of every life can be said to be infinite, of course, but the sidelining of women's deaths and highlighting of men's, especially in the context of a protest by women soccer players, is a crystallization of why #SayHerName is a necessary corrective. Even in the midst of it, Black women seem to disappear.

Secondly, as effective as Black Lives Matters is as a movement and a discourse, one of the ways it is ideologically constrained is through the rearticulation of the movement and its ideas, with particular organizations or individuals, especially when these organizations and individuals support policies and ideas that have generally negative connotations publicly. (This, in addition to expected hamfisted arguments that occur when, for example, a plane, paid for by a small fan group, flew over the Manchester City-Burnley restart match with the phrase "WHITE LIVES MATTER, BURNLEY,"[87] or when British media personality Katie Hopkins tweeted out that for #whiteoutwednesday, she would be "posting a picture of my arse. Thank you").[88] That is, while some organizations have taken on the name and are sympathetic with the original principles, they also take stands that are not in line with Black Lives Matter as articulated by the original women and, as a result, allow detractors to dismiss the entire movement. And some of those who are not in favor of Black Lives Matter also articulate ideas that were not origin points for the movement but allow detractors to then easily dismiss the movement.

One obvious example is when George Floyd's background is utilized to discount the movement as a whole, making his criminal record a reason to dismiss concerns about police brutality. In a letter to the editor of the *Northern Echo*, Joe Mulroy claims to be ashamed of the Premier League's use of BLM, because it ultimately gives honor to a "6ft six serial criminal . . . [who] . . . has spent years in jail for several different offences, one of which was forcing his way into a pregnant woman's home, putting a gun to her belly holding her hostage while five other members of his gang ransacked the house."[89] Not only has the narrative of this crime been disputed, but such an argument dismisses the entire Black Lives Matter philosophy, and it does so by arguing, in effect, that some Black lives don't matter.[90]

A second example—and one most people will be familiar with in ongoing cultural debates—was referred to above, when player Rachel Hill explains after being criticized for not kneeling that she did not kneel because of what the flag means for military family members and to her. In essence, while the kneeling by Colin Kaepernick was designed specifically to respect the flag while protesting police brutality and racism,[91] Hill reinforces the articulation of taking a knee with disrespect for the flag.[92] (On the other hand, Molly McElwee wrote about the incident in *The Telegraph* and noted that the uncomfortable position taking a knee put players into was precisely the point. That is, we all need to have a more complex understanding of race, nationalism, and the meaning of our actions).[93]

In a somewhat similar manner, when MLS restarted in Dallas in a game pitting Dallas FC against Nashville SC, several fans booed the players who took a knee. While Dallas defender Reggie Cannon called the booing "absolutely disgusting," because players were taking a stand for something they believed in, the fans once again took the idea of "taking a knee" as disrespect for the flag and the nation.[94]

Early on, when Black Lives Matter was placed on Premier League jerseys, Ben Bradley, MP (Member of Parliament) for Mansfield, called the action a "political stunt" and questioned why the Premier League was supporting a group that was "attacking police officers and war memorials."[95] Bradley went on to note that the Premier League has not "read the small print of what it's backing,"[96] constructing what appears to be a legal compact between a movement, its specific details (e.g., "attack the police"), and the Premier League. A compact and "small print," I stress, that do not exist. Bradley argues that the Premier League should return its attention to "Kick It out," "an organization who do amazing work fighting racism in sport and do it in a sensible and peaceful way—rather than back those who aim to dismantle capitalism and British Institutions."[97] In effect, Bradley not only articulates ideas with BLM that are not essential components (although perhaps held by individuals) and stresses a need for more civility in discussions of racism.

In a similar fashion, by September, many administrators in the Premier League were also trying to draw a distinction between antiracism and BLM because, they argue, BLM was an organization. Premier League chief executive Richard Masters, for example, told a British Parliamentary committee, "We are drawing a clear distinction between a moral cause and a political movement."[98] In the same essay, former Wolves and QPR midfielder Karly Henry, wrote, "The divisive Black Lives Matter organization, however DOES NOT" provide an inclusive and politically neutral antiracism movement. In July, Crystal Palace and England midfielder Andros Townsend openly "disowned Black Lives Matter" by saying he had no interest in their "far-left ideology" and criticized Black Lives Matter of London for its "promotion of policies" intended to "end capitalism," as well as its "anti-Semitism."[99] Editorialist Calvin Robinson of *The Telegraph* argued that the Premier League should never have "gotten into bed with Black Lives Matter," because it (aligning the movement with Black Lives Matter UK) is "anti-capitalist" and "anti-democratic."[100] He goes on to call BLM an abhorrent group with anti-Semitic messages; BLM is, Robinson notes, a group that "defiles British values and should be ignored and disregarded as the opportunistic and extremist Marxist organization it is."[101] Elsewhere, Raheem Kassam, the former editor of Breitbart News London, called the inclusion of BLM in the Premier League "real time cultural Marxism."[102] Again, the stress here is to push BLM aside in favor of a more civil discourse that does not raise particularly difficult issues.

While not articulating BLM with nefarious beliefs, former England striker and director of football at Queens Park Rangers, Les Ferdinand, argued that both the slogan and taking a knee were publicity stunts that diluted antiracism messages.[103] After Queens Park Rangers and their opponent Coventry did not have any players kneel before their championship league match, Ferdinand defended their behavior by saying BLM was a dilution of the message, rather than a message itself, thereby erasing, rather than highlighting, the potential of the phrase as articulated by its founders and others. Indeed, in a larger sense, the Premier League took something of the same stance. In June, Premier League CEO Richard Masters said of BLM that "it is perfectly possible to support BLM the sentiment without being seen to support any political organization."[104] After the start of the new season, however, they moved away from the phrase "Black lives matter" and argued that they did so because they were "aware of the risk posed by groups that seek to hijack popular causes."[105] While in July 2020, editorialist Oliver Holt expressed hope that the Premier League would keep "Black Lives Matter," he expressed concern that the League, suffering from some criticism of specific "policies" of the BLM movement, would move to a tamer, more marketable expression of its concern. Indeed, to a small degree, the league tried to make a distinction between the expression and movement of Black Lives Matter, from the organization in London operating under its name.[106] Ultimately, however, they gave up on attempting to retrieve it. By September, when the new season started, the league had dropped the BLM badge and replaced it with their "No Room for Racism" patch, the name of a program that had been in place for several years prior to the emergence of BLM as a Premier League ally.[107] To say there is no room for racism is very different from saying "Black Lives Matter." The former, fitting in with the neoliberal marketplace, is an assertion that there should be ho hindrance to fair competition by individuals in any market (including the market of the pitch); to say "Black Lives Matter" is to acknowledge that the system currently works systemically against Black lives; it acts as a challenge to the existing market system. The latter is overtly politically; the former, while implicitly supporting the neoliberal marketplace, is a way for sports to "attempt to preserve the [false] division from politics."[108]

Ultimately, then, with a great deal of cultural momentum behind it and multiple attempts to try to nuance the complexity of Black Lives Matter as a movement, the disciplinary mechanisms around it functioned to encourage a reversion to earlier, more civil, programs against racism. As Alissa Richardson argues in her essay "Dismantling Respectability," one element of BLM as a movement was, in fact, to push against the constraints imposed by respectability politics.[109] It is not that the existing programs were negative; it is more that what we see here is a constraining of the meaning of the movement in such a way that the complexity of its questions, the discomfort asking them might produce, is evacuated as the phrase is taken on to have other, nondominant views. It is anticapitalist, pro-Marxist, antidemocratic. Its take on racism is evacuated nearly completely.

Moving Forward

The intersection of the relaunching of soccer leagues and the deaths of George Floyd and Jacob Blake provided a cultural nodal point for the articulation and rearticulation of Blackness, racism, and police brutality. The global (or at least somewhat international) coalition that built around the phrase "Black Lives Matter" offered an important opportunity in the war of positions over the discourses of humanity and race. While this was clearly a moment in which publics were reminded about the racism faced by the Black population in everyday life, and while the phrase "Black Lives Matter" certainly allowed a moment of rearticulation of Blackness in public life, it was also a rearticulation that faced ideological clawback.

That said, if one role of criticism is not only to highlight these moments of opportunity and the progressive change they bring but also to help move this forward, then it behooves critics to illuminate the ways a phrase like Black Lives Matter is ultimately disciplined to some degree back into dominant meanings. As I have pointed out, while Black Lives Matter was founded by Black women who were interested in highlighting the value of all Black lives (across gender, across sexuality, across age, etc.), the articulation of Black Lives Matter in the world of US and British soccer was cordoned off in several ways. First, as I have noted, in terms of the victims of police brutality who became the icons or motivating factors, George Floyd and Jacob Blake stood in, rather than any women, including Breonna Taylor, whose murder occurred at a similar time. Black lives may matter, but in the visuals offered in the world of soccer, it is (assumedly) straight Black men whose lives are highlighted.

Secondly, while Black Lives Matter is a movement and a philosophy that asks us to rethink the value and meaning of Black life, when it is articulated with particular organizations and particular politics, it becomes less of a rethinking of race or a rearticulation of the police state, and more of a containment of the idea within a leftist, Marxist organization. It is far easier to disagree with an organization with unfavorable politics than to do the difficult task of rethinking the meaning of lives, of Blackness. With the Premier League making the decision to replace Black Lives Matter with "No Room for Racism,"[110] it, in effect, gave up the goal of encouraging a rethinking of the value of Black lives ontologically and morally. Of course, very few would argue that there should be room for racism, but this expression plays very differently than the assertion that Black lives matter. "No Room for Racism" does not force a questioning of whiteness, of heteronormativity, or gender binarism, in quite the same way.

Conclusion

A Few Minutes of Extra Time

> How is soccer like God? Each inspires devotion among believers and distrust among intellectuals. . . . The scorn of many conservative intellectuals comes from their conviction that soccer worship is precisely the superstition people deserve. . . . In contrast, many leftist intellectuals denigrate soccer because it castrates the masses and derails their revolutionary ardor. Bread and circus, circus without the bread: hypnotized by the ball, which exercises a perverse fascination, workers forget who they are and let themselves be led about like sheep by their class enemies.
>
> —Eduardo Galeano, *Soccer in Sun and Shadow*

I recall the first time I read the quotation above from Eduardo Galeano, the poet laureate of soccer. I was bemused by the words. However, the more I've immersed myself both as a fan and as a critic, the more I've come to appreciate them. While I don't agree with everything Galeano has to say, he provides a lot to play off of when I think about the role of soccer for the individual and for its public. In this brief section, I'm going to refer back to Galeano as I work through some concluding thoughts.

It's been strange to work on the book this year, at this particular moment in history. Like a lot of people, I've been in my home a lot, reading, writing, building a home gym, baking bread, worrying about the world. While the pandemic has seemed unrelenting and altered all of our worlds (even forcing a soccer hiatus for awhile), we were also faced here in the United States with the psychodrama of a president who lost an election and seemed about to refuse to step down, and then an insurrection by his followers just before the inauguration of a new president.

It's been a moment in history that has forced a lot of us to rethink our priorities, to question what we find important, and where we find our pleasures and comforts. It is also a moment in which one might ask, "Is writing about soccer all that important?" If we take Galeano's "intellectuals" seriously, then the answer is, of course, yes. If soccer is one of our "breads and circuses," if it is a superstition, then it would clearly play a role in these politics in one way or another.

Hopefully, though, I have made it clear that I take neither the conservative nor the leftist intellectual position, at least not in the overstated way they appear to Galeano. Instead, I have suggested that while I do believe the conditions of soccer fandom enable a different affect than other sports, helping create an ecstatic public, I also believe this leads to a much more powerful cohesion among soccer fans that can be deployed on the left, on the right, for progressives and for conservatives. Soccer fandom creates or fosters a power in the fan, but it is not one with predetermined ends. That said, soccer fans, because they are members of our shared larger ideological world, rely on some of the same logics that permeate culture. These logics do not determine what we think, but they do give us the "common sense" upon which we must act and react. In that way, the discourse of fandom is often going to lean toward a conservatism of common sense.

The Neoliberal Logic

In her relatively recent work, *In the Ruins of Neoliberalism*, Wendy Brown attempts to explain how we arrived at the current political situation (i.e., she was attempting to understand the results of the 2016 election in the United States). Long a theorist of neoliberalism, Brown asserts early in the book that she wants to be clear that she is not claiming that neoliberalism caused the hard right conservatism in the West, but rather that "nothing is untouched by a neoliberal mode of reason and valuation and that neoliberalism's attack on democracy has everywhere inflected law, political culture, and political subjectivity."[1] While Brown's treatise is a masterful walk through political philosophy, I mainly invoke her to help think about the ways that the neoliberal mode of reason shapes all of our commonsense understandings, including those in sport and entertainment. The logic of neoliberalism affects the former hooligans' understanding of their role in the economy; it influences the way we place value on franchise; the way a player understands his role in "coming out" as gay (e.g., "It's all my responsibility, after all. People are in fact not hostile toward homosexuals"); it influences the logic of equal pay; it shapes the ways we shift from Black Lives Matter to equality for all; it influences, indeed, the way entire leagues discuss their successes and failures. I have attempted to do so in a way that does more than simply say, "See! Neoliberalism is there as well." While I believe that Brown is correct and that nothing is untouched by a neoliberal mode of reason, simply pointing that out is not enough. If neoliberalism has in broad strokes become the common sense of contemporary culture, it is one task of cultural critics to trace out these logics in detail, as a way of laying them bare and allowing for a resistance to them. While sometimes this can be tricky (e.g., I simultaneously want to support arguments for equal pay while dismantling the logic on which they are being built), such dismantling serves a powerful purpose.

Neoliberalism at the Intersections

While working on this project, I at times feared that my choices of bodies of discourse would appear as if I were pursuing a Whitman's sampler method of critical reading, I ultimately decided that illustrating the intersections of various identities and discourses is vital to any critical project. That said, the chapters did fall into three different areas with similar themes, each ultimately illustrating some of the ways that cultural discourse around soccer and neoliberalism necessarily links or intersects with a great number of other identity categories. Hence, I underlined the connections between these commonsense cultural discourses within particular contexts and multiple ways in which they intersected with race, class, gender, sexuality, and nationality. In some cases, these intersections are overtly "about" these categories. Thus, the arguments over equal pay for women and the arguments over Black Lives Matter necessarily deal with gender and race, respectively, and the ways they intersect with neoliberalism. Again, I would want to highlight that there are multiple other categories that could have been drawn forth; I made particular choices given my own particular interests.

In terms of specific areas of critical thematics, the first two chapters provide insights into how "neoliberalism" has become so commonsensical that it is a loose script through which people understand their biographies. The hooligan erasure of racism and violence, the embrace of skilled training and economic success within the existing economy, Robbie Roger's coming to understand that the world is not homophobic, that his life will be normal . . . these are stories where actions are understood through a neoliberal script. Similarly, the next two chapters explored the way the translation of the sport (i.e., what English teams can meet to a US viewer, what the Mexican league means as it is translated into the US), again revealed different patterns of neoliberalism, an understanding that success is a matter of the correct economic and psychic actions, in an arena without constraint. The final two chapters, highlighting two different but timely social movements ("Equal Pay," Black Lives Matter") illustrate how movements that in some sense were reactions against neoliberal assumptions ultimately are (more than partially) assumed back into its logic. The cases are different, then, but the lesson is similar throughout.

Sensate Ecstasy and the Ecstatic Public

When I began this project, I wanted to stress Simon Critchley's notion of "sensate ecstasy."[2] While I am not a critic who has been extremely influenced by recent theoretical moves in affect theory, in the case of soccer fandom, it seems unavoidable to touch upon how affect influences the fan base and their experiences in and through the discourses. In the quotation that starts this conclusion, Galeano mentions the ways soccer fans are hypnotized by soccer and the ways leftist critics turn on soccer for serving as a distraction, as bread and circuses quelling any revolutionary spirit or progressive voice. Indeed, Terry Eagleton, perhaps predictably, authored an opinion piece for *The Guardian* over a decade ago, entitled "Football: A Dear Friend to Capitalism."[3] Eagleton argues that football, along with television in general, answers the "age-old dilemma of our political masters: What should we do with them when they're not working?"[4] Football, for Eagleton is the "Breads and circuses" of capitalism, the new "opium of the people," an "austere religious faith [that] determines what you wear, whom you associate with, what anthems you sing and what shrine of transcendent truth you worship at."[5] If that were not damning enough, Eagleton concludes by observing, "If every rightwing think tank came up with a scheme to distract the populace from political injustice and compensate them for lives of hard labour, the solution in each case would be the same: football."[6] While I appreciate the ways any form of entertainment can distract individuals from taking care of social ills, can encourage fans to utilize finances and energies in places other than the search for social justice, I also assume that while the sensate ecstasy of soccer does require some agreement, and some drawing upon hegemonic logics, it is not closed down but leaves space for critique and transition. While it, of course, in part is a form of distraction, it is also a place of meaning, a place where values are debated, where family and cohesion are formed.

In my mind, in what I hope to have shown through my own analysis and by multiple examples of other "soccer scholars," is that while soccer does have a powerful affective dimension for its fans, it does not necessarily lead to a distraction that works against political action. Indeed, as others have shown, if anything, it establishes a sense of identity and "public" that is ripe for use in political projects. Rather than necessarily a distraction, soccer fandom becomes a location for identity and argument. While, as I have illustrated, these arguments are not necessarily progressive (indeed, I have illustrated the way they are deeply entwined with the logic of neoliberalism), there is a power in these connections. To be more aware of this power, to be more aware of the pressures toward being clawed back to ideological common sense, is to be more aware of how one can critique this type of regression, to open bodies of discourse up further.

I close, then, still a fan who is emotionally tied into the sport, emotionally drawn to others, part of a diaspora without origin. Hopefully, though, I am drawn to the middle of this identity with a stronger sense of how these feelings of sensate ecstasy ultimately work to interpellate me into particular ideologies and discourses. And hopefully, the act of criticism makes me more aware of the discourses I assume, making me and others better at the act of everyday critical thinking. Ultimately, this is a baseline for what critical cultural studies can hope for.

Notes

Introduction

Epigraph 1. Simon Critchley, *What We Think about When We Think about Soccer* (New York: Penguin Books, 2017), 27.

Epigraph 2. Laurent Dubois, *The Language of the Game: How to Understand Soccer*, 1st ed. (New York: Basic Books, 2018), 17.

Epigraph 3. Wendy Brown, *In the Ruins of Neoliberalism: The Rise of Antidemocratic Politics in the West*, Wellek Library Lectures (New York: Columbia University Press, 2019), 8.

1. Benedict R. O'G Anderson, *Imagined Communities: Reflections on the Origin and Spread of Nationalism*, rev. ed. (London: Verso, 2016); James Boyd White, *Heracles' Bow: Essays on the Rhetoric and Poetics of the Law* (Madison: University of Wisconsin Press, 1989); Maurice Charland, "Constitutive Rhetoric: The Case of the *Peuple Québécois*," *Quarterly Journal of Speech* 73, no. 2 (May 1987): 133–50.

2. Michael Silk and Emma Chumley, "Memphis United? Diaspora, S(t)imulated Spaces and Global Consumption Economies," in *Manchester United: A Thematic Study*, ed. David L. Andrews, 249–64 (London: Routledge, 2004).

3. As in every book about this sport, I had to make a choice between "football" or "soccer." I have chosen chiefly to utilize "soccer" given that I am writing in the context of the United States. That said, when I quote others, I leave the term "football" alone if that is the term used. I do not think there will be any confusion because my sole focus is on the one sport.

4. Critchley, *What We Think about When We Think about Soccer*, 26.

5. The United Soccer League at the time was the third tier of professional soccer in the United States, under Major League Soccer (first) and the North American Soccer League. The Professional Development League (PDL) existed on the fourth tier. While the NASL is now defunct, and USL Championship has moved up to second tier, MLS remains the top-tier soccer league in the United States.

6. Given my almost mystical passion for soccer, it was with great wonder that after I wrote my friend Robert to get the details of this game for this section of the introduction, he noted that the game had occurred exactly ten years to the day of my asking him for the information. While I know better, it does make it hard *not* to believe that there is something special in the attraction.

7. Loosely from a shortened Italian word for "boss," a capo is a fan who helps organize the ongoing chants and cheers. While most supporter groups utilize capos in MLS Soccer and in other leagues around the world, some specific fan groups (e.g., the Columbus Crew) and entire leagues (e.g., the Premier League) leave it up to spontaneous moments within the crowd itself to lead to chants or cheers emerging.

8. James Montague, *1312: Inside the Ultras* (London: Ebury Press, 2020), 203.

9. Critchley, *What We Think about When We Think about Soccer*, 26. Italics in original.

10. In chapter 1, I problematize the metaphor of addiction in terms of how it has been used in terms of soccer fandom.

11. "American Outlaws."

12. Jonathan Wilson, *Inverting the Pyramid: The History of Soccer Tactics*, 2nd trade pbk. ed., 10th anniversary ed. (New York: Nation Books, 2018).

13. "Speedway Soccer," n.d.

14. Nick Hornby, *Fever Pitch*, 1st Riverhead trade pbk. ed (New York: Riverhead Books, 1998).

15. Critchley, *What We Think about When We Think about Soccer*, 26.

16. Critchley, *What We Think about When We Think about Soccer*, 48.

17. Critchley, *What We Think about When We Think about Soccer*, 113.

18. Critchley, *What We Think about When We Think about Soccer*, 169.

19. H. Lloyd Goodall, *Divine Signs: Connecting Spirit to Community* (Carbondale: Southern Illinois University Press, 1996).

20. Critchley, *What We Think about When We Think about Soccer*, 71.

21. Michael Serazio, *The Power of Sports: Media and Spectacle in American Culture*, Postmillenial Pop (New York: New York University Press, 2019), 4.

22. Critchley, *What We Think about When We Think about Soccer*, 168.

23. Daniel A. Grano and Michael L. Butterworth, "Rhetoric, Sport and the Political: An Introduction," in *Sport, Rhetoric, and Political Struggle*, ed. Daniel A. Grano and Michael L. Butterworth (New York: Peter Lang, 2019), 11.

24. Byung-Chul Han and Erik Butler, *The Burnout Society* (Stanford, CA: Stanford University Press, 2015).

25. Han and Butler, *Burnout Society*, 8.

26. Han and Butler, *Burnout Society*, 11.

27. Robert Asen, "Neoliberalism, the Public Sphere, and a Public Good," *Quarterly Journal of Speech* 103, no. 4 (October 2, 2017): 329.

28. Asen, "Neoliberalism, the Public Sphere, and a Public Good," 331.

29. Asen, "Neoliberalism, the Public Sphere, and a Public Good," 332.

30. Asen, "Neoliberalism, the Public Sphere, and a Public Good," 345.

31. Asen, "Neoliberalism, the Public Sphere, and a Public Good," 334.

32. Brown, *In the Ruins of Neoliberalism*, 8.

33. Michel Foucault, Michel Senellart, and Michel Foucault, *The Birth of Biopolitics: Lectures at the Collège de France, 1978–79*, 1st pbk ed., repr., Lectures at the Collège de France (New York: Picador, 2010).

34. Wendy Brown, *Undoing the Demos: Neoliberalism's Stealth Revolution*, 1st pbk. ed., Near Futures (New York: Zone Books, 2017), 30.

35. Brown, *Undoing the Demos*, 17.

36. The clearest articulation of this argument about faith risking the self in favor of the whole can be found in Ivan Ascher, *Portfolio Society: On the Capitalist Mode of Prediction* (New York: Zone Books, 2016).

37. Andrei S. Markovits and Steven L. Hellerman, *Offside: Soccer and American Exceptionalism* (Princeton: Princeton University Press, 2001), xii.

38. David L. Andrews and Michael Silk, "Introduction," 3, in Michael L. Silk and David L. Andrews, eds., *Sport and Neoliberalism: Politics, Consumption, and Culture*, Sporting (Philadelphia: Temple University Press, 2012), 1–15.

39. Abraham Iqbal Khan, *Curt Flood in the Media: Baseball, Race, and the Demise of the Activist-Athlete* (Jackson: University Press of Mississippi, 2012), 14.

40. Daniel A. Grano, "Football after Fragmentation: Brain Banking, Chronic Traumatic Encephalopathy, and Racial Biosociality in the NFL," *Communication and Critical/Cultural Studies* 17, no. 4 (October 1, 2020): 39.

41. Jay Coakley, "Ideology Doesn't Just Happen: Sports and Neoliberalism," *Curitiba* 1 (n.d.): 69.

42. Grano and Butterworth, "Rhetoric, Sport and the Political," 1.

43. Grano and Butterworth, "Rhetoric, Sport and the Political," 8.

44. Serazio, *Power of Sports*, 35.

45. Asen, "Neoliberalism, the Public Sphere, and a Public Good," 329.

46. As a preapology to the reader, while I am inspired by soccer as well, I hope my own writing is clear rather than beautiful.

47. Eduardo Galeano, *Soccer in Sun and Shadow* (New York: Nation Books, 2013).

48. Hornby, *Fever Pitch*.

49. Galeano, *Soccer in Sun and Shadow*, 149.

50. Hornby, *Fever Pitch*, 223.

51. Galeano, *Soccer in Sun and Shadow*, 149.

52. Critchley, *What We Think about When We Think about Soccer*, 1.

53. Peter L. Berger, *The Sacred Canopy: Elements of a Sociological Theory of Religion* (New York: Anchor Books, 1990).

54. Critchley, *What We Think about When We Think about Soccer*, 34.

55. Serazio, *Power of Sports*, 29.

56. Dubois, *Language of the Game*.

57. Dubois, *Language of the Game*, 2.

58. Dubois, *Language of the Game*, 164.

59. Dubois, *Language of the Game*, 238.

60. Bill Buford, *Among the Thugs*, 1st Vintage Departures ed., Vintage Books Vintage Departures (New York: Vintage Departures, 1993).

61. Franklin Foer, *How Soccer Explains the World: An Unlikely Theory of Globalization* (New York; London: HarperPerennial, 2010); David Goldblatt, *The Age of Football: Soccer and the 21st Century* (New York: Macmillan, 2020); Simon Kuper and Stefan Szymanski, *Soccernomics: Why England Loses; Why Germany, Spain, and France Win; and Why One Day Japan, Iraq, and the United States Will Become Kings of the World's Most Popular Sport*, 2018 World Cup ed. (New York: Nation Books, 2018).

62. Dubois, *Language of the Game*, 270–71.

Chapter 1

Epigraph. Andy Nicholls, *Scally: Confessions of a Category C Football Hooligan* (Ramsbottom, UK: Milo, 2002).

1. Buford, *Among the Thugs*.

2. Foer, *How Soccer Explains the World*, 100.

3. Patrick Potter, *Ultras: A Way of Life (London: Carpet Bombing Culture*, 2019).

4. Montague, *1312*.

5. While Montague provides a more current and comprehensive view of ultras around the globe, Franklin Foer takes a similar tack a decade earlier, providing an engaging narrative of his encounter with supporters of Red Star Belgrade and noting their work for Milosevic. See Foer, *How Soccer Explains the World*, especially chapter 1.

6. Potter, *Ultras*.

7. This despite the fact that most MLS supporter groups have more stylistically in common with Italian supporter groups.

8. Keith Richards and James Fox, *Life*, 1st Back Bay pbk. ed. (New York: Back Bay Books, 2011). See also Michael G. Kammen, *Mystic Chords of Memory: The Transformation of Tradition in American Culture*, 1st Vintage Books ed. (New York: Vintage Books, 1993); Maurice Halbwachs and Lewis A. Coser, *On Collective Memory*, The Heritage of Sociology (Chicago: University of Chicago Press, 1992); Kendall R. Phillips, "The Failure of Memory: Reflections on Rhetoric and Public Remembrance," *Western Journal of Communication* 74, no. 2 (April 2010): 208–23; John Bodnar, *Remaking America: Public Memory, Commemoration, and Patriotism in the Twentieth Century*, 1st pbk. printing (Princeton: Princeton University Press, 1994). This is overkill for such a minor point, but each of the authors listed deftly investigates public memory with this point as an assumption.

9. John Fiske and John Hartley, *Reading Television*, 2nd ed., New Accents (London: Routledge, 2003), 85. While the same claims, of course, have been made in multiple ways, I remain indebted to the metaphor of clawback. The idea, of course, is that ideas or fashions, in order to have currency and popularity, must resonate with existing languages and ideology. As a result, ideas tend back toward the center, with change occurring slowly.

10. Clifford John T. Stott and Geoff Pearson, *Football "Hooliganism": Policing and the War on the "English Disease."* (London: Pennant Books, 2007). Stott and Pearson provide a history and an explanation for hooliganism, as well as a discussion of how well it has been "cured" in the United Kingdom.

11. Tim Crabbe and Adam Brown, "'You're Not Welcome Anymore': The Football Crowd, Class and Social Exclusion," in *British Football and Social Exclusion*, ed. Stephen Wagg (London: Routledge, 2004), 26–46.

12. For some examples of the Leicester school, see Patrick Murphy, John Williams, and Eric Dunning, *Football on Trial: Spectator Violence and Development in the Football World* (London: Routledge, 1990); John Williams, Eric Dunning, and Patrick Murphy, *Hooligans Abroad: The Behaviour and Control of English Fans in Continental Europe*, 2nd ed., repr. (London: Routledge, 1992); Eric Dunning, Patrick Murphy, and John Williams, *The Roots of Football Hooliganism: An Historical and Sociological Study* (London: Routledge, 1992). Their work has been argued and contended with by numerous others, including Gary Armstrong, *Football Hooligans: Knowing the Score*, Explorations in Anthropology (Oxford: Berg, 1998); Anthony King, "Football Hooliganism and the Practical Paradigm," *Sociology of Sport Journal* 16, no. 3 (September 1999): 269–73; Clifford Stott and Steve Reicher, "How Conflict Escalates: The Inter-Group Dynamics of Collective Football Crowd 'Violence,'" *Sociology* 32, no. 2 (May 1998): 353–77; Peter E. Marsh, Elisabeth Rosser, and Rom Harré, *The Rules of Disorder*, Social Worlds of Childhood (London: Routledge, 1995).

13. Shaun Best, "The Leicester School of Football Hooliganism: An Evaluation," *Soccer & Society* 11, no. 5 (September 2010): 573–87.

14. Jon Dart, "Confessional Tales from Former Football Hooligans: A Nostalgic, Narcissistic Wallow in Football Violence," *Soccer & Society* 9, no. 1 (January 2008): 42–55.

15. Dart, "Confessional Tales from Former Football Hooligans," 45.

16. Dart, "Confessional Tales from Former Football Hooligans," 51.

17. Steve Redhead, "Hit and Tell: A Review Essay on the Soccer Hooligan Memoir," *Soccer & Society* 5, no. 3 (January 2004): 393.

18. Redhead, "Hit and Tell," 396.

19. Anthony King, "Violent Pasts: Collective Memory and Football Hooliganism," *Sociological Review* 49, no. 4 (November 2001): 568–85.

20. King, "Violent Pasts," 581.

21. Richard Gregg, "The Ego-Function of the Rhetoric of Protest," *Philosophy and Rhetoric* 4, no. 2 (1971): 71–91.

22. King, "Violent Pasts," 583.

23. John King, *The Football Factory* (London: Vintage, 1997).

24. Buford, *Among the Thugs*.

25. Mickey Francis and Peter Walsh, *Guvnors* (Bury, UK: Milo Books, 1999), xii.

26. Tony O'Neill, *Red Army General: Leading Britain's Biggest Hooligan Gang* (Lytham, UK: Milo, 2004), ix.

27. Martin King, *Hoolifan: Thirty Years of Hurt* (Edinburgh: Mainstream, 2002), 15.

28. Francis and Walsh, *Guvnors*.

29. Francis and Walsh, *Guvnors*, ix.

30. O'Neill, *Red Army General*, viii.

31. Cass Pennant, *Cass* (London: John Blake, 2008), i.

32. Jason Marriner, *Life as a Chelsea Headhunter* (Clacton-on-Sea, UK: Apex, 2009).

33. King, *Hoolifan*.

34. Francis and Walsh, *Guvnors*.

35. Cass Pennant and Martin King, *Terrace Legends* (London: John Blake, 2005).

36. Nicholls, *Scally*. Underlined in original.

37. Francis and Walsh, *Guvnors*, x.

38. "Firms" are groups that participate in football hooliganism. Some were very clearly defined, some less so.

39. Francis and Walsh, *Guvnors*, 111.

40. O'Neill, *Red Army General*, 4.

41. O'Neill, *Red Army General*, 86.

42. King, *Football Factory*, 102.

43. King, *Hoolifan*, 177.

44. Pennant, *Cass*, ii.

45. Pennant and King, *Terrace Legends*, 173.

46. Pennant and King, *Terrace Legends*, 261.

47. Buford, *Among the Thugs*, 21.

48. Buford, *Among the Thugs*, 88.

49. Buford, *Among the Thugs*, 167.

50. Buford, *Among the Thugs*, 205.

51. Buford, *Among the Thugs*, 217.

52. James Bannon, *Running with the Firm: My Double Life as an Undercover Hooligan*, 1.

53. Bannon, *Running with the Firm*, 139.

54. Bannon, *Running with the Firm*, 142.

55. Francis and Walsh, *Guvnors*, 3.

56. Marriner, *Life as a Chelsea Headhunter*, 72.

57. Buford, *Among the Thugs*, 116.

58. This is the term used to signify the hooligans who were, loosely, in charge, organizing the overall effort.

59. Pennant and King, *Terrace Legends*, 2.

60. Pennant and King, *Terrace Legends*, 142.

61. Pennant and King, *Terrace Legends*, 186.

62. Francis and Walsh, *Guvnors*, 5.
63. O'Neill, *Red Army General*, 92.
64. Francis and Walsh, *Guvnors*, 59.
65. O'Neill, *Red Army General*, ix.
66. O'Neill, *Red Army General*, 92–93.
67. King, *Football Factory*, 54, 154–55.
68. Rob Randles, *Road End Hooligans* (Monee, IL: independently published, 2017), 14.
69. Pennant and King, *Terrace Legends*, 17.
70. Marriner, *Life as a Chelsea Headhunter*, 102.
71. E. Summerson Carr, *Scripting Addiction: The Politics of Therapeutic Talk and American Sobriety* (Princeton: Princeton University Press, 2011), 12.
72. Carr, *Scripting Addiction*, 14.
73. Carr, *Scripting Addiction*, 180.
74. In a somewhat inverted fashion, Joshua Hanan illustrates how those with Attention Deficit Disorder diagnoses learn to talk about the use of pharmaceuticals (or their nonuse) in terms of how successful they allow them to be as neoliberal subjects. In short, one must find routes to overcome one's flaws to be able to work successfully as an individual in a "normal" fashion. See Joshua S. Hanan, "Subjects of Technology: An Auto-Archeology of Attention Deficit Disorder in Neoliberal Time(s)," *Cultural Studies ↔ Critical Methodologies* 19, no. 2 (April 2019): 105–15.
75. Pennant, *Cass*, 58.
76. Francis and Walsh, *Guvnors*, xii.
77. Francis and Walsh, *Guvnors*, 134.
78. O'Neill, *Red Army General*, ix.
79. Buford, *Among the Thugs*, 301.
80. Bannon, *Running with the Firm*, 1.
81. Bannon, *Running with the Firm*, 259–60.
82. Nicholls, *Scally*, 17.
83. Marriner, *Life as a Chelsea Headhunter*, 17. Emphasis mine.
84. Pennant and King, *Terrace Legends*, 19.
85. Pennant and King, *Terrace Legends*, 110.
86. Pennant and King, *Terrace Legends*, 169.
87. King, *Hoolifan*, 112.
88. King, *Hoolifan*, 198–200.
89. Francis and Walsh, *Guvnors*, 100.
90. O'Neill, *Red Army General*, 241.
91. Pennant and King, *Terrace Legends*, 143.
92. Pennant and King, *Terrace Legends*, 202.
93. King, *Hoolifan*, 149.
94. Pennant, *Cass*, 206.
95. Nicholls, *Scally*, 137.
96. King, *Football Factory*, 23, 46, 169.
97. Buford, *Among the Thugs*, 129–58.
98. O'Neill, *Red Army General*, 76.
99. O'Neill, *Red Army General*, 91.
100. King, *Hoolifan*, 51.
101. King, *Hoolifan*, 51.

102. King, *Hoolifan*, 134. "Icky" was a top lad with the Headhunters. "Black Willie" was a hooligan within Chelsea ranks.

103. Marriner, *Life as a Chelsea Headhunter*, 44.

104. Marriner, *Life as a Chelsea Headhunter*, 57.

105. Nicholls, *Scally*, 30.

106. Nicholls, *Scally*, 39.

107. Nicholls, *Scally*, 147.

108. Nicholls, *Scally*, 147.

109. Nicholls, *Scally* 148–49.

110. Nicholls, *Scally*, 153–54.

111. Francis and Walsh, *Guvnors*, 10.

112. Francis and Walsh, *Guvnors*, 32.

113. Francis and Walsh, *Guvnors*, 33.

114. Francis and Walsh, *Guvnors*, 59.

115. Pennant, *Cass*, 11.

116. Pennant, *Cass*, 72.

117. Pennant, *Cass*, 29.

118. Pennant, *Cass*, 55.

119. Pennant, *Cass*, 56.

120. Francis and Walsh, *Guvnors*, 64.

121. O'Neill, *Red Army General*, 61.

122. King, *Football Factory*, 62, 79–80.

123. King, *Hoolifan*, 75.

124. King, *Hoolifan*, 214.

125. Pennant and King, *Terrace Legends*.

126. Bannon, *Running with the Firm*, 67.

127. Bannon, *Running with the Firm*, 229.

128. Stephen Dillon, *Fugitive Life: The Queer Politics of the Prison State* (Durham, NC: Duke University Press, 2018), 23.

129. See, for example, Francis and Walsh, *Guvnors*, 60.

130. Pennant and King, *Terrace Legends*, 198.

131. O'Neill, *Red Army General*, 168.

132. Marriner, *Life as a Chelsea Headhunter*, 22.

133. Pennant and King, *Terrace Legends*, 15.

134. King, *Hoolifan*, 126.

135. Pennant, *Cass*, 91.

136. Randles, *Road End Hooligans*, 85.

137. I have not been able to discover how "common" the story of post-hooligan economic success is in "real" terms, only that it is the common narrative of the literature.

138. Carr, *Scripting Addiction*, 180.

139. Francis and Walsh, *Guvnors*, 104–05.

140. Francis and Walsh, *Guvnors*, 194.

141. Nicholls, *Scally*, 77, 107, 191.

142. Pennant and King, *Terrace Legends*, 44, 73, 83, 123, 147, 213.

143. O'Neill, *Red Army General*, 35.

144. King, *Hoolifan*, 142.

145. Pennant, *Cass*, 47.

146. Pennant, *Cass*, 347–48.

147. Brown, *In the Ruins of Neoliberalism*, 93.

148. Melinda Cooper, *Family Values: Between Neoliberalism and the New Social Conservatism*, Near Futures (New York: Zone Books, 2017), 268.

149. Brown, *Undoing the Demos*, 167.

150. John Clark, "Football and Working Class Fans: Tradition and Change," in *Football Hooliganism: The Wider Context*, ed. Roger Ingham (London: Interaction, 1978), 36–70.

151. Years ago I looked at a literal case in which "apology" was offered in public to circumvent the anti-Semitic discourse of Professor Griff, a member of hip-hop group Public Enemy. John M. Sloop, "'Apology Made to Whoever Pleases': Cultural Discipline and the Grounds of Interpretation," *Communication Quarterly* 42, no. 4 (September 1994): 345–62. In the case of the hooligans, however, we find something more interesting, because they each overtly refuse the idea of apology, although their apologia and disciplining works as apology by other terms.

152. Montague, *1312*.

153. Goldblatt, *Age of Football*.

154. "MLS Lifts Ban on Anti-Nazi Symbol Following Fan Protests," NBCSports.

Chapter 2

Epigraph 1. Donald McRae, "In Football It's Impossible to Come Out," *The Guardian*, March 29, 2013.

Epigraph 2. Greg Beacham, "Robbie Rogers, Openly Gay U.S. Soccer Player, Joins L.A. Galaxy in Return to MLS," *Huffington Post*, May 25, 2013.

1. One of the best metatellings of this story is Davy Lane, "The Life and Death of Justin Fashanu," *Roads and Kingdoms*.

2. "£1m Football Star: I AM GAY," *The Sun*, October 22, 1990.

3. "John Fashanu: My Gay Brother Is an Outcast," *The Voice*, October 30, 1990.

4. Useful overviews of Robbie Rogers's journey include "Los Angeles Galaxy Welcome New Addition Robbie Rogers," *San Jose Mercury News*, May 26, 2013; and, Greg Beacham, "Gay Soccer Player Robbie Rogers Joins LA Galaxy," Southern California Public Radio, May 26, 2013.

5. For the sake of those who are not soccer fans, soccer teams in most leagues can loan their players to other teams (in their own league or in other leagues) for specific periods of time (usually a full season). While the team who loans out the player continues to own their contract, the team who is "borrowing" the player pays all (or sometimes most) of their pay. At the end of the prescribed term, the player returns to the team who owns their contract. The team can then either keep the player or put them back out on loan.

6. I note here the way that Justin Fashanu's narrative arrives to help set the context for the meaning of the Rogers case. In a relatively recent essay, Daniel Grano makes the case that past sports "heroes" and figures are brought back time and time again in different contexts to intervene in contemporary political issues. See Daniel Grano, "Muhammad Ali versus the 'Modern Athlete': On Voice in Mediated Sports Culture," *Critical Studies in Media Communication* 26 (2009): 191–211.

7. In the following the distinction between largely "US."-based narratives and UK-based narratives about the case is crude but convenient. Such a distinction is, of course, ultimately a false one in an age of internet access and global circulation. Moreover, some of the sources draw upon here have different narratives for readers in different countries. Instead of clear-cut lines, then, are the contours of two narratives that "make sense" within the sports cultures

of each national context. "Context" here is loosely defined as Lawrence Grossberg does in *Cultural Studies in the Future Tense* (Durham, NC: Duke University Press, 2010), 257. Grossberg, noting that cultural studies attempt to understand the way power infiltrates, contaminates, limits and empowers possibilities for lives, argues that one must understand the creation of meaning in how people actually live their lives (and interpret the world). Obviously, then, context could get down to the most micro definition in terms of space/time/location/identity. Here that meaning is broadened to provide the ways one event encourages two largely different understandings based chiefly on the "national sports culture" of the interpreter.

8. See arguments made by Rita Felski, *The Limits of Critique* (Chicago: University of Chicago Press, 2015); and Bruno Latour, "Why Has Critique Run Out of Steam? From Matters of Fact to Matters of Concern," *Critical Inquiry* 30 (2004): 225–48.

9. Felski, *Limits of Critique*, 40.

10. Judgments about these public confessionals of celebrities and personalities are oddly negative and dismissive about their potential to queer public cultures and how their declarations might enable others to see themselves as something other than disgusting or shameful or sinful. In many academic treatments, critics lodge accusations against celebrities and personalities that they would never direct at others struggling to marshal the resources necessary to brace themselves against the cruelties of strangers and kin emboldened by culturally sanctioned heterosexisms.

11. See, for example, a memorial issue for Eve Kosofsky Sedgwick in *Criticism* 52 (2010), the essays in dialogue with Robyn Wiegman in *Feminist Theory* 15 (2014), and the special issue on antinormativity in *differences* 26 (2015). Claire Sisco King demonstrates the critical necessity of preserving the antinomy of reparative and paranoid reading strategies in "American Queerer: Norman Rockwell and the Art of Queer Feminist Critique," *Women's Studies in Communication* 39 (2016).

12. Isaac West, "Queer Generosities," *Western Journal of Communication* 77 (2013): 539.

13. Grossberg, *Cultural Studies in the Future Tense*, 20–30.

14. There are, of course, multiple examples. We provide a few examples here. See, for example, Nick Trujillo, "Hegemonic Masculinity on the Mound: Media Representations of Nolan Ryan and American Sports Culture," *Critical Studies in Media Communication* 8 (1991): 290–308; R. W. Connell, *Which Way Is Up?: Essays on Sex, Class, and Culture* (Sydney: Allen & Unwin, 1983); Michael L. Butterworth, "'Katie Was Not Only a Girl, She Was Terrible': Katie Hnida, Body Rhetoric, and Football at the University of Colorado," *Communication Studies* 59 (2008): 259–70; Thomas P. Oates, "The Erotic Gaze in the NFL Draft," *Communication & Critical/Cultural Studies* 4 (2007): 74–90.

15. William P. Cassidy, *Sports Journalism and Women Athletes: Coverage of Coming Out Stories* (Basingstoke: Palgrave Macmillan, 2019).

16. There are multiple examples, several of which are highlighted here just to provide some direction. See, for example, Michael L. Butterworth, "The Politics of the Pitch: Claiming and Contesting Democracy through the Iraqi National Soccer Team," *Communication & Critical/Cultural Studies* 4 (2007): 194; Barbara Cox and Shona Thompson, "Multiple Bodies: Sportswomen, Soccer and Sexuality," *International Review for the Sociology of Sport* 35 (2000): 5–20; Jayne Caudwell, "Sporting Gender: Women's Footballing Bodies as Sites/Sights for the (Re) Articulation of Sex, Gender, and Desire," *Sociology of Sport Journal* 20 (2003): 371–86; Judith Halberstam, *Female Masculinities* (Durham, NC: Duke University Press, 1998); Adi Adams and Eric Anderson, "Exploring the Relationship between Homosexuality and Sport among the Teammates of a Small, Midwestern Catholic College

Soccer Team," *Sport, Education and Society* 17 (2012): 347–60; Ellis Cashmore and Jamie Cleland, "Glasswing Butterflies: Gay Professional Football Players and Their Culture," *Journal of Sports and Social Issues* 35 (2011): 420–36; Lindsey Mean, "Identity and Discursive Practice: Doing Gender on the Football Pitch," *Discourse and Society* 12 (2001): 791; Gert Hekma, "'As Long as They Don't Make an Issue of It . . . ': Gay Men and Lesbians in Organized Sports in the Netherlands," *Journal of Homosexuality* 35 (1998): 10; Adi Adams, Eric Anderson, and Mark McCormack, "Establishing and Challenging Masculinity: The Influence of Gendered Discourses in Organized Sport, " *Journal of Language and Social Psychology* 29 (2010): 278–300.

17. We would certainly want to mark Jamie Cleland's analysis of internet message boards dedicated to discussion of association. In this analysis Cleland finds that fans express some readiness for an openly gay player. See Jamie Cleland, "Discussing Homosexuality on Association Football Fan Message Boards: A Changing Cultural Context," *International Review for the Sociology of Sport* 18 (2013): 1–16.

18. Indeed, in an earlier study on the discourse about the body of track star Caster Semenya, I found numerous constraints around gender, sexuality, and cisgenderism. John M. Sloop, "'This Is Not Natural': Caster Semenya's Gender Threats," *Critical Studies in Media Communication* 29, no. 2 (June 2012): 81–96.

19. The gender dimension here is important, as there are multiple out female athletes in soccer and in other sports. While there are some obvious reasons for this (some problematic, including the assumption that "sporting women" do not fit heteronormative assumptions, while male athletes are hyper examples of heteronormativity, the existence of this dynamic needs to be underline.

20. In Susan Hubert's review of Ellen DeGeneres's coming-out process, there is some movement between text and context, but ultimately the focus rests on industrial logics and interests, as well as emphasizing it as a televisual spectacle where the context, figured as homophobia and heterosexism, dominates the analysis. "What's Wrong with This Picture? The Politics of Ellen's Coming Out Party," *Journal of Popular Culture* 33, no. 2 (1999): 31–36. Bonnie Dow's critique of the discourse surrounding DeGeneres's coming-out emphasizes how the confessional framing of the events set into motion a constraining set of subjectivities and limited frames for processing nonheterosexual sexualities. "*Ellen*, Television, and the Politics of Gay and Lesbian Visibility," *Critical Studies in Media Communication* 18 (2001): 123–40. Helene Shugart revisits these claims and bolsters them in her reading of how Rosie O'Donnell's coming-out narrative neutralized her sexuality by emphasizing her childlike fandom, middle-class persona and dress, and her love for her adopted children. "On Misfits and Margins: Narrative, Resistance, and the Poster Child Politics of Rosie O'Donnell," *Communication & Critical/Cultural Studies* 2 (2005): 52–76.

21. John Hughson and Marcus Free, "Football's 'Coming Out': Soccer and Homophobia in England's Tabloid Press," *Media International Australia*, no. 140 (2011): 117–25.

22. Joah G. Iannotta and Mary Jo Kane, "Sexual Stories as Resistance Narratives in Women's Sports: Reconceptualizing Identity Performance," *Sociology of Sport Journal* 19 (2002): 347–62.

23. Andrew Billings, Leigh Moscowitz, Coral Rae, Natalie Brown-Devlin, "The Art of Coming Out: Traditional and Social Media Frames Surrounding the NBA's Jason Collins," *Journalism & Mass Communication Quarterly* 92 (2015): 142–60.

24. Marie Hardin, Kathleen Kuehn, Hillary Jones, Jason Genovese, and Murali Balaji, "'Have You Got Game?' Hegemonic Masculinity and Neo-Homophobia in U.S. Newspaper Sports Columns," *Communication, Culture & Critique* 2 (2009): 182–200.

25. Tom Boellstorff, "When Marriage Falls: Queer Coincidence in Straight Time," *GLQ* 13 (2007): 227–48. In this essay, Boellstorff proposes coincidental temporalities as an alternative to straight time. Straight time, according to Boellstorff, aligns with the paranoid position, as the present is "hopelessly compromised by its copresence with systems of domination" (231). In its place, Boellstorff offers up coincidence as an alternative understanding of temporalities, the queering of temporalities where overlapping temporalities and spatialities coexist without hegemonic incorporation.

26. Diana Fisher, "Immigrant Closets: Tactical-Micro-Practices-in-the-Hyphen," *Journal of Homosexuality* 45 (2003): 171–292.

27. Isaac West and Jeff Bennett, "Tomorrow Be-Longs to Us," in *Queer Praxis: Questions for LGBTQ Worldmaking*, ed. Dustin Bradley Goltz and Jason Zingsheim, 249–59 (New York: Peter Lang, 2015).

28. Rogers, Robbie H., "The Next Chapter," robbiehrogers, March 23, 2013. All of the quotations following are in this statement.

29. Critchley, *What We Think about When We Think about Soccer*, 161.

30. Kevin Baxter, "It's Just Another Day in Soccer," *Los Angeles Times*, June 2, 2013, C1.

31. Graham Parker, "Robbie Rogers to Return to US Soccer with LA Galaxy," *The Guardian*, May 25, 2013.

32. "Support for Former US International Who Says He Is Gay," *Haaretz*, February 17, 2013.

33. "Coming Out," *Daily News* (New York), February 16, 2013, Sports55.

34. Rick Freeman, "Pro Soccer Player Robbie Rogers Says He is Gay," Fox News.com, February 16, 2013.

35. "Football Unites to Back Rogers," *Sunday Times*, February 17, 2013, Sport 5.

36. James Masters, "U.S. Soccer Star 'Comes Out' as Gay," CNN.com, February 15, 2013.

37. "Robbie Rogers Returns to MLS, the World of Twitter Responds," MLSsoccer.com, May 26, 2013.

38. David Kent, "Former Leeds Winger Rogers Comes Out but Announces His Retirement Aged Just 25," *Daily Mail*, February 15, 2013.

39. Orrin Schwarz, "Rogers Makes News on Two Major Fronts," *Chicago Daily Herald*, February 16, 2013, Sports 1.

40. "Robbie Rogers Comes Out, then 'Retires' on His Own Terms," *Montreal Gazette*, February 19, 2013.

41. Wayne Besen, "Robbie Rogers' Coming Out Doesn't Mean He Should Quit Pro Soccer," *Huffington Post*, February 23, 2013.

42. Steve Clare, "Robbie Rogers—Please Come Back and Play," *Huffington Post*, February 25, 2013.

43. Piers Edwards, "Robbie Rogers' Retirement Reasons Could Bring Change," CNN, March 29, 2013.

44. Neil W., "Rogers: Footballers Can't Be Openly Gay," Professional Footballers' Association, March 29, 2013; "Neil Warnock: Robbie Rogers Could Have Come Out at Leeds and Been Accepted," *Independent*, March 29, 2013; Paul Collins, "Warnock Insists Rogers Would Have Been Supported Had He Come Out at Leeds," *Daily Mail*, March 30, 2013.

45. Steve Busfield, "Robbie Rogers Trains with LA Galaxy after Coming Out and Quitting Soccer," *The Guardian*, May 1, 2013.

46. Beth Harris, "Rogers Makes Galaxy Debut as Openly Gay Athlete," *San Diego Union-Tribune*, May 26, 2013.

47. Greg Beacham, "Robbie Rogers, Openly Gay U.S. Soccer Player, Joins L.A. Galaxy in

Return to MLS," *Huffington Post*, May 25, 2013. See also "Robbie Rogers Set for Debut with L.A. Galaxy," *The Province*, May 26, 2013; Billy Witz, "Rogers Says He's Ready for a Role as a Pioneer," *New York Times*, May 26, 2013, SP 1; Dave Zirin, "Soccer Star Robbie Rogers: Out, Proud, and Now Un-Retired!," *The Nation*, May 26, 2013.

48. Greg Beacham, "Gay Soccer Player Robbie Rogers Joins LA Galaxy," Southern California Public Radio, May 16, 2013.

49. "Football: Openly Gay Rogers Makes Unforgettable MLS Debut," *Interaksyon*, May 27, 2013.

50. Philip Johnson, "L.A. Galaxy Player Becomes the First Openly Gay Athlete in Major League Soccer," *Business Insider*, May 28, 2013.

51. Jason Kandel, "Gay Soccer Player Robbie Rogers Joins LA Galaxy," NBC Los Angeles, May 25, 2013.

52. Stefan Bondy, "Rogers Out, and Back In," *Daily News* (New York), May 26, 2013, Sports 70.

53. Billy Witz, "Gay Athlete Ready for Role as a Pioneer," *International Herald Tribune*, May 27, 2013, Sports 12. See also "The Future's Bright for the Two Robbies," *Irish Examiner*, May 29, 2013.

54. "Trailblazer: Game Changer," *Nightline* (ABC News transcript), April 29, 2013; "Trailblazer: Joining the Team," *Nightline* (ABC News transcript), May 25, 2013.

55. Billy Witz, "Milestone for Gay Athletes as Rogers Plays for Galaxy," *New York Times*, May 27, 2013.

56. Greg Beacham, "Gay Soccer Player Robbie Rogers Joins LA Galaxy," *89.3 KPCC*, May 25, 2013.

57. "Monday Postgame: Why LA Galaxy's Robbie Rogers Is the Right Trailblazer," MLSsoccer.com, May 27, 2013.

58. Eliott C. McLaughlin and Jill Martin, "Robbie Rogers Takes Field as 1st Openly Gay Male Player in U.S. Pro Sports Match," CNN, May 27, 2013.

59. Phil Collin, "Los Angeles Galaxy Welcome New Addition Robbie Rogers," *San Jose Mercury News*, May 26, 2013. See also Leon Watson, "Robbie Rogers Receives a Standing Ovation on His Return to U.S. Soccer as He Becomes the First Openly Gay Athlete in Professional Men's Team Sport," *Mail Online*, May 27, 2013; Beth Harris, "Rogers Makes Galaxy Debut as Openly Gay Athlete," *San Diego Union-Tribune*, May 26, 2013.

60. Mary Alta Feddeman, "Coming Out: Robbie Rogers, Stephen Bickford, and a New Future for Gay Athletes," *IndyWeek*, June 7, 2013.

61. Stefan Bondy, "Robbie Rogers out, and Then Back in with Galaxy," *Daily News* (New York), May 25, 2013.

62. Jason Collins, "Why NBA Center Jason Collins Is Coming Out," *Sports Illustrated* April 29, 2013.

63. Kevin Baxter, "It's Just Another Day in Soccer," *Los Angeles Times*, June 2, 2013, C1.

64. Robbie Rogers and Eric Marcus, *Coming out to Play* (New York: Penguin Books, 2014).

65. Kyle R. King, "Three Waves of Gay Male Athlete Coming Out Narratives," *Quarterly Journal of Speech* 103, no. 4 (October 2, 2017): 384–86.

66. "MLS Commissioner Don Garber on Robbie Rogers: 'A Courageous Man and a Terrific Soccer Player,'" MLSsoccer.com, May 25, 2013.

67. Graham Parker, "Mike Magee on Fire for Chicago but Robbie Rogers Struggles in LA," *The Guardian*, June 20, 2013.

68. Jason Kandel, "Gay Soccer Player Robbie Rogers Joins L.A. Galaxy," nbclosangeles.com, May 25, 2013.

69. Harris, "Rogers Makes Galaxy Debut as Openly Gay Athlete."

70. Barry Moran, "Keano's Praise for New Gay Colleague," *The Sun*, May 28, 2013, News 13.

71. Grossberg, *Cultural Studies in the Future Tense*, 225.

72. Grossberg, *Cultural Studies in the Future Tense*, 257.

73. "USA Star Rogers: I Am Gay," *Daily Mirror*, February 16, 2013, Sport 62.

74. "Football Unites to Back Rogers," *Sunday Times* (London), February 17, 2013, Sport 5.

75. "Rogers: Footballers."

76. Adam Sherwin, "'Banter' Prevents Players from Coming Out, Says Robbie Rogers," *The Independent*, March 29, 2013.

77. Collins, "Warnock."

78. Donald McRae, "Football: 'In Football It's Impossible to Come Out' Exclusive," *The Guardian*, March 30, 2013, Sports 1.

79. David Kent, David McCormack, and Suzannah Hills, "Former Leeds Football Player Comes Out as Gay and Announces His Retirement from the Sport Aged Just 25," *Daily Mail*, February 16, 2013. See also Leon Watson, "Robbie Rogers Receives a Standing Ovation on His Return to U.S. Soccer," *Daily Mail*, May 27, 2013.

80. Wayne Dhesi, "The British Obsession with Gay Footballers," *Huffington Post*, May 14, 2013.

81. "Robbie Rogers Contemplates Returning to U.S. Soccer," *Daily Mail*, April 15, 2013. See also "Admission from Ex-Leeds United Midfielder Rogers Turns Spotlight on Attitudes," *Yorkshire Evening Post*, February 15, 2013; Kent, "Former Leeds."

82. "Robbie Rogers Contemplates"; see also "Admission"; Kent, McCormack, and Hills, "Former Leeds."

83. "Robbie Rogers Contemplates."

84. Masters, "U.S. Soccer Star 'Comes Out' as Gay."

85. Robbie Rogers with Eric Marcus, *Coming Out to Play* (New York: Penguin, 2014), 123.

86. Rogers with Marcus, *Coming Out to Play*, 125.

87. Witz, "Rogers Says."

88. "Robbie Rogers Returns (Thank God)," *The Offside Rules*, May 2013. This site is evidently no longer extant.

89. Witz, "Milestone."

90. John Branch, "Not the Moment, Not the Man," *New York Times*, May 27, 2013.

91. Abraham Iqbal Khan, "Michael Sam, Jackie Robinson, and the Politics of Respectability," *Communication & Sport* (2015): 1–21.

92. David Goldblatt, *The Age of Football: Soccer and the 21st Century*. (New York: W. W. Norton, 2020), 147.

93. "Robbie Rogers: FIFA Fails to Support Gays," *USA Today*, January 20, 2015.

94. Lindsey Gaston, Rory Magrath, and Eric Anderson, "From Hegemonic to Inclusive Masculinities in English Professional Football: Marking a Cultural Shift," *Journal of Gender Studies* 27, no. 3 (April 3, 2018).

95. Edward M. Kian, "A Case Study on Message-Board and Media Framing of Gay Male Athletes on a Politically Liberal Web Site," *International Journal of Sport Communication* 8, no. 4 (December 2015): 500–518.

96. Edward M. Kian, Eric Anderson, and Danny Shipka, "'I Am Happy to Start the Conversation': Examining Sport Media Framing of Jason Collins' Coming Out and Playing in the NBA," *Sexualities* 18, no. 5–6 (September 2015): 618–40.

97. Samantha King, "What's Queer about (Queer) Sport Sociology Now? A Review Essay," *Sociology of Sport Journal* 25, no. 4 (December 2008): 426.

98. McDonald points out that this move to homonormativity is, of course, not exclusive to men or soccer. She illustrates how the WNBA marketing departments, along with a compliant mass-media industry, mobilized images of traditional beauty, liberal feminism, and the idealized family. See Mary McDonald, "Out-of-Bounds Plays," in *Sports and Neoliberalism: Politics, Consumption and Culture*, ed. Michael L. Silk and David L. Andrews (Philadelphia: Temple University Press, 2012), 217.

99. Cody Shulak, "Comment," in "Robbie Rogers Joining LA Galaxy, Will Make History."

100. Reardon Steele, "Comment" in Branch, "Note"; and Richard W. Desiderio, "Comment," in Branch, "Note."

101. Grossberg, Cultural Studies in the Future Tense," 257.

102. Two recent examples are Jason Collins, who came out and then went into retirement from the NBA, and Michael Sam, a football player who signed with the NFL but was never able to make the roster to an actual game.

Chapter 3

Epigraph. Matt Jones, "How to Pick an English Premier League Team," *World Soccer Talk* (blog), July 2, 2012.

1. After the three-year contract, NBC renewed its deal with the Premier League. However, certain games each week now appeared only on a premium app (NBC Sports Gold) for several seasons, then on The Peacock. Nonetheless, the amount of coverage of games is immense.

2. Ernest Hemingway, with an introduction by Seán A. Hemingway, *The Sun Also Rises*, Hemingway Library ed. (New York: Scribner, 2016).

3. William Gibson, *Pattern Recognition* (Rutherford, NJ: Berkley, 2003).

4. It is somehow appropriate that no one knows whether Shaw said this first. The attribution is generally to a *Reader's Digest* issue (November 1942), although it is not found in any of his published works.

5. Richard Giulianotti and Roland Robertson, *Globalization and Football: A Critical Sociology*, 1st ed. (Thousand Oaks, CA: SAGE, 2009), 172.

6. Critchley, *What We Think about When We Think about Soccer*, 26.

7. Critchley, *What We Think about When We Think about Soccer*, 61.

8. While the claim for family tradition can be found in multiple places, I found myself touched by the simplicity of Elton John's statement about his attachment to Watford. "It's in your blood: Watford were my dad's team, therefore Watford were my team." Elton John, *ME: Elton John Official Autobiography* (New York: St. Martin's Griffin, 2020), 26.

9. Lawrence Wenner, "Playing Dirty: On Reading Media Texts and the Sports Fan in the 21st Century," in *Sports Mania: Essays on Fandom and the Media in the 21st Century*, ed. Lawrence Hugenberg, Paul Haridakis, and Adam Earnheardt (Jefferson, NC: McFarland, 2008), 24.

10. Billy Baker, "The Biggest Threat Facing Middle-Age Men Isn't Smoking or Obesity. It's Loneliness." *Boston Globe*, March 9, 2017.

11. Dubois, *Language of the Game*, 17.

12. Franklin Foer, *How Soccer Explains the World: An Unlikely Theory of Globalization* (New York; London: HarperPerennial, 2010), 244–46.

13. Richard Giulianotti, *Football: A Sociology of the Global Game* (Cambridge, UK: Polity Press, 1999), xii.

14. John Urry and Jonas Larsen, *The Tourist Gaze 3.0*, 3rd ed., Theory, Culture & Society (Los Angeles: Sage, 2011).

15. Giulianotti, *Football*, 148.

16. Giulianotti, *Football*, 150.

17. Giulianotti and Robertson, *Globalization and Football*, 24.

18. Giulianotti and Robertson, *Globalization and Football*, 34.

19. Giulianotti and Robertson, *Globalization and Football*, 35.

20. Roger Bennett, "An In-Depth Look at America's Premier League Allegiances," ESPN.com, September 24, 2013.

21. David Rowe and Callum Gilmour, "Sport, Media, and Consumption in Asia: A Merchandised Milieu," *American Behavioral Scientist* 53, no. 10 (June 2010): 1530–48.

22. Duffy, "English Premier League: A Primer for New Soccer Fans Picking a Club."

23. Ellen Peacock, "It's Time America to Pick Your English Premier League Team," *Fado* (blog), September 1, 2015; Eric Celeste, "Soccer's Sorting Hat," *American Airlines Magazine*"; James Kilpatrick, "Which MLS Team Should You Support? Find Your Premier League Team's Equivalent," Sky Sports.

24. Peacock, "It's Time America to Pick Your English Premier League Team"; Celeste, "Soccer's Sorting Hat."

25. Duffy, "English Premier League."

26. Peacock, "It's Time America to Pick Your English Premier League Team."

27. Ben Burrows, "What NFL Team Is like Your Premier League Side? Here's Who You Should Root for This Season," *Mirror*, September 7, 2017.

28. New team owner Assem Allam wanted to change the name from its historic "Hull City Association Football Club" to "Hull City Tigers," arguing that the team would be easier to market with such a name. He clearly misunderstood fan attachment to tradition. As the fans rose up against the name change, the Football Association, which has to approve all such changes, denied the request.

29. Burrows, "What NFL Team Is like Your Premier League Side?"

30. Jared Leeper, "American Guide to Choosing a Premier League Team 2017–18 Edition."

31. Nick Schwartz, "Your Guide to Picking a Favorite Premier League Team," *For The Win* (blog), August 15, 2013. Piers Morgan is a very vocal Arsenal fan who often is critical of Manchester United.

32. Andrei Markovits and Lars Rensman, *Gaming the World: How Sports Are Reshaping Global Politics and Culture* (Princeton, NJ: Princeton University Press, 2014), 201.

33. Markovits and Rensman, *Gaming the World*, 216.

34. Wenner, "Playing Dirty."

35. Julius Lasin, "Choosing a Premier League Team Based on Your Favorite Rapper."

36. Lasin, "Choosing a Premier League Team Based on Your Favorite Rapper."

37. Goldblatt, *Age Of Football*, 34–43.

38. Kuper and Szymanski, *Soccernomics*, 27.

39. Markovits and Rensman, *Gaming the World*, 216.

40. Anne Coulter, "Coulter: Any Growing Interest in Soccer a Sign of Nation's Moral Decay."

41. Kilpatrick, "Which MLS Team Should You Support?"

42. In yet another example of how contingent these connections are, Henry is currently the manager of the Montreal Impact of MLS.

43. Foer, *How Soccer Explains the World*, 244–46.

44. Duffy, "English Premier League"; see also Celeste, "Soccer's Sorting Hat."

45. Duffy, "English Premier League."

46. Jonathan Segur, "An English Premier League Primer," *Rolling Stone* (blog), August 15, 2014.

47. Peacock, "It's Time America to Pick Your English Premier League Team."

48. Sam's Army, "Love Soccer but Need a Team? No Problem—Barstool's Guide to Picking an EPL Club," *Barstool Sports* (blog).

49. Jones, "How to Pick an English Premier League Team."

50. David Fleenor, "How to Pick Your English Premier League Team."

51. Bennett, "In-Depth Look at America's Premier League Allegiances."

52. Dubois, *Language of the Game*, 262.

53. Hornby, *Fever Pitch*, 179.

54. Hornby, *Fever Pitch*, 179.

55. See, for example, Davey Edmondson, "English Premier League: Each Club's Most Famous Fans," Bleacher Report.

56. Schwartz, "Your Guide to Picking a Favorite Premier League Team." In the case of Jackson, the former owner was friends with Jackson and had put a statue of Jackson (since removed) outside of the stadium to commemorate Jackson's one-time visit.

57. Fleenor, "How to Pick Your English Premier League Team."

58. Bill Simmons, "Page 2: Choosing My EPL Team," ESPN.com.

59. For instance, in the summer of 2016, I attended a Chelsea friendly at the University of Michigan. While at the game, I saw, for the first time in my life, several young men wearing brand-new Leicester City FC jerseys. This was, of course, the year that Leicester had surprised everyone by winning the Premier League. In Michigan multiple people chided the young men, asking if they had been lifelong fans of the team.

60. Duffy, "English Premier League."

61. Peacock, "It's Time America to Pick Your English Premier League Team"; for warnings about not choosing relegation-threatened teams, see Fleenor, "How to Pick Your English Premier League Team."

62. Schwartz, "Your Guide to Picking a Favorite Premier League Team." Indeed, since that guide was written, Sunderland avoided relegation a few times, then were relegated to the Championship League one season, and then were relegated to League One a season thereafter.

63. As something of a sidebar, while I was drafting this chapter, an article appeared on Deadspin that was reporting on the contents of an academic article presented at a conference entitled "A Fair Shake for the Fair-Weather Fan" by Marcus Hedahl, Nate Olson, Kyle Fruh, and Luke Maring. The authors argued that fair-weather fans were good for the sport because they forced teams to treat fans with respect and therefore tried to incentivize them, rather than allowing the owners to know they have a full supporters group that will purchase tickets and goods regardless of how the team performs or how the fans are treated. See Reed Tucker, "Maybe Fair-Weather Fans Are Actually Good for Sports," Deadspin.

64. Crabbe and Brown, "You're Not Welcome Anymore."

65. As a result of sanctions placed on Abramovich after Russia's invasion of the Ukraine, he was forced to sell the team, which was purchased by a consortium headed up by Los Angeles Dodgers owner Todd Boehly.

66. Duffy, "English Premier League; Segura and Segura, "English Premier League Primer"; Peacock, "It's Time America to Pick Your English Premier League Team."

67. Bennett, "An In-Depth Look at America's Premier League Allegiances."

68. Burrows, "What NFL Team Is like Your Premier League Side?"

69. Burrows, "What NFL Team Is like Your Premier League Side?"

70. Simmons, "Page 2: Choosing My EPL Team."

71. Schwartz, "Your Guide to Picking a Favorite Premier League Team."

72. Simon Kuper, *Soccer against the Enemy: How the World's Most Popular Sport Starts and Fuels Revolutions and Keeps Dictators in Power* (New York: Basic Books, 2010), 216.

73. Segura, "English Premier League Primer."

74. Aaron Gordon, "A VICE Sports Guide to How to Pick an English Premier League Team Guide," Vice.com.

75. Army, "Love Soccer but Need a Team?"; Simmons, "Page 2: Choosing My EPL Team."

76. Giulianotti, *Football.*

77. Verner Møller and Jakob Genz, "Commercial Sport—Debordian Spectacle or Barthesian Mythology?," *Catalan Journal of Communication & Cultural Studies* 6, no. 2 (October 1, 2014): 261.

78. Fiske and Hartley, *Reading Television,* 85.

79. Montague, *1312,* 265.

80. Dubois, *Language of the Game,* 17.

81. Goldblatt, *Age of Football,* 399.

Chapter 4

Epigraph. Joani Cruz, "Five Hateful Comparisons between Liga MX and MLS," *CE Noticias Financieras,* August 2, 2020.

1. Tracey Schoenadal, "Hispanic Audiences, Millennials, and a College Education," *YouGovSport* (blog), June 20, 2019.

2. This chapter is looking to the discourse around Liga MX and MLS, both men's soccer leagues. While the National Women's Soccer League is holding steady in size, and while Liga MX has recently established a female league—Liga MX Femenil—I am placing my focus on the men's leagues simply because at this time they are far more popular and hence grab more attention.

3. While numerous leagues are now available to US viewers, given the multiple digital and streaming outlets available, MLS and the Premier League continue to have the most "mainstream" coverage (although not, as I show below, the highest ratings of soccer in the United States.

4. For comparison's sake, the average NFL game in 2020 was 15.4 million, and this number was down slightly from previous years. See Rick Porter, "NFL Ratings Slip in 2020, Remain Dominant on Broadcast," *Hollywood Reporter,* January 6, 2021.

5. Connor Fleming, "U.S. Viewership of Liga MX Playoffs Smashes EPL and MLS Ratings," The18.

6. Jabari Young, "Major League Soccer Increased Viewership This Season. Now It Has to Convince Networks It's Worth $300 Million per Year," CNBC, December 18, 2021.

7. "What Is the Most Popular Football League in the United States?," LADS Podcast.

8. Dan Adu-Gyamfi, "How to Watch Liga MX in English on US TV and Streaming," *World Soccer Talk* (blog), December 1, 2019.

9. Christopher Harris, "MLS Fails to Close TV Ratings Gap with Premier League and Liga MX," *World Soccer Talk* (blog), April 10, 2019.

10. Graham Ruthven, "MLS Is Pulling Fans into Stadiums, but TV Audiences Remain Underwhelming," *The Guardian,* August 25, 2020.

11. Mark Asher Goodman, "Fear and Desire: TV Ratings, Revenue, and MLS' Relationship with the Latinx Community," American Soccer Analysis.

12. Dubois, *Language of the Game*, 241.

13. Foer, *How Soccer Explains the World*, 5.

14. Goldblatt, *Age of Football*, 31.

15. The Seattle Sounders actually won in 2022, after I drafted this chapter.

16. Erik Siemers, "The Evolution of MLS Expansion Fees," *St. Louis Business Journal*, August 22, 2019.

17. Joe Prince-Wright, "MLS, Mexico Impress in Study of Global Attendance Figures," *ProSoccerTalk | NBC Sports* (blog), April 16, 2019.

18. "Univision's TUDN to Exclusively Telecast Liga MX Guardianes 2020 Final Featuring Leon vs. UNAM," *News Bites*, December 15, 2020.

19. Perry Kostidakis, "La Liga Games in the US 'Not Fair for Anyone,' Says Liga MX President," CNN Digital, October 12, 2018.

20. "Economic Strength Strengthens Liga MX-MLS," *CE Noticias Financieras*, November 27, 2019.

21. Jon Marthaler, "Soccer Insider: In the U.S., Most Eyes Glued to Mexico's Liga MX," *Star Tribune (Minneapolis)*, July 21, 2017.

22. Kevin Baxter, "Mexico's Liga MX Has the Lion's Share of Soccer Viewers in the U.S.," *Los Angeles Times*, April 30, 2016.

23. Baxter "Mexico's Liga MX Has the Lion's Share of Soccer Viewers in the U.S."

24. Cruz, "Five Hateful Comparisons between Liga MX and MLS."

25. "MLS Grew, but Still Doesn't Reach Liga MX," *CE Noticias Financieras*, December 19, 2020.

26. "Carlos Vela, the Mexican Looking to Dethrone the Liga MX in Concacaf," *CE Noticias Financieras*, February 28, 2020.

27. Julia Poe, "Former Liga MX Players Weigh in on Unprecedented Shift of Interest in MLS," *Orlando Sentinel*, January 20, 2020, sec. Sports.

28. Francisco González, "La Liga MX at Risk," *CE Noticias Financieras*, December 21, 2020.

29. Jon Marthaler, "Gap between Best of MLS and Mexican Soccer Starting to Close," *(Minneapolis) Star Tribune*, April 28, 2018.

30. "Liga MX . . . Stagnant," *CE Noticias Financieras*, March 11, 2020.

31. "MLS, Liga MX Launch Leagues Cup Competition," *Sports Illustrated*, May 29, 2019.

32. Fred Figuero, "Arriola, Outsider to Relaunch Liga MX," *CE Noticias Financieras*, December 8, 2020.

33. Cruz, "Five Hateful Comparisons between Liga MX and MLS."

34. "Hand in Hand, Liga MX vs. MLS," *CE Noticias Financieras*, January 23, 2020. While MLS does negotiate a television contract for the league as a whole, individual teams are also allowed to negotiate local contracts for games that are not televised nationally.

35. "The Crisis of Owners in the Liga MX," *CE Noticias Financieras*, November 15, 2019.

36. Neil deMause, "Is MLS a Ponzi Scheme?," Deadspin; Neil deMause, "If MLS Isn't a Ponzi Scheme, Maybe It's the WeWork of Sports?," *Field of Schemes* (blog); Billy Haisley, "MLS, Which Is Definitely Not a Ponzi Scheme, Wants to Expand by Adding Three New Teams for $200 Million Each," Deadspin.

37. Cruz, "Five Hateful Comparisons between Liga MX and MLS."

38. Erendira Palma Hernández, "Current Crisis, an Opportunity for Liga MX to Reinvent Itself," *CE Noticias Financieras*, June 13, 2020.

39. Poe, "Former Liga MX Players Weigh in on Unprecedented Shift of Interest in MLS."

40. Elihū Hernández, "MLS and Liga MX, the Eternal Comparison," *CE Noticias Financieras*, March 23, 2020.

41. Jon Marthaler, "CONCACAF Champions League Needs Better Tournament to Juice Interest," *Star Tribune*, February 16, 2019.

42. "Hand in Hand, Liga MX vs. MLS."

43. Javier Aguirre, "Liga MX Lacks Dissemination, Getting into the Libertadores Would Be Wonderful," *CE Noticias Financieras*, November 29, 2019.

44. "Vermeer Heats the LAFC-UANL Matchup by Saying That in Europe You See MLS and Not Liga MX," *CE Noticias Financieras*, February 27, 2020.

45. "Vermeer Heats the LAFC-UANL Matchup by Saying That in Europe You See MLS and Not Liga MX."

46. Cruz, "Five Hateful Comparisons between Liga MX and MLS."

47. "Liga MX Appoints Genius Sports Group as Exclusive Long-Term Official Data, Streaming and Integrity Partner," *Dow Jones Institutional News*, November 24, 2020.

48. "Internationalization, Inexperience in Liga MX," *CE Noticias Financieras*, July 24, 2020.

49. Kuper, *Soccer against the Enemy*, 25.

50. Goldblatt, *Age of Football*, 286.

51. Han and Butler, *Burnout Society*.

52. Han and Butler, *Burnout Society*, 8.

53. Asen, "Neoliberalism, the Public Sphere, and a Public Good," 331.

54. Asen, "Neoliberalism, the Public Sphere, and a Public Good," 345.

55. Asen, "Neoliberalism, the Public Sphere, and a Public Good," 334.

Chapter 5

Epigraph 1. Amanda Gonzalez, "US Women's National Team Stars Fighting for Equal Pay on Soccer Field," *Hilltop Views* (blog), April 5, 2016.

Epigraph 2. Rachel Bachman, "U.S. Soccer Offers Women Equal Pay in Some Matches—and They Reply, Do Better," *Wall Street Journal*, March 8, 2020, sec. Life, A1.

Epigraph 3. Andrew Das, "Pay Disparity in U.S. Soccer? It's Complicated," *New York Times*, April 21, 2016, sec. Sports.

1. The USSF is the nonprofit body that governs American soccer at the international, professional, and amateur levels, including overseeing the women's and men's national teams.

2. Markovits and Hellerman, *Offside*, 160.

3. I want to stress here at the outset that I of course strongly support arguments for equal pay. While it will be necessary for me to point out the complicated nature of the arguments concerning it, I want nothing in my tale to be seen as anything but supportive of the equal pay arguments.

4. An excellent summary of the lawsuit and the historic relation between the USWNT and USSF can be found at "USWNT Lawsuit versus U.S. Soccer Explained," ESPN.com, June 3, 2020.

5. Anne M. Peterson, "Goal Reached: US Women's Soccer Team Gets New Contract," AP NEWS, April 6, 2017.

6. While the next two words in the chapter are "Simply put," even the parameters I spell out are oversimplifying the case, in that the pay rate has built-in annual changes, there are routes by which some women could play for only a few games, etc. In short, the outline I provide is a broad way; the details are seemingly endless.

7. Allen Smith, "Female Soccer Stars Bring EEOC Wage Discrimination Complaint," SHRM, April 1, 2016.

8. Graham Hays, "USWNT's Unequal Pay Claim Rejected by Judge," ESPN.com, May 1, 2020.

9. Andrew Das, "U. S. Soccer and Women's Stars Reach Deal on Working Conditions," *New York Times*, December 1, 2020, sec. Sports.

10. By the time of this book's publication, the team has reached an "equal pay" agreement with US Soccer. This does not alter the argument of this chapter, which focuses on the public justifications for equal pay.

11. For a philosophical argument in favor of equal pay for the USWNT along the principle of equality, see Alfred Archer and Martine Prange, "'Equal Play, Equal Pay': Moral Grounds for Equal Pay in Football," *Journal of the Philosophy of Sport* 46, no. 3 (September 2, 2019): 416–36.

12. Khan, *Curt Flood in the Media*, 15.

13. Dubois, *Language of the Game*, 120.

14. Dubois, *Language of the Game*, 127–36.

15. Markovits and Rensman, *Gaming the World*, 157–58.

16. Gail J. Newsham, *In a League of Their Own! The Dick, Kerr Ladies 1917–1965* (Trowbridge, UK: Paragon, 2018).

17. For other very useful histories of the women's game, see Tim Tate, *Women's Football: The Secret History* (London: John Blake, 2016); Jean Williams, *The History of Women's Football* (Barnsley: Pen and Sword History, 2021).

18. The teams were organized either by factories or associated athletic clubs and football clubs.

19. I admit that I find myself having to keep from relaying many of the narratives Newsham provides, lest I get sidetracked from my task in this chapter.

20. For an additional history of women and soccer, see Tate, *Women's Football.*

21. Hortense J. Spillers, *Black, White, and in Color: Essays on American Literature and Culture* (Chicago: University of Chicago Press, 2003), xiii.

22. Hornby, *Fever Pitch*, 11.

23. Goldblatt, *Age of Football*, 145.

24. Goldblatt, *Age of Football*, 364.

25. Goldblatt, *Age of Football*, 308.

26. Jafar Panahi, dir., *Offside* (Sony Pictures Home Entertainment, 2007).

27. Quoted in Lindsey Meân, "Identity and Discursive Practice: Doing Gender on the Football Pitch," *Discourse & Society* 12, no. 6 (November 2001): 791.

28. Meân, "Identity and Discursive Practice."

29. Goldblatt, *Age of Football*, 23.

30. American "exceptionalism" has many meanings, of course, some more technical than others. Here, I'm simply referring to the ideology that sees the US as "different" and "better" than other national cultures, that sees its orientation and behaviors as an "exception" (and as an improvement over) others. Markovits and Hellerman observe that US "sports exceptionalism" is deeply rooted in other exceptionalisms but refers to the way the US has highlighted sports other than does a majority of the rest of the world.

31. Brian D. Bunk, *From Football to Soccer: The Early History of the Beautiful Game in the United States*, Sport and Society (Urbana: University of Illinois Press, 2021).

32. Eileen Narcotta-Welp, "Opening the Soccer Frontier: The Beautiful Game's American Past and Potential for the Future," in *Soccer Frontiers: The Global Game in the United States, 1863–1913*, ed. Chris Bolsman and George Kioussis (Knoxville: University of Tennessee Press, 2021), 298.

33. Moira Donegan, "USA's Formidable Women's Team Is No Accident. It's a Product of Public Policy," *The Guardian*, July 6, 2019.

34. Donegan, "USA's Formidable Women's Team Is No Accident."

35. Markovits and Hellerman, *Offside*, 163.

36. Rachel Allison, *Kicking Center: Gender and the Selling of Women's Professional Soccer*, Critical Issues in Sport and Society (New Brunswick, NJ: Rutgers University Press, 2018), 15.

37. Markovits and Rensman, *Gaming the World*, 158.

38. Goldblatt, *Age of Football*, 145.

39. Goldblatt, *Age of Football*, 307.

40. Using the database Proquest, I searched for "US Women's Soccer Equal Pay" and limited the sources to newspapers, wire feeds, reports, magazines, and trade journals. This excluded "Dissertations & Theses," "Blogs, Podcasts, & Websites," "Other Sources," and "Scholarly Journals." In effect, I was wanting to get a mix of "objective" news accounts about the issues, as well as public editorials. While some of the other sources (e.g., "Blogs, Podcasts, & Websites") would have their own interesting stories to tell, my assumption is that they were drawing upon some of the same news sources that my analysis draws upon.

41. Allison, *Kicking Center*, 64–65.

42. Dianne Feinstein, "Feinstein Supports Equal Pay for U.S. Women's Soccer Team," United States Senator for California.

43. Kevin Baxter, "On the Matter of the USWNT and Equal Pay, It's Complicated," *Los Angeles Times*, July 14, 2019, sec. Soccer.

44. Rachel Bachman, "Judge Says U.S. Women's Soccer Team Paid Less per Game than Men," *Wall Street Journal*, November 8, 2019, sec. US.

45. "Equal Pay for Equal Work—and Not Just for Soccer Stars," *Los Angeles Times*, August 5, 2019, sec. Opinion.

46. Nancy Armour, "US Soccer Insults All Women with Its 'Argument' in Equal Pay Lawsuit," *USA Today*, March 10, 2020.

47. Barry Svrluga, "Perspective: U.S. Women's Soccer Players Deserve Equal Pay, and It Shouldn't Take a Lawsuit," *Washington Post*, March 8, 2019.

48. Jesse Jackson, "'Equal Pay, Equal Pay, Equal Pay,'" *Chicago Sun-Times*, July 8, 2019.

49. "Congressman Morelle Fights to Secure Equal Pay for United States Women's National Soccer Team," Representative Joseph Morelle, July 27, 2019. www.morelle.house.gov.

50. Erin Flynn, "USWNT's Equal Pay Fight Echoes Challenges of Female Sports Pioneers," Western Michigan University, July 29, 2019.

51. Flynn, "USWNT's Equal Pay Fight Echoes Challenges of Female Sports Pioneers."

52. Baxter, "On the Matter of the USWNT."

53. Rachel Bachman, "U.S. Soccer Federation President Resigns in Wake of Sponsor, Player Backlash," *Wall Street Journal*, March 13, 2020, sec. Life.

54. Armour, "US Soccer Insults All Women with Its 'Argument' in Equal Pay Lawsuit."

55. Rachel Bachman, "U.S. Soccer Federation Says Male Players Carry 'More Responsibility'; Backlash Follows," *Wall Street Journal*, March 12, 2020, sec. Life.

56. Rachel Bachman, "U.S. Women's Soccer Players Sought Lawsuit Talks," *Wall Street Journal*, June 27, 2019, sec. Life.

57. Svrluga, "Perspective: U.S. Women's Soccer Players Deserve Equal Pay, and It Shouldn't Take a Lawsuit."

58. Ben Gartland, "U.S. Women's Soccer Deserves Equal Pay," *The DePaulia* (blog), April 10, 2016.

59. Bachman, "U.S. Women's Soccer Players Sought Lawsuit Talks."

60. Carli Lloyd, "Why I'm Fighting for Equal Pay," *New York Times*, April 10, 2016, sec. Sports.

61. Bachman, "Judge Says Women's Soccer Team Paid Less per Game than Men."

62. Rachel Bachman, "U.S. Women's Soccer Team Moves to Speed Appeal in Equal Pay Case," *Wall Street Journal*, May 9, 2020, sec. Life.

63. Janet Adamy, "Hillary Clinton Joins U.S. Women's Soccer Player in Call for Equal Pay," *Wall Street Journal*, April 12, 2016, sec. Politics.

64. Andrew Das, "Can U.S. Soccer and Its Women's Team Make Peace on Equal Pay?," *New York Times*, May 2, 2020, sec. Sports.

65. "The U.S. Women's Soccer Team Has More than Earned Equal Pay," *Washington Post*, July 8, 2019.

66. "The U.S. Women's Soccer Team Has More than Earned Equal Pay."

67. Goldblatt, *Age of Football*, 399.

68. Kevin Draper, "Pushed by Consumers, Some Sponsors Join Soccer's Fight over Equal Pay," *New York Times*, August 5, 2019, sec. Sports.

69. Baxter, "On the Matter of the USWNT."

70. "Equal Pay and the U.S. Women's Soccer Team," *Medicine Hat News*, July 15, 2019.

71. Maddy Birch, "Women's National Team Has Earned Right to Be Paid More," LancasterOnline, April 26, 2020.

72. Brown, *Undoing the Demos*, 31.

73. Rachel Bachman, "U.S. Women's Team Sues Soccer Federation, Alleging Gender Discrimination," *Wall Street Journal*, March 8, 2019.

74. Matthew Futterman, "U.S. Soccer Files Defense against Equal-Pay Complaint," *Wall Street Journal*, June 1, 2016, sec. Life.

75. Adam Kilgore, "U.S. Women's Soccer Players Raise Stakes in Debate over How Pay Scales Are Set," *Washington Post*, March 31, 2016, sec. D. C. United/Soccer.

76. Kilgore, "U.S. Women's Soccer Players Raise Stakes in Debate over How Pay Scales Are Set."

77. Kilgore, "U.S. Women's Soccer Players Raise Stakes in Debate over How Pay Scales Are Set."

78. "The U.S. Women's Soccer Team Has More than Earned Equal Pay."

79. "The U.S. Women's Soccer Team Has More than Earned Equal Pay."

80. Gartland, "U.S. Women's Soccer Deserves Equal Pay."

81. "U.S. Women's Soccer Team Should Get Equal Pay," *Wilkes-Barre Citizens' Voice*, April 3, 2016.

82. Pat DiDomenico, "Lessons for Employers: The Equal Pay Lawsuit by U.S. Women's Soccer Team," *TCA Regional News*, April 8, 2016.

83. Ben Gartland, "U.S. Women's Soccer Deserves Equal Pay," *The DePaulia* (blog), April 10, 2016.

84. For an interesting philosophical justification of equal pay, see Archer and Prange, "'Equal Play, Equal Pay.'"

85. Cheryl Cooky and Dunja Antunovic, "'This Isn't Just about Us': Articulations of Feminism in Media Narratives of Athlete Activism," *Communication & Sport* 8, no. 4–5 (August 2020): 698.

Chapter 6

Epigraph 1. Amos Barshad, "Premier League Embraces Optics of Anti-Racism; but Many in Soccer Say Much More Must Be Done," *National Post*, August 21, 2020, sec. A.

Epigraph 2. Calvin Robinson, "The Premier League Should Have Thought Twice before Getting into Bed with Black Lives Matter," *The Telegraph*, July 1, 2020.

1. Anoop Mirpuri, "Why Can't Kobe Pass (the Ball)? Race and the NBA in an Age of Neoliberalism," in *Commodified and Criminalized: New Racism and African Americans in Contemporary Sports*, ed. David J. Leonard and C. Richard King (Lanham, MD: Rowman and Littlefield, 2011), 95–120.

2. "Herstory," Black Lives Matter.

3. "About," Black Lives Matter.

4. "About."

5. "Herstory."

6. Allissa V. Richardson, "Dismantling Respectability: The Rise of New Womanist Communication Models in the Era of Black Lives Matter," *Journal of Communication* 69, no. 2 (April 1, 2019): 193–213.

7. Carolyn Elerding, "The Social Media Agon as Differencing Machine: A Materialist Feminist Perspective," *Communication, Culture and Critique* 11, no. 1 (March 1, 2018): 162–78.

8. Catherine L. Langford and Montené Speight, "#BlackLivesMatter: Epistemic Positioning, Challenges, and Possibilities," *Journal of Contemporary Rhetoric* 5, no. 3/4 (2015): 86.

9. Danielle Sarver Coombs and Anne C. Osborne, "Negotiating Insider–Outsider Status in Ethnographic Sports Research," *Sport in Society* 21, no. 2 (February 2018): 243–59.

10. Dubois, *Language of the Game*, 195.

11. Hornby, *Fever Pitch*, 182.

12. Buford, *Among the Thugs*, 136.

13. Foer, *How Soccer Explains the World*, 48.

14. Jacco van Sterkenburg and Annelies Knoppers, "Sport as a Contested Racial/Ethnic Discourse: Processes of Racialization in Dutch Sport Media and Sport Policy," *Journal of Multicultural Discourses* 7, no. 2 (July 2012): 119–36.

15. Tom Bassam, "Sharp Rise in Football Racism as Incidents Go Up by More than 50% in One Year," *The Guardian*, January 30, 2020. "Reporting Statistics," Kick It Out.

16. Bassam, "Sharp Rise in Football Racism as Incidents Go Up by More than 50% in One Year."

17. "The Damning List of Racist Incidents Which Marred Football in 2019," *The Independent*, December 23, 2019.

18. "The Damning List of Racist Incidents Which Marred Football in 2019."

19. Ravi Ubha, "Premier League: Racist and Homophobic Incidents Tarnish 'Best League in the World,'" CNN, December 10, 2019.

20. Barnaby Lane, "15 Racist Incidents from across the World of Soccer That Made 2019 One of the Sport's Most Shameful Years Ever," Business Insider.

21. Jacob Steinberg, "From Parks to Premier League: The Shocking Scale of Racism in English Football," *The Guardian*, April 12, 2019, sec. Football.

22. Stan Stejskal et al., "MLS Players Share Their Thoughts and Experiences on Racism in America," The Athletic, June 9, 2020.

23. Stejskal et al., "MLS Players Share Their Thoughts and Experiences on Racism in America."

24. Jeff Kassouf, "Amid Nationwide Protests, Black NWSL Players Train with Feelings Many Teammates Are Only Just Beginning to Understand," June 12, 2020.

25. Ryan McDonald, "Utah Royals FC, NWSL, Players Respond to Allegation of Racial Slurs at Rio Tinto Stadium Directed at Portland Thorns FC Goalkeeper Adrianna Franch," *Deseret News*, September 9, 2019.

26. As I illustrate in the next chapter, even making this claim completely ignores the large number of Mexican Americans who are soccer fans but follow Mexico's Liga MX rather than the US league or European leagues. For the most part, they are invisible in English-language US news.

27. Dubois, *Language of the Game*, 196. See also Goldblatt, *Age of Football*, 86–88, for a discussion of football fan culture's relationship to the Arab Spring.

28. Potter, *Ultras*, 82.

29. Potter, *Ultras*, 145.

30. Foer, *How Soccer Explains the World*, 7.

31. Potter, *Ultras*, 20.

32. Goldblatt, *Age of Football*, 24. Goldblatt explores the politics of different ultras throughout his work.

33. Ryan Kelly, "MLS Flag Ban: What Is the Iron Front Symbol & Why Was It Barred from Soccer Stadiums?"

34. Clearly, what I indicated by "mainstream" is a very biased function of my search. Using Proquest, I search for "soccer" and "Black Lives Matter," using English as my language, and selected magazines, newspapers, and wire feeds. The idea here was to get some "centralized" idea of how the discussion was taking place, knowing full well how problematic some of these searches can be. I stopped at two hundred articles as a large enough number to provide a good sense of the public "discussion."

35. Tim Daniels, "Premier League to Replace Player Names on Kits with 'Black Lives Matter,'" Bleacher Report.

36. Barnaby Lane, "Premier League Players Took a Knee for the First 10 Seconds of the League's Return in a Powerful Show of Solidarity with the Black Lives Matter Movement," Business Insider, June 18, 2020.

37. Because of the pandemic delay, the conclusion of one season was pushed right up next to the start of the following season.

38. Paul MacInnes, "Premier League Drops Black Lives Matter Badge from Shirts for Own Campaign," *The Guardian*, September 10, 2020.

39. Andrew Das, Twitter post, June 27, 2020, 12:02 p.m. Interestingly, the *USA Today* telling of the story misquotes the statement in some ways that could lend to analysis itself. See Scott Gleeson, "NWSL Players Wear 'Black Lives Matter' Shirts, Kneel before First Game of Challenge Cup," *USA Today*.

40. Asif Burhan, "Megan Rapinoe Is Proud Her Teammates Now Stand with Her in Kneeling," *Forbes*, January 13, 2021.

41. Luis Miguel Echegaray, "MLS Black Players for Change's Mission, Plans after Orlando," *Sports Illustrated*, August 6, 2020.

42. Mike McGrath, "How Europe's Other Big Leagues Have Approached Black Lives Matter," *The Telegraph*, July 2, 2020.

43. Paul Gittings, "Jadon Sancho's 'Justice for George Floyd' Protest," CNN, May 31, 2020.

44. "McKennie: U.S. Might Not Accept Me for Skin Color," ESPN.com, October 12, 2020.

45. Esteban Suárez, "The Black Referee in Mexico Overcoming Racism on the Soccer Field," AL DÍA News, July 13, 2020.

46. For this chapter, I searched for the phrases "Black Lives Matter" and "Soccer" to develop my reading list, regardless of where they took me in terms of leagues. The majority of the discourse took me to discussions of the Premier League, Major League Soccer, and the

National Women's Soccer League. However, I will also discuss the meaning of the phrase in other leagues that are mentioned as well.

47. Marc Stein, "Led by N.B.A., Boycotts Disrupt Pro Sports in Wake of Blake Shooting," *New York Times*, June 24, 2020.

48. Anne M. Peterson, "Black Players for Change Lead Protest at MLS Is Back Tourney," AP NEWS, July 9, 2020.

49. Andy Clayton, "NWSL Becomes First U.S. Pro League to Return to Action, All Players Take a Knee during National Anthem," *Daily News* (New York).

50. Jonathan Liew, "Black Lives Matter Has Exposed Sport's Underlying Failure to Deal with Racism," *The Guardian*, June 13, 2020.

51. Liew, "Black Lives Matter Has Exposed Sport's Underlying Failure to Deal with Racism."

52. Daniel Blackham, "Thierry Henry Kneels for 8 Minutes and 46 Seconds during MLS Match in George Floyd Tribute," Express.co.uk, July 10, 2020.

53. Calum Trenaman, "Thierry Henry Kneels during Match to Honor George Floyd," CNN, July 10, 2020.

54. Fiona Sun, "Black Lives Matter in Hong Kong Too: African Migrants Say Racism Leaves Them Feeling Alienated, Shunned," *South China Morning Post*, June 27, 2020.

55. "Man City Thump Arsenal 3–0 as Premier League Returns," *La Prensa Latina Media* (blog), June 18, 2020.

56. "'BlackLivesMatter': Liverpool Stars Take a Knee to Show Support," Vanguard, June 1, 2020.

57. Todd D. Mielwski, "Forward Madison FC Says Sunday Home Game Postponed to Spotlight 'Fight against Racial Injustice and Systemic Oppression,'" Madison.com, August 28, 2020.

58. Neil M Davidson, "Major League Soccer Players Boycott Training in Apparent Labour Impasse," TSN, June 1, 2020.

59. Peterson, "Black Players for Change Lead Protest at MLS Is Back Tourney."

60. Peterson, "Black Players for Change Lead Protest at MLS Is Back Tourney."

61. Tyler Lauletta, "MLS Players Kneel in Solidarity before First Match of Restart," Insider, July 8, 2020.

62. "Premier League Renames Players to 'Black Lives Matter,'" *CE Noticias Financieras*, June 13, 2020, English ed.

63. "'BlackLivesMatter': Liverpool Stars Take a Knee to Show Support."

64. Ian Winrow and James Gray, "Players to Wear Black Lives Matter on the Back of Shirts," *I*, June 12, 2020.

65. "'BlackLivesMatter': Liverpool Stars Take a Knee to Show Support."

66. Jill Martin, Leah Asmelash, and David Close, "These Teams and Athletes Refused to Play in Protest of the Jacob Blake Shooting," CNN, August 28, 2020.

67. Mark Guidi, "Former Rangers Star Rod Wallace Says on August 1, Scottish Football Has to Show That Black Lives Matter," *Sunday Post* (blog), June 28, 2020.

68. Musa Okwonga, "The Premier League Is Returning—and Bringing with It a Statement on Black Lives Matter," *Washington Post*, June 16, 2020.

69. Segun Odegbami, "Black Lives Matter," *Complete Sports* (blog), August 1, 2020.

70. Odegbami, "Black Lives Matter."

71. Peterson, "Black Players for Change Lead Protest at MLS Is Back Tourney."

72. Guidi, "Former Rangers Star Rod Wallace Says on August 1, Scottish Football Has to Show That Black Lives Matter."

73. Sam Dean, "Patrick van Aanholt Ready to Take a Knee for Black Lives Matter When Premier League Returns," *The Telegraph*, June 11, 2020.

74. Okwonga, "The Premier League Is Returning—and Bringing with It a Statement on Black Lives Matter."

75. "Premier League Renames Players to 'Black Lives Matter.'"

76. "Premier League Renames Players to 'Black Lives Matter.'"

77. Barshad, "Premier League Embraces Optics of Anti-Racism; But Many in Soccer Say Much More Must Be Done." The "Rooney Rule" is an NFL policy, adopted in 2003 and named after former Pittsburgh Steelers owner Dan Rooney, that requires NFL teams with head coaching, general manager, or equivalent front-office position openings to interview at least one underrepresented minority.

78. Melissa Reddy, "Football Needs to Show That Black Lives Matter on Boards Too," *The Independent*, July 30, 2020.

79. Oliver Holt, "Allowing Logos Has to Be More than Just a Sop to Players," *Mail Online*, July 4, 2020.

80. Antonio Rüdiger, "This Article Will Not Solve Racism in Football," *The Players' Tribune*, May 27, 2021.

81. Chris Porter, "Marcus Rashford, Black Lives Matter and a British Premier Who Is Out of His League," *The Conversation*.

82. Jennifer L. Borda and Bailey Marshall, "Creating a Space to #SayHerName: Rhetorical Stratification in the Networked Sphere," *Quarterly Journal of Speech* 106, no. 2 (April 2, 2020): 133–55.

83. Kimberlé Crenshaw et al., *Say Her Name: Resisting Police Brutality against Black Women* (Columbia Law School. New York: African American Policy Forum, Center for Intersectionality and Social Policy Studies, 2016).

84. John Branch, "The Anthem Debate Is Back. But Now It's Standing That's Polarizing," *New York Times*, July 4, 2020, sec. Sports.

85. Branch, "The Anthem Debate Is Back."

86. Alisha Haridasani Gupta, "Since 2015: 48 Black Women Killed by the Police. And Only 2 Charges," *New York Times*, September 24, 2020, sec. U.S.

87. Barshad, "Premier League Embraces Optics of Anti-Racism; but Many in Soccer Say Much More Must Be Done."

88. Jack Beresford, "Katie Hopkins Reveals Tweet to That Got Her Permanently Banned from Twitter," *Irish Post*, June 24, 2020.

89. Joe Mulroy, "In the First Premier League Games They Knelt for Black Lives Matter, Surely This Is Totally Wrong," *Northern Echo*, June 19, 2020.

90. Jessica Lee, "EXCLUSIVE: Investigating George Floyd's Criminal Record," Snopes.com, August 31, 2020. While in the largest sense, Floyd's criminal record is irrelevant to how he was treated and the value of his life, some memes have not only exaggerated his record but in doing so have made the actions of the police officers at the moment of his death appear more justified.

91. Eric Reid, "Why Colin Kaepernick and I Decided to Take a Knee," *New York Times*, September 25, 2017, sec. Opinion. In this opinion piece for the *New York Times*, Kaepernick's San Francisco 49ers teammate explains that while Kaepernick had been sitting during the national anthem, a visit and discussion with retired Green Beret and NJL player Nate Boyer made them consider that taking a knee would be better, because "it's a respectful gesture. I remember thinking our posture was like a flag flown at half-mast to mark a tragedy. It baffles me that our protest is still being misconstrued as disrespectful to the country, flag, and military personnel. We chose it [kneeling] because it's just the opposite."

92. Branch, "Anthem Debate Is Back. But Now It's Standing That's Polarizing."

93. Molly McElwee, "Taking a Knee during National Anthems Is Distracting and Uncomfortable—but That Is Precisely the Point," *The Telegraph*, July 7, 2020.

94. Aimee Lewis, "FC Dallas' Reggie Cannon Criticizes Booing of Players Kneeling during National Anthem," CNN.com, August 13, 2020.

95. Andrew Topping, "MP Blasts Premier League over Black Lives Matter Campaign," NottinghamshireLive, June 14, 2020.

96. Topping, "MP Blasts Premier League over Black Lives Matter Campaign."

97. Topping, "MP Blasts Premier League over Black Lives Matter Campaign."

98. Mitch Phillips, "Premier League, NFL and Cricket Wrestle with BLM Response," *National Post.*

99. Ben Rumsby, "Andros Townsend Disowns Black Lives Matter Movement after Crystal Palace Criticise Its Political Agendas," *The Telegraph*, July 2, 2020.

100. Robinson, "Premier League Should Have Thought Twice before Getting into Bed with Black Lives Matter."

101. Robinson, "Premier League Should Have Thought Twice before Getting into Bed with Black Lives Matter."

102. Spencer Neale, "'Cultural Marxism': Premier League Clubs Wear 'Black Lives Matter' on Jerseys as Matches Restart," *Washington Examiner*, June 17, 2020.

103. Sridhar Shrivathsa, "Soccer-Players Must Keep Taking a Knee to Highlight BLM, Says Ex-QPR Defender Onuoha," *National Post*, September 26, 2020.

104. Simon Evans, "Soccer-Premier League CEO Says Black Lives Matter a Moral Cause, Not a Political One," Reuters.

105. Holt, "Allowing Logos Has to Be More than Just a Sop to Players."

106. Matt Lawton, "Black Lives Matter Logo to Stay on Shirts," *The Times*, July 2, 2020.

107. Holt, "Allowing Logos Has to Be More than Just a Sop to Players."

108. Grano and Butterworth, "Rhetoric, Sport and the Political," 1.

109. Richardson, "Dismantling Respectability."

110. Joe Tanner, "Premier League Players to Wear 'No Room for Racism' Badges on Kits, Replacing Black Lives Matter Logo," Sky Sports, September 10, 2020.

Conclusion

Epigraph. Galeano, *Soccer in Sun and Shadow*, 36–37.

1. Brown, *In the Ruins of Neoliberalism*, 8.

2. Critchley, *What We Think about When We Think about Soccer*.

3. Terry Eagleton, "Football: A Dear Friend to Capitalism," *The Guardian*, June 15, 2010.

4. Eagleton, "Football: A Dear Friend to Capitalism."

5. Eagleton, "Football: A Dear Friend to Capitalism."

6. Eagleton, "Football: A Dear Friend to Capitalism."

Bibliography

"£1m Football Star: I AM GAY." *The Sun*, October 22, 1990.

"About." Black Lives Matter.

Adams, Adi, and Eric Anderson. "Exploring the Relationship between Homosexuality and Sport among the Teammates of a Small, Midwestern Catholic College Soccer Team." *Sport, Education and Society* 17, no. 3 (June 2012): 347–63.

Adams, Adi, Eric Anderson, and Mark McCormack. "Establishing and Challenging Masculinity: The Influence of Gendered Discourses in Organized Sport." *Journal of Language and Social Psychology* 29, no. 3 (September 2010): 278–300.

Adamy, Janet. "Hillary Clinton Joins U.S. Women's Soccer Player in Call for Equal Pay." *Wall Street Journal*, April 12, 2016, sec. Politics.

"Admission from Ex-Leeds United Midfielder Rogers Turns Spotlight on Attitudes," *Yorkshire Evening Post*, February 15, 2013.

Adu-Gyamfi, Dan. "How to Watch Liga Mx in English on US TV and Streaming." *World Soccer Talk* (blog), December 1, 2019.

Agrobinsonla. "Quiz: Which Premier League Team Should I Support?" Proprofs.com.

Aguirre, Javier. "Liga MX Lacks Dissemination, Getting into the Libertadores Would Be Wonderful." *CE Noticias Financieras*, November 29, 2019.

Allison, Rachel. *Kicking Center: Gender and the Selling of Women's Professional Soccer*. Critical Issues in Sport and Society. New Brunswick, NJ: Rutgers University Press, 2018.

"American Outlaws," n.d. Theamericanoutlaws.com.

Anderson, Benedict R. O'G. *Imagined Communities: Reflections on the Origin and Spread of Nationalism*. Rev. ed. London: Verso, 2016.

Archer, Alfred, and Martine Prange. "'Equal Play, Equal Pay': Moral Grounds for Equal Pay in Football." *Journal of the Philosophy of Sport* 46, no. 3 (September 2, 2019): 416–36.

Armour, Nancy. "US Soccer Insults All Women with Its 'Argument' in Equal Pay Lawsuit." March 10, 2020. Usatoday.com.

Armstrong, Gary. *Football Hooligans: Knowing the Score*. Explorations in Anthropology. Oxford: Berg, 1998.

Army, Sam's. "Love Soccer but Need a Team? No Problem—Barstool's Guide to Picking an EPL Club." *Barstool Sports* (blog).

Ascher, Ivan. *Portfolio Society: On the Capitalist Mode of Prediction*. New York: Zone Books, 2016.

Asen, Robert. "Neoliberalism, the Public Sphere, and a Public Good." *Quarterly Journal of Speech* 103, no. 4 (October 2, 2017): 329–49.

Bachman, Rachel. "Judge Says U.S. Women's Soccer Team Paid Less per Game than Men." *Wall Street Journal*, November 8, 2019, sec. US.

———. "U.S. Soccer Federation President Resigns in Wake of Sponsor, Player Backlash." *Wall Street Journal*, March 13, 2020, sec. Life.

———. "U.S. Soccer Federation Says Male Players Carry 'More Responsibility'; Backlash Follows." *Wall Street Journal*, March 12, 2020, sec. Life.

———. "U.S. Soccer Offers Women Equal Pay in Some Matches—and They Reply, Do Better." *Wall Street Journal*, March 8, 2020, sec. Life.

———. "U.S. Women's Soccer Players Sought Lawsuit Talks." *Wall Street Journal*, June 27, 2019, sec. Life.

———. "U.S. Women's Soccer Team Moves to Speed Appeal in Equal Pay Case." *Wall Street Journal*, May 9, 2020, sec. Life.

———. "U.S. Women's Team Sues Soccer Federation, Alleging Gender Discrimination." *Wall Street Journal*, March 8, 2019.

Baker, Billy. "The Biggest Threat Facing Middle-Age Men Isn't Smoking or Obesity. It's Loneliness." *Boston Globe*, March 9, 2017.

Bannon, James. *Running with the Firm: My Double Life as an Undercover Hooligan*. London: Ebury, 2014.

Barshad, Amos. "Premier League Embraces Optics of Anti-Racism; but Many in Soccer Say Much More Must Be Done." *National Post*, August 21, 2020, sec. A.

Bassam, Tom. "Sharp Rise in Football Racism as Incidents Go Up by More than 50% in One Year." *The Guardian*, January 30, 2020.

Baxter, Kevin. "It's Just Another Day in Soccer." *Los Angeles Times*, June 2, 2013.

———. "Mexico's Liga Mx Has the Lion's Share of Soccer Viewers in the U.S." *Los Angeles Times*, April 30, 2016.

———. "On the Matter of the USWNT and Equal Pay, It's Complicated." *Los Angeles Times*, July 14, 2019, sec. Soccer.

Beacham, Greg. "Gay Soccer Player Robbie Rogers Joins LA Galaxy." Southern California Public Radio, May 16, 2013.

———. "Robbie Rogers, Openly Gay U.S. Soccer Player, Joins L.A. Galaxy in Return to MLS." *Huffington Post*, May 25, 2013.

Bennett, Roger. "An In-Depth Look at America's Premier League Allegiances." ESPN.com, September 24, 2013.

Beresford, Jack. "Katie Hopkins Reveals Tweet That Got Her Permanently Banned from Twitter." *Irish Post*, June 24, 2020.

Berger, Peter L. *The Sacred Canopy: Elements of a Sociological Theory of Religion*. New York: Anchor Books, 1990.

Besen, Wayne. "Robbie Rogers' Coming Out Doesn't Mean He Should Quit Pro Soccer." *Huffington Post*, February 22, 2013.

Best, Shaun. "The Leicester School of Football Hooliganism: An Evaluation." *Soccer & Society* 11, no. 5 (September 2010): 573–87.

Billings, Andrew C., Leigh M. Moscowitz, Coral Rae, and Natalie Brown-Devlin. "The Art of Coming Out: Traditional and Social Media Frames Surrounding the NBA's Jason Collins." *Journalism & Mass Communication Quarterly* 92, no. 1 (March 2015): 142–60.

Birch, Maddy. "Women's National Team Has Earned Right to Be Paid More." Lancaster-Online, April 26, 2020.

Blackham, Daniel. "Thierry Henry Kneels for 8 Minutes and 46 Seconds during MLS Match in George Floyd Tribute." *Express.co.uk*, July 10, 2020.

"'Blacklivesmatter': Liverpool Stars Take a Knee to Show Support." *Vanguard*, June 1, 2020.

Bodnar, John. *Remaking America: Public Memory, Commemoration, and Patriotism in the Twentieth Century*. 1st pbk. print. Princeton: Princeton University Press, 1994.

Boellstorff, T. "When Marriage Falls: Queer Coincidences in Straight Time." *GLQ: A Journal of Lesbian and Gay Studies* 13, no. 2–3 (January 1, 2007): 227–48.

Bolster, John. "Monday Postgame: Why LA Galaxy's Robbie Rogers Is the Right Trailblazer." MLSsoccer.com, May 27, 2013.

Bondy, Stefan. "Robbie Rogers Out, and Then Back in with Galaxy." *Daily News* (New York).

———. "Rogers Out and Back In." *Daily News* (New York), May 26, 2013.

Borda, Jennifer L., and Bailey Marshall. "Creating a Space to #sayhername: Rhetorical Stratification in the Networked Sphere." *Quarterly Journal of Speech* 106, no. 2 (April 2, 2020): 133–55.

Branch, John. "Note the Moment, Not the Man." *New York Times*, May 27, 2013, sec. Sports.

———. "The Anthem Debate Is Back. But Now It's Standing That's Polarizing." *New York Times*, July 4, 2020, sec. Sports.

Brown, Wendy. *In the Ruins of Neoliberalism: The Rise of Antidemocratic Politics in the West*. Wellek Library Lectures. New York: Columbia University Press, 2019.

———. *Undoing the Demos: Neoliberalism's Stealth Revolution*. First paperback ed. Near Futures. New York: Zone Books, 2017.

Buford, Bill. *Among the Thugs*. 1st Vintage Departures ed. New York: Vintage Departures, 1993.

Bunk, Brian D. *From Football to Soccer: The Early History of the Beautiful Game in the United States*. Sport and Society. Urbana: University of Illinois Press, 2021.

Burhan, Asif. "Megan Rapinoe Is Proud Her Teammates Now Stand with Her in Kneeling." *Forbes*, January 13, 2021.

Burrows, Ben. "What NFL Team Is like Your Premier League Side? Here's Who You Should Root for This Season." *Mirror*, September 7, 2017.

Busfield, Steve. "Robbie Rogers Trains with LA Galaxy after Coming Out and Quitting Soccer." *The Guardian*, May 1, 2013, sec. Football.

Butterworth, Michael L. "'Katie Was Not Only a Girl, She Was Terrible': Katie Hnida, Body Rhetoric, and Football at the University of Colorado." *Communication Studies* 59, no. 3 (August 12, 2008): 259–73.

———. "The Politics of the Pitch: Claiming and Contesting Democracy through the Iraqi National Soccer Team." *Communication and Critical/Cultural Studies* 4, no. 2 (June 2007): 184–203.

"Carlos Vela, the Mexican Looking to Dethrone the Liga MX in Concacaf." *CE Noticias Financieras*, February 28, 2020.

Carr, E. Summerson. *Scripting Addiction: The Politics of Therapeutic Talk and American Sobriety*. Princeton: Princeton University Press, 2011.

Cashmore, Ellis, and Jamie Cleland. "Glasswing Butterflies: Gay Professional Football Players and Their Culture." *Journal of Sport and Social Issues* 35, no. 4 (November 2011): 420–36.

Cassidy, William P. *Sports Journalism and Women Athletes: Coverage of Coming Out Stories*. Basingstoke: Palgrave Macmillan, 2019.

Caudwell, Jayne. "Sporting Gender: Women's Footballing Bodies as Sites/Sights for the (Re) Articulation of Sex, Gender, and Desire." *Sociology of Sport Journal* 20, no. 4 (December 2003): 371–86.

Celeste, Eric. "Soccer's Sorting Hat." *American Airlines Magazine*. Accessed August 18, 2020. Page no longer extant.

Charland, Maurice. "Constitutive Rhetoric: The Case of the Peuple Québécois." *Quarterly Journal of Speech* 73, no. 2 (May 1987): 133–50.

Clare, Steve. "Robbie Rogers—Please Come Back and Play." *Huffington Post*, February 25, 2013.

Clark, John. "Football and Working Class Fans: Tradition and Change." In *Football Hooliganism: The Wider Context*, edited by Roger Ingham, 37–60. London: Interaction, 1978.

Clayton, Andy. "NWSL Becomes First U.S. Pro League to Return to Action, All Players Take a Knee during National Anthem." *Daily News* (New York).

Cleland, Jamie. "Discussing Homosexuality on Association Football Fan Message Boards: A Changing Cultural Context." *International Review for the Sociology of Sport* 50, no. 2 (March 2015): 125–40.

Coakley, Jay. "Ideology Doesn't Just Happen: Sports and Neoliberalism." *Curitiba* 1 (n.d.): 67–84.

Collin, Phil. "Los Angeles Galaxy Welcome New Addition Robbie Rogers." *Mercury News* (blog), May 26, 2013.

Collins, Jason. "Why NBA Center Jason Collins Is Coming Out Now." *Sports Illustrated*, April 29, 2013.

Collins, Paul. "Neil Warnock Insists Rogers Would Have Been Supported Had He Come Out While at Leeds." *Mail Online*.

"Coming Out." *Daily News* (New York), February 16, 2013.

Connell, Raewyn. *Which Way Is Up? Essays on Sex, Class, and Culture*. Sydney: Allen & Unwin, 1983.

Cooky, Cheryl, and Dunja Antunovic. "'This Isn't Just about Us': Articulations of Feminism in Media Narratives of Athlete Activism." *Communication & Sport* 8, no. 4–5 (August 2020): 692–711.

Coombs, Danielle Sarver, and Anne C. Osborne. "Negotiating Insider–Outsider Status in Ethnographic Sports Research." *Sport in Society* 21, no. 2 (February 2018): 243–59.

Cooper, Melinda. *Family Values: Between Neoliberalism and the New Social Conservatism*. Near Futures. New York: Zone Books, 2017.

Coulter, Anne. "Coulter: Any Growing Interest in Soccer a Sign of Nation's Moral Decay." Clarionledger.

Cox, Barbara, and Shona Thompson. "Multiple Bodies: Sportswomen, Soccer and Sexuality." *International Review for the Sociology of Sport* 35, no. 1 (March 2000): 5–20.

Crabbe, Tim, and Adam Brown. "'You're Not Welcome Anymore': The Football Crowd, Class and Social Exclusion." In *British Football and Social Exclusion*, edited by Stephen Wagg, 26–46. London: Routledge, 2004.

Crenshaw, Kimberlé, Andrea J. Ritchie, Rachel Anspach, Rachel Gilmer, and Luke Harris. *Say Her Name: Resisting Police Brutality against Black Women*. Columbia Law School. New York: African American Policy Forum, Center for Intersectionality and Social Policy Studies, 2016.

Critchley, Simon. *What We Think about When We Think about Soccer*. New York: Penguin Books, 2017.

"The Crisis of Owners in the Liga MX." *CE Noticias Financieras*, November 15, 2019.

Cruz, Joani. "Five Hateful Comparisons between Liga MX and MLS." *CE Noticias Financieras*, August 2, 2020.

"The Damning List of Racist Incidents Which Marred Football in 2019." *The Independent*, December 23, 2019.

Daniels, Tim. "Premier League to Replace Player Names on Kits with 'Black Lives Matter.'" Bleacher Report.

Dart, Jon. "Confessional Tales from Former Football Hooligans: A Nostalgic, Narcissistic Wallow in Football Violence." *Soccer & Society* 9, no. 1 (January 2008): 42–55.

Das, Andrew. "Can U.S. Soccer and Its Women's Team Make Peace on Equal Pay?" *New York Times*, May 2, 2020, sec. Sports.

———. "Pay Disparity in U.S. Soccer? It's Complicated." *New York Times*, April 21, 2016, sec. Sports.

———. "U.S. Soccer and Women's Stars Reach Deal on Working Conditions." *New York Times*, December 1, 2020, sec. Sports.

Davidson, Neil M. "Major League Soccer Players Boycott Training in Apparent Labour Impasse". *Toronto Star*, June 1, 2020.

Dean, Sam. "Patrick Van Aanholt Ready to Take a Knee for Black Lives Matter When Premier League Returns." *The Telegraph*, June 11, 2020.

deMause, Neil. "If MLS Isn't a Ponzi Scheme, Maybe It's the Wework of Sports?" *Field of Schemes* (blog), November 5, 2019.

———. "Is MLS a Ponzi Scheme?" Deadspin.

Dhesl, Wayne. "The British Obsession with Gay Footballers." *Huffington Post*, December 6, 2017.

DiDomenico, Pat. "Lessons for Employers: The Equal Pay Lawsuit by U.S. Women's Soccer Team." *TCA Regional News*, April 8, 2016.

Dillon, Stephen. *Fugitive Life: The Queer Politics of the Prison State*. Durham, NC: Duke University Press, 2018.

Donegan, Moira. "USA's Formidable Women's Team Is No Accident. It's a Product of Public Policy." *The Guardian*, July 6, 2019.

Dow, Bonnie. "Ellen, Television, and the Politics of Gay and Lesbian Visibility." *Critical Studies in Media Communication* 18, no. 2 (June 2001): 123–40.

Draper, Kevin. "Pushed by Consumers, Some Sponsors Join Soccer's Fight over Equal Pay." *New York Times*, August 5, 2019, sec. Sports.

Dubois, Laurent. *The Language of the Game: How to Understand Soccer*. 1st ed. New York: Basic Books, 2018.

Duffy, Ty. "The English Premier League: A Primer for New Soccer Fans Picking a Club." https://m.bjkkby.com.

Dunning, Eric, Patrick Murphy, and John Williams. *The Roots of Football Hooliganism: An Historical and Sociological Study*. London: Routledge, 2015.

Eagleton, Terry. "Football: A Dear Friend to Capitalism." *The Guardian*, June 15, 2010.

Echegaray, Luis Miguel. "MLS Black Players for Change's Mission, Plans after Orlando." *Sports Illustrated*, August 6, 2020.

"Economic Strength Strengthens Liga MX-MLS." *CE Noticias Financieras*, November 27, 2019.

Edds, Robin. "Which English Premier League Team Should You Support?" BuzzFeed.

Edmondson, Davey. "English Premier League: Each Club's Most Famous Fans." Bleacher Report.

Edwards, Piers. "Robbie Rogers' Retirement Reasons Could Bring Change." CNN, March 29, 2013.

Elerding, Carolyn. "The Social Media Agon as Differencing Machine: A Materialist Feminist Perspective." *Communication, Culture and Critique* 11, no. 1 (March 1, 2018): 162–78.

"Equal Pay and the U.S. Women's Soccer Team." *Medicine Hat News*, July 15, 2019.

"Equal Pay for Equal Work—and Not Just for Soccer Stars." *Los Angeles Times*, August 5, 2019, sec. Opinion.

Evans, Simon. "Premier League CEO Says Black Lives Matter a Moral Cause, Not a Political One." Reuters, June 30, 2020.

Fashanu, John. "John Fashanu: My Gay Brother Is an Outcast." *The Voice*, October 30, 1990.

Feddeman, Mary Alta. "Coming Out: Robbie Rogers, Stephen Bickford and a New Future for Gay Athletes." INDY Week, June 7, 2013.

Feinstein, Diane. "Feinstein Supports Equal Pay for U.S. Women's Soccer Team." United States Senator for California." www.feinstein.senate.gov.

Felski, Rita. *The Limits of Critique*. Chicago: University of Chicago Press, 2015.

Figuero, Fred. "Arriola, Outsider to Relaunch Liga MX." *CE Noticias Financieras*, December 8, 2020.

Fisher, Diana. "Immigrant Closets: Tactical-Micro-Practices-in-the-Hyphen." *Journal of Homosexuality* 45, no. 2–4 (September 23, 2003): 171–92.

Fiske, John, and John Hartley. *Reading Television*. 2nd ed. New Accents. London: Routledge, 2003.

Fleenor, David. "How to Pick Your English Premier League Team—Soccer365." Soccer365.

Fleming, Connor. "U.S. Viewership of Liga MX Playoffs Smashes EPL and MLS Ratings." The18.

Flynn, Erin. "USWNT's Equal Pay Fight Echoes Challenges of Female Sports Pioneers." Western Michigan University, July 29, 2019.

Foer, Franklin. *How Soccer Explains the World: An Unlikely Theory of Globalization*. New York: HarperPerennial, 2010.

"Football: Openly Gay Rogers Makes Unforgettable MLS Debut." Interaksyon. May 27, 2013.

"Football Unites to Back Rogers." (London) *Sunday Times*, February 17, 2013.

Foucault, Michel, Michel Senellart, and Michel Foucault. *The Birth of Biopolitics: Lectures at the Collège de France, 1978—79*. 1st pbk ed. [Repr.]. Lectures at the Collège de France. New York: Picador, 2010.

Fox, Ragan Cooper. "Gay Grows Up: An Interpretive Study on Aging Metaphors and Queer Identity." *Journal of Homosexuality* 52, no. 3–4 (May 15, 2007): 33–61.

Francis, Mickey, and Peter Walsh. *Guvnors*. Bury, UK: Milo Books, 1999.

Futterman, Matthew. "U.S. Soccer Files Defense against Equal-Pay Complaint." *Wall Street Journal*, June 1, 2016, sec. Life.

Galeano, Eduardo. *Soccer in Sun and Shadow*. New York: Nation Books, 2013.

Gartland, Ben. "U.S. Women's Soccer Deserves Equal Pay." *The DePaulia* (blog), April 10, 2016.

Gaston, Lindsey, Rory Magrath, and Eric Anderson. "From Hegemonic to Inclusive Masculinities in English Professional Football: Marking a Cultural Shift." *Journal of Gender Studies* 27, no. 3 (April 3, 2018): 301–12.

Gibson, William. *Pattern Recognition*. Rutherford, NJ: Berkley, 2003.

Gittings, Paul. "Jadon Sancho's 'Justice for George Floyd' Protest." CNN. May 31, 2020.

Giulianotti, Richard. *Football: A Sociology of the Global Game*. Cambridge, UK: Polity Press, 1999.

Giulianotti, Richard, and Roland Robertson. *Globalization and Football: A Critical Sociology*. 1st ed. Thousand Oaks, CA: SAGE, 2009.

Gleeson, Scott. "NWSL Players Wear 'Black Lives Matter' Shirts, Kneel before First Game of Challenge Cup." *USA Today*, June 27, 2020.

Goldblatt, David. *The Age of Football: Soccer and the 21st Century*. New York: Macmillan, 2020.

Gonzalez, Amanda. "US Women's National Team Stars Fighting for Equal Pay on Soccer Field." *Hilltop Views* (blog), April 5, 2016.

González, Francisco. "La Liga MX at Risk." *CE Noticias Financieras*, December 21, 2020.

Goodall, H. Lloyd. *Divine Signs: Connecting Spirit to Community*. Carbondale: Southern Illinois University Press, 1996.

Goodman, Mark Asher. "Fear and Desire: TV Ratings, Revenue, and MLS' Relationship with the Latinx Community." American Soccer Analysis. September 24, 2019.

Gordon, Aaron. "A VICE Sports Guide to How to Pick an English Premier League Team Guide." Vice.

Grano, Daniel A. "Football after Fragmentation: Brain Banking, Chronic Traumatic Encephalopathy, and Racial Biosociality in the NFL." *Communication and Critical/Cultural Studies* 17, no. 4 (October 1, 2020): 339–59.

———. "Muhammad Ali versus the 'Modern Athlete': On Voice in Mediated Sports Culture." *Critical Studies in Media Communication* 26, no. 3 (August 2009): 191–211.

Grano, Daniel A., and Michael L. Butterworth. "Rhetoric, Sport and the Political: An Introduction." In *Sport, Rhetoric, and Political Struggle*, edited by Daniel A. Grano and Michael L. Butterworth, 1–22. New York: Peter Lang, 2019.

Gregg, Richard B. "The Ego-Function of the Rhetoric of Protest." *Philosophy and Rhetoric*, Vol. 4, no. 2 (Spring 1971), 71–91.

Grossberg, Lawrence. *Cultural Studies in the Future Tense*. Durham, NC: Duke University Press, 2010.

Guidi, Mark. "Former Rangers Star Rod Wallace Says on August 1, Scottish Football Has to Show That Black Lives Matter." *Sunday Post* (blog). June 28, 2020.

Gupta, Alisha Haridasani. "Since 2015: 48 Black Women Killed by the Police. And Only 2 Charges." *New York Times*, September 24, 2020, sec. U.S.

Haisley, Billy. "MLS, Which Is Definitely Not a Ponzi Scheme, Wants to Expand by Adding Three New Teams for $200 Million Each." Deadspin.

Halberstam, Judith. *Female Masculinity*. Twentieth anniversary ed. Durham, NC: Duke University Press, 2018.

Halbwachs, Maurice, and Lewis A. Coser. *On Collective Memory*. The Heritage of Sociology. Chicago: University of Chicago Press, 1992.

Hanan, Joshua S. "Subjects of Technology: An Auto-Archeology of Attention Deficit Disorder in Neoliberal Time(s)." *Cultural Studies ↔ Critical Methodologies* 19, no. 2 (April 2019): 105–15.

"Hand in Hand, Liga MX vs. MLS." *CE Noticias Financieras*. January 23, 2020.

Hardin, Marie, Kathleen M. Kuehn, Hillary Jones, Jason Genovese, and Murali Balaji. "'Have You Got Game?' Hegemonic Masculinity and Neo-Homophobia in U.S. Newspaper Sports Columns." *Communication, Culture & Critique* 2, no. 2 (June 2009): 182–200.

Harris, Beth. "Rogers Makes Galaxy Debut as Openly Gay Athlete." *San Diego Union-Tribune*, May 27, 2013.

Harris, Christopher. "MLS Fails to Close TV Ratings Gap with Premier League and Liga MX." *World Soccer Talk* (blog), April 10, 2019.

Hays, Graham. "USWNT's Unequal Pay Claim Rejected by Judge." ESPN.com, May 1, 2020.

Hekma, Gert. "'As Long as They Don't Make an Issue of It . . .': Gay Men and Lesbians in Organized Sports in the Netherlands." *Journal of Homosexuality* 35, no. 1 (February 12, 1998): 1–23.

Hemingway, Ernest. With an introduction by Seán A. Hemingway. *The Sun Also Rises*. Hemingway Library ed. New York: Scribner, 2016.

Hernández, Erendira Palma. "Current Crisis, an Opportunity for Liga MX to Reinvent Itself." *CE Noticias Financieras*, June 13, 2020.

Hernández, Elihú. "MLS and Liga MX, the Eternal Comparison." *CE Noticias Financieras*, March 23, 2020.

"Herstory." Black Lives Matter.

Holt, Oliver. "Allowing Logos Has to Be More than Just a Sop to Players." *Mail Online*, July 4, 2020.

Hornby, Nick. *Fever Pitch*. 1st Riverhead trade pbk. ed. New York: Riverhead Books, 1998.

Hubert, Susan J. "What's Wrong with This Picture? The Politics of Ellen's Coming Out Party." *Journal of Popular Culture* 33, no. 2 (September 1999): 31–36.

Hughson, John, and Marcus Free. "Football's 'Coming Out': Soccer and Homophobia in England's Tabloid Press." *Media International Australia* 140, no. 1 (August 2011): 117–25.

Iannotta, Joah G., and Mary Jo Kane. "Sexual Stories as Resistance Narratives in Women's Sports: Reconceptualizing Identity Performance." *Sociology of Sport Journal* 19, no. 4 (December 2002): 347–69.

Ingham, Roger, ed. *Football Hooliganism: The Wider Context*. London: Inter-Action Inprint, 1978.

"Internationalization, Inexperience in Liga MX." *CE Noticias Financieras*, July 24, 2020.

Jackson, Jesse. "'Equal Pay, Equal Pay, Equal Pay.'" *Chicago Sun-Times*, July 8, 2019.

John, Elton. *Me: Elton John Official Autobiography*, New York: Henry Holt, 2020.

Johnson, Philip. "L.A. Galaxy Player Becomes the First Openly Gay Athlete in Major League Soccer," May 28, 2013, *Business Insider*.

Jones, Matt. "How to Pick an English Premier League Team." *World Soccer Talk* (blog), July 2, 2012.

Kammen, Michael G. *Mystic Chords of Memory: The Transformation of Tradition in American Culture*. 1st Vintage Books ed. New York: Vintage Books, 1993.

Kandel, Jason. "Gay Soccer Player Robbie Rogers Joins LA Galaxy." *NBC Los Angeles* (blog), May 25, 2013.

Kassouf, Jeff. "Amid Nationwide Protests, Black NWSL Players Train with Feelings Many Teammates Are Only Just Beginning to Understand." The Equalizer. June 12, 2020.

Kelly, Ryan. "MLS Flag Ban: What Is the Iron Front Symbol & Why Was It Barred from Soccer Stadiums?" Goal.

Kent, David. "Robbie Rogers, Once of Leeds, Comes Out as Gay and Retires Aged 25." *Daily Mail*, February 15, 2013.

Kent, David, David McCormack, and Suzannah Hills. "Former Leeds Football Player Comes Out as Gay and Announces His Retirement from the Sport Aged Just 25." *Mail Online*, February 16, 2013.

Khan, Abraham Iqbal. *Curt Flood in the Media: Baseball, Race, and the Demise of the Activist-Athlete*. Jackson: University Press of Mississippi, 2012. Ebook Central, Proquest.

———. "Michael Sam, Jackie Robinson, and the Politics of Respectability." *Communication & Sport* 5, no. 3 (June 2017): 331–51.

Kian, Edward M. "A Case Study on Message-Board and Media Framing of Gay Male Athletes on a Politically Liberal Web Site." *International Journal of Sport Communication* 8, no. 4 (December 2015): 500–18.

Kian, Edward M, Eric Anderson, and Danny Shipka. "'I Am Happy to Start the Conversation': Examining Sport Media Framing of Jason Collins' Coming Out and Playing in the NBA." *Sexualities* 18, no. 5–6 (September 2015): 618–40.

Kilgore, Adam. "U.S. Women's Soccer Players Raise Stakes in Debate over How Pay Scales Are Set." *Washington Post*, March 31, 2016, sec. D.C. United/Soccer.

Kilpatrick, James. "Which MLS Team Should You Support? Find Your Premier League Team's Equivalent." Sky Sports.

King, Anthony. "Football Hooliganism and the Practical Paradigm." *Sociology of Sport Journal* 16, no. 3 (September 1999): 269–73. https://doi.org/10.1123/ssj.16.3.269.

———. "Violent Pasts: Collective Memory and Football Hooliganism." *Sociological Review* 49, no. 4 (November 2001): 568–85.

King, Claire Sisco. "American Queerer: Norman Rockwell and the Art of Queer Feminist Critique." *Women's Studies in Communication* 39, no. 2 (April 2, 2016): 157–76.

King, John. *The Football Factory*. London: Vintage, 1997.

King, Kyle R. "Three Waves of Gay Male Athlete Coming Out Narratives." *Quarterly Journal of Speech* 103, no. 4 (October 2, 2017): 372–94.

King, Martin. *Hoolifan: Thirty Years of Hurt*. Edinburgh: Mainstream, 2002.

King, Samantha. "What's Queer about (Queer) Sport Sociology Now? A Review Essay." *Sociology of Sport Journal* 25, no. 4 (December 2008): 419–42.

Kostidakis, Perry. "La Liga Games in the US 'Not Fair for Anyone,' Says Liga MX President." CNN Digital, October 12, 2018.

Kuper, Simon. *Soccer against the Enemy: How the World's Most Popular Sport Starts and Fuels Revolutions and Keeps Dictators in Power*. New York: Basic Books, 2010.

Kuper, Simon, and Stefan Szymanski. *Soccernomics: Why England Loses; Why Germany, Spain, and France Win; and Why One Day Japan, Iraq, and the United States Will Become Kings of the World's Most Popular Sport*. 2018 World Cup ed. New York: Nation Books, 2018.

Lane, Barnaby. "15 Racist Incidents from Across the World of Soccer That Made 2019 One of the Sport's Most Shameful Years Ever." Business Insider.

———. "Premier League Players Took a Knee for the First 10 Seconds of the League's Return in a Powerful Show of Solidarity with the Black Lives Matter Movement." Business Insider, June 18, 2020.

Lane, Davey. "The Life and Death of Justin Fashanu." Roads & Kingdoms. February 25, 2014.

Langford, Catherine L., and Montené Speight. "#BlackLivesMatter: Epistemic Positioning, Challenges, and Possibilities." *Journal of Contemporary Rhetoric* 5, no. 3/4 (2015): 78–89.

Lasin, Julius. "Choosing a Premier League Team Based on Your Favorite Rapper." Complex.

Latour, Bruno. "Why Has Critique Run Out of Steam? From Matters of Fact to Matters of Concern." *Critical Inquiry* 30, no. 2 (January 2004): 225–48.

Lauletta, Tyler. "MLS Players Kneel in Solidarity before First Match of Restart." Insider. July 8, 2020.

Lawton, Matt. "Black Lives Matter Logo to Stay on Shirts." (London) *The Times*. July 2, 2020.

Lee, Jessica. "EXCLUSIVE: Investigating George Floyd's Criminal Record." Snopes.com, August 31, 2020.

Leeper, Jared. "American Guide to Choosing a Premier League Team 2017–18 Edition."

Lewis, Aimee. "FC Dallas' Reggie Cannon Criticizes Booing of Players Kneeling during National Anthem." CNN.com. August 13, 2020.

Liew, Jonathan. "Black Lives Matter Has Exposed Sport's Underlying Failure to Deal with Racism." *The Guardian*, June 13, 2020.

"Liga MX . . . Stagnant." *CE Noticias Financieras*. March 11, 2020.

"Liga MX Appoints Genius Sports Group as Exclusive Long-Term Official Data, Streaming and Integrity Partner." Dow Jones Institutional News. November 24, 2020.

Lloyd, Carli. "Why I'm Fighting for Equal Pay." *New York Times*, April 10, 2016, sec. Sports.

MacInnes, Paul. "Premier League Drops Black Lives Matter Badge from Shirts for Own Campaign." *The Guardian*, September 10, 2020.

Magrath, Rory. "'To Try and Gain an Advantage for My Team': Homophobic and Homosexually Themed Chanting among English Football Fans." *Sociology* 52, no. 4 (August 2018): 709–26.

"Man City Thump Arsenal 3–0 as Premier League Returns." La Prensa Latina. June 18, 2020.

Markovits, Andrei, and Lars Rensman. *Gaming the World: How Sports Are Reshaping Global Politics and Culture*. Princeton: Princeton University Press, 2014.

Markovits, Andrei S., and Steven L. Hellerman. *Offside: Soccer and American Exceptionalism*. Princeton: Princeton University Press, 2001.

Marriner, Jason. *Life as a Chelsea Headhunter*. Clacton-on-Sea, UK: Apex, 2009.

Marsh, Peter E., Elisabeth Rosser, and Rom Harré. *The Rules of Disorder*. Social Worlds of Childhood. London: Routledge, 1995.

Marthaler, Jon. "Concacaf Champions League Needs Better Tournament to Juice Interest." *Star Tribune (Minneapolis)*, February 16, 2019.

———. "Gap between Best of MLS and Mexican Soccer Starting to Close." *Star Tribune (Minneapolis)*, April 28, 2018.

———. "Soccer Insider: In the U.S., Most Eyes Glued to Mexico's Liga MX." *Star Tribune (Minneapolis)*, July 21, 2017.

Martin, Jill, Leah Asmelash, and David Close. "These Teams and Athletes Refused to Play in Protest of the Jacob Blake Shooting." CNN, August 28, 2020.

Masters, James. "U.S. Soccer Star 'Comes Out' as Gay." CNN, February 18, 2013.

McDonald, Mary. "Out-of-Bounds Plays." In *Sports and Neoliberalism: Politics, Consumption and Culture*, edited by Michael L. Silk and David L. Andrews, 211–24. Philadelphia: Temple University Press, 2012.

McDonald, Ryan. "Utah Royals FC, NWSL, Players Respond to Allegation of Racial Slurs at Rio Tinto Stadium Directed at Portland Thorns FC Goalkeeper Adrianna Franch." *Deseret News*, September 9, 2019.

McElwee, Molly. "Taking a Knee during National Anthems Is Distracting and Uncomfortable—but That Is Precisely the Point." *The Telegraph*, July 7, 2020.

McGrath, Mike. "How Europe's Other Big Leagues Have Approached Black Lives Matter." *The Telegraph*, July 2, 2020.

"McKennie: U.S. Might Not Accept Me for Skin Color." ESPN.com, October 12, 2020.

McLaughlin, Eliott C. and Jill Martin. "Robbie Rogers Becomes 1st Openly Gay Man in U.S. Pro Soccer." CNN. May 25, 2013.

McRae, Donald. "In Football It's Imposible to Come Out." *The Guardian*, March 29, 2013.

Meân, Lindsey. "Identity and Discursive Practice: Doing Gender on the Football Pitch." *Discourse & Society* 12, no. 6 (November 2001): 789–815.

Mendola, Nicholas. "The New Fan's 2016–17 Guide to Finding a Favorite Premier League Club." *ProSoccerTalk* (blog), *NBC Sports*, August 12, 2016.

Mielwski, Todd D. "Forward Madison Fc Says Sunday Home Game Postponed to Spotlight 'Fight against Racial Injustice and Systemic Oppression.'" Madison.com, August 28, 2020.

Mirpuri, Anoop. "Why Can't Kobe Pass (the Ball)? Race and the NBA in an Age of Neoliberalism." In *Commodified and Criminalized: New Racism and African Americans in Contemporary Sports*, edited by David J. Leonard and C. Richard King, 95–120. Lanham, MD: Rowman and Littlefield, 2011.

"MLS, Liga MX Launch Leagues Cup Competition." *Sports Illustrated*, May 29, 2019.

"MLS Commissioner Don Garber on Robbie Rogers: 'A Courageous Man and a Terrific Soccer Player.'" MLSsoccer.com. May 25, 2013.

"MLS Grew, but Still Doesn't Reach Liga MX." *CE Noticias Financieras*, December 19, 2020.

"MLS Lifts Ban on Anti-Nazi Symbol Following Fan Protests." NBCSports. September 25, 2019.

"MLS Players by Ethnicity 2019." Statista.

Møller, Verner, and Jakob Genz. "Commercial Sport—Debordian Spectacle or Barthesian Mythology?" *Catalan Journal of Communication & Cultural Studies* 6, no. 2 (October 1, 2014): 257–71.

Montague, James. *1312: Inside the Ultras*. London: Ebury Press, 2020.

Moran, Barry. "Keano's Praise for New Gay Colleague." *The Sun*, May 28, 2013.

Morelle, Joseph (Representative). "Congressman Morelle Fights to Secure Equal Pay for United States Women's National Soccer Team," www.morelle.house.gov, July 27, 2019.

Mulroy, Joe. "'In the First Premier League Games They Knelt for Black Lives Matter, Surely This Is Totally Wrong.'" *Northern Echo*, June 19, 2020.

Murphy, Patrick, John Williams, and Eric Dunning. *Football on Trial: Spectator Violence and Development in the Football World*. London: Routledge, 1990.

Narcotta-Welp, Eileen. "Going Solo: The Spectre of the 1999ers and Hope Solo as the 'Conscious Pariah.'" *Sport in Society* 21, no. 7 (July 3, 2018): 996–1012.

———. "Opening the Soccer Frontier: The Beautiful Game's American Past and Potential for the Future." In *Soccer Frontiers: The Global Game in the United States, 1863–1913*, edited by Chris Bolsman and George Kioussis. Knoxville: University of Tennessee Press, 2021.

Neale, Spencer. "'Cultural Marxism': Premier League Clubs Wear 'Black Lives Matter' on Jerseys as Matches Restart." *Washington Examiner*, June 17, 2020.

Newsham, Gail J. *In a League of Their Own! The Dick, Kerr Ladies 1917–1965*. Trowbridge, UK: Paragon, 2018.

Nicholls, Andy. *Scally: Confessions of a Category C Football Hooligan*. Ramsbottom, UK: Milo, 2002.

Oates, Thomas P. "The Erotic Gaze in the NFL Draft." *Communication and Critical/Cultural Studies* 4, no. 1 (March 2007): 74–90.

Oates, Thomas Patrick. *Football and Manliness: An Unauthorized Feminist Account of the NFL*. Feminist Media Studies. Urbana: University of Illinois Press, 2017.

Odegbami, Segun. "Black Lives Matter." *Complete Sports* (blog), August 1, 2020.

Okwonga, Musa. "The Premier League Is Returning—and Bringing with It a Statement on Black Lives Matter." *Washington Post*, June 16, 2020.

O'Neill, Tony. *Red Army General: Leading Britain's Biggest Hooligan Gang*. Lytham, UK: Milo, 2004.

Panahi, Jafar, dir. *Offside*. Sony Pictures Home Entertainment, 2007.

Parker, Graham. "Mike Magee on Fire for Chicago but Robbie Rogers Struggles in LA." *The Guardian*, June 20, 2013.

———. "Robbie Rogers to Return to US Soccer with La Galaxy." *The Guardian*, May 25, 2013, sec. Football.

Peacock, Ellen. "It's Time America to Pick Your English Premier League Team." *Fado* (blog), September 1, 2015.

Pennant, Cass. *Cass*. London: John Blake, 2008.

Pennant, Cass, and Martin King. *Terrace Legends*. London: John Blake, 2005.

Petermon, Jade D., and Leland G. Spencer. "Black Queer Womanhood Matters: Searching for the Queer Herstory of Black Lives Matter in Television Dramas." *Critical Studies in Media Communication* 36, no. 4 (August 8, 2019): 339–56.

Peterson, Anne M. "Black Players for Change Lead Protest at MLS Is Back Tourney." AP NEWS, July 9, 2020.

———. "Goal Reached: US Women's Soccer Team Gets New Contract." AP NEWS, April 6, 2017.

Phillips, Kendall R. "The Failure of Memory: Reflections on Rhetoric and Public Remembrance." *Western Journal of Communication* 74, no. 2 (April 2010): 208–23.

Phillips, Mitch. "Premier League, NFL and Cricket Wrestle with BLM Response." National Post. September 11, 2020.

Poe, Julia. "Former Liga MX Players Weigh in on Unprecedented Shift of Interest in MLS." *Orlando Sentinel*, January 20, 2020, sec. Sports.

Porter, Chris. "Marcus Rashford, Black Lives Matter and a British Premier Who Is Out of His League." The Conversation.

Porter, Rick. "NFL Ratings Slip in 2020, Remain Dominant on Broadcast." *Hollywood Reporter*, January 6, 2021.

Potter, Patrick. *Ultras: A Way of Life: The Fight for the Soul of Modern Football*. London: Carpet Bombing Culture 2019.

"Premier League Renames Players to 'Black Lives Matter.'" *CE Noticias Financieras*, June 13, 2020, English ed.

Prince-Wright, Joe. "MLS, Mexico Impress in Study of Global Attendance Figures." *ProSoccer-Talk* (blog), *NBC Sports*, April 16, 2019.

"Pro Soccer Player Robbie Rogers Says He Is Gay." Fox News, March 25, 2015.

Randles, Rob. *Road End Hooligans*. Monee, IL: indepedently published, 2017.

Reddy, Melissa. "Football Needs to Show That Black Lives Matter on Boards Too." *The Independent*, July 30, 2020.

Redhead, Steve. "Hit and Tell: A Review Essay on the Soccer Hooligan Memoir." *Soccer & Society* 5, no. 3 (January 2004): 392–403.

Reid, Eric. "Why Colin Kaepernick and I Decided to Take a Knee." *New York Times*, September 25, 2017, sec. Opinion.

"Reporting Statistics." Kick It Out.

Richards, Keith, and James Fox. *Life*. 1st Back Bay pbk. ed. New York: Back Bay Books, 2011.

Richardson, Allissa V. "Dismantling Respectability: The Rise of New Womanist Communication Models in the Era of Black Lives Matter." *Journal of Communication* 69, no. 2 (April 1, 2019): 193–213.

Riordan, John. "The Future's Bright for the Two Robbies." *Irish Examiner*, May 29, 2013, sec. IE-Sport/COLUMNISTS.

"Robbie Rogers Comes Out, Then 'Retires' on His Own Terms." *Montreal Gazette*, February 19, 2013.

"Robbie Rogers Contemplates Returning to U.S. Soccer to Become First Gay Athlete in Professional Men's Team Sport." *Mail Online*, April 15, 2013.

"Robbie Rogers Returns (Thank God)." Offside Rules. May 2013. This is no longer extant.

"Robbie Rogers Returns to MLS, the World of Twitter Responds." MLSsoccer.com, May 26, 2013.

"Robbie Rogers Set for Debut with L.A. Galaxy." The Province. May 26, 2013.

Robinson, Calvin. "The Premier League Should Have Thought Twice before Getting into Bed with Black Lives Matter." *The Telegraph*, July 1, 2020.

Robinson, Joshua, and Matthew Futterman. "U.S. Women's Soccer Team Stars Allege Pay Discrimination." *Wall Street Journal*, April 1, 2016, sec. Life.

Rogers, Robbie. "Robbie Rogers: FIFA Fails to Support Gays." *USA Today*.

———. "Robbie Rogers . . . the Next Chapter." Leeds United Mad. September 3, 2020.

Rogers, Robbie, and Eric Marcus. *Coming Out to Play*. New York: Penguin Books, 2014.

Rowe, David, and Callum Gilmour. "Sport, Media, and Consumption in Asia: A Merchandised Milieu." *American Behavioral Scientist* 53, no. 10 (June 2010): 1530–48.

Rüdiger, Antonio. "This Article Will Not Solve Racism in Football." *Players' Tribune*, May 27, 2021.

Rumsby, Ben. "Andros Townsend Disowns Black Lives Matter Movement after Crystal Palace Criticise Its Political Agendas." *The Telegraph*, July 2, 2020.

Ruthven, Graham. "MLS Is Pulling Fans into Stadiums, but TV Audiences Remain Underwhelming." *The Guardian*, August 25, 2020.

Schoenadal, Tracy. "Hispanic Audiences, Millennials, and a College Education." *YouGovSport* (blog), June 20, 2019.

Schwartz, Nick. "Your Guide to Picking a Favorite Premier League Team." *For the Win* (blog), August 15, 2013.

Schwarz, Orrin. "Rogers Makes News on Two Major Fronts." *Chicago Daily Herald*, February 16, 2013.

Scott, Nate. "Your Guide to Picking a Favorite Premier League Team." *For the Win* (blog), August 4, 2015.

Segura, Jonathan. "An English Premier League Primer." *Rolling Stone* (blog), August 15, 2014.

Serazio, Michael. *The Power of Sports: Media and Spectacle in American Culture*. Postmillenial Pop. New York: New York University Press, 2019.

Sherwin, Adam. "'Banter' Prevents Players from Coming Out, Says Robbie Rogers." *The Independent*, March 29, 2013.

Shrivathsa, Sridhar. "Soccer-Players Must Keep Taking a Knee to Highlight BLM, Says Ex-QPR Defender Onuoha." *National Post*, September 26, 2020.

Shugart, Helene A. "On Misfits and Margins: Narrative, Resistance, and the Poster Child Politics of Rosie O'Donnell." *Communication and Critical/Cultural Studies* 2, no. 1 (March 2005): 52–76.

Siemers, Erik. "The Evolution of MLS Expansion Fees." *St. Louis Business Journal*, August 22, 2019.

Silk, Michael, and Emma Chumley. "Memphis United? Diaspora, S(t)imulated Spaces and Global Consumption Economies." In *Manchester United: A Thematic Study*, edited by David L. Andrews, 249–64. London: Routledge, 2004.

Silk, Michael L., and David L. Andrews, eds. *Sport and Neoliberalism: Politics, Consumption, and Culture*. Sporting. Philadelphia: Temple University Press, 2012.

Simmons, Bill. "Page 2: Choosing My EPL Team." ESPN.com.

Sloop, John M. "'Apology Made to Whoever Pleases': Cultural Discipline and the Grounds of Interpretation." *Communication Quarterly* 42, no. 4 (September 1994): 345–62.

———. "'This Is Not Natural': Caster Semenya's Gender Threats." *Critical Studies in Media Communication* 29, no. 2 (June 2012): 81–96.

Smith, Allen. "Female Soccer Stars Bring EEOC Wage Discrimination Complaint." SHRM, April 1, 2016.

"Speedway Soccer." Speedwaysoccer.com.

Spillers, Hortense J. *Black, White, and in Color: Essays on American Literature and Culture*. Chicago: University of Chicago Press, 2003.

Stein, Marc. "Led by N.B.A., Boycotts Disrupt Pro Sports in Wake of Blake Shooting." *New York Times*, August 26, 2020.

Steinberg, Jacob. "From Parks to Premier League: The Shocking Scale of Racism in English Football." *The Guardian*, April 12, 2019, sec. Football.

Stejskal, Stan, Felipe Cardenas, Matt Pentz, Pablo Maurer, and Joshua Kloke. "MLS Players Share Their Thoughts and Experiences on Racism in America." *The Athletic*, June 9, 2020.

Sterkenburg, Jacco van, and Annelies Knoppers. "Sport as a Contested Racial/Ethnic Discourse: Processes of Racialization in Dutch Sport Media and Sport Policy." *Journal of Multicultural Discourses* 7, no. 2 (July 2012): 119–36.

Stott, Clifford, and Geoff Pearson. *Football "Hooliganism": Policing and the War on the "English Disease."* London: Pennant Books, 2007.

Stott, Clifford, and Steve Reicher. "How Conflict Escalates: The Inter-Group Dynamics of Collective Football Crowd 'Violence.'" *Sociology* 32, no. 2 (May 1998): 353–77.

Suárez, Esteban. "The Black Referee in Mexico Overcoming Racism on the Soccer Field." AL DÍA News, July 13, 2020.

Sun, Fiona. "Black Lives Matter in Hong Kong Too: African Migrants Say Racism Leaves Them Feeling Alienated, Shunned." *South China Morning Post*, June 27, 2020.

Svrluga, Barry. "Perspective | U.S. Women's Soccer Players Deserve Equal Pay, and It Shouldn't Take a Lawsuit." *Washington Post*. March 8, 2019.

Tanner, Joe. "Premier League Players to Wear 'No Room for Racism' Badges on Kits, Replacing Black Lives Matter Logo." Sky Sports, September 10, 2020.

Tate, Tim. *The Secret History of Women's Football*. London: John Blake, 2013.

———. *Women's Football: The Secret History*. London: John Blake, 2016.

Taylor, Mark. "Katie Hopkins Slammed by Premier League Star over Offensive Black Lives Matter Comments." *(London) Daily Star*, June 5, 2020.

Topping, Andrew. "MP Blasts Premier League over Black Lives Matter Campaign." NottinghamshireLive, June 14, 2020.

"Trailblazer: Joining the Team." *Nightline (ABC)*, May 25, 2013.

"Trailblazer: Game Changer." *Nightline (ABC)*, April 29, 2013.

Trenaman, Calum. "Thierry Henry Kneels during Match to Honor George Floyd." CNN. July 10, 2020.

Trujillo, Nick. "Hegemonic Masculinity on the Mound: Media Representations of Nolan Ryan and American Sports Culture." *Critical Studies in Mass Communication* 8, no. 3 (September 1991): 290–308.

Tucker, Reed. "Maybe Fair-Weather Fans Are Actually Good for Sports." Deadspin.

Ubha, Ravi. "Premier League: Racist and Homophobic Incidents Tarnish 'Best League in the World.'" CNN. December 10, 2019.

"Univision's TUDN to Exclusively Telecast Liga MX Guardianes 2020 Final Featuring Leon vs. UNAM." News Bites. December 15, 2020.

Urry, John, and Jonas Larsen. *The Tourist Gaze 3.0*. 3rd ed. Theory, Culture & Society. Los Angeles: Sage, 2011.

"The U.S. Women's Soccer Team Has More than Earned Equal Pay." *Washington Post*, July 8, 2019.

"U.S. Women's Soccer Team Should Get Equal Pay." *Wilkes-Barre Citizens' Voice*. April 3, 2016.

"USA Star Rogers: I Am Gay." *Daily Mirror*, February 17, 2013.

"USWNT Lawsuit versus U.S. Soccer Explained." ESPN.com. June 3, 2020.

"Vermeer Heats the LAFC-UANL Matchup by Saying That in Europe You See MLS and Not Liga MX." *CE Noticias Financieras*, February 27, 2020.

Vertelney, Seth. "Liga MX Is Television Ratings King in United States." Goal.com.

W., Neil. "Rogers: Footballers Can't Be Openly Gay," March 29, 2013. Professional Footballers Association.

Warnock, Neil. "Neil Warnock: Robbie Rogers Could Have Come Out at Leeds and Been Accepted." *The Independent*, March 29, 2013.

Watson, Leon. "Robbie Rogers Receives a Standing Ovation on His Return to U.S. Soccer as He Becomes the First Openly Gay Athlete in Professional Men's Team Sport." *Mail Online*, May 27, 2013.

Watts, Rebecca. "The Florida Gator Nation Online." In *Sports Mania: Essays on Fandom and The Media in the 21st Century*, edited by Lawrence Hugenberg, Paul Haridakis, and Adam Earnheardt, 243–56. Jefferson, NC: McFarland, 2008.

Wenner, Larwence. "Playing Dirty: On Reading Media Texts and the Sports Fan in the 21st Century." In *Sports Mania: Essays on Fandom and the Media in the 21st Century*, edited by Lawrence Hugenberg, Paul Haridakis, and Adam Earnheardt, 12–32. Jefferson, NC: McFarland, 2008.

Werner, Karel. "Religious Practice and Yoga in the Time of the Vedas, Upaniṣads and Early Buddhism," Annals of the Bhandarkar Oriental Research Institute 56 (2021): 179–94.

West, Isaac. "Queer Generosities." *Western Journal of Communication* 77, no. 5 (October 2013): 538–41.

West, Isaac, and Jeffrey Bennett. "Tomorrow Belongs to Us." In *Queer Praxis: Questions for LGBTQ Worldmaking*, edited by Dustin Bradley Goltz and Jason Zingsheim, 249–59. New York: Peter Lang, 2015.

"What Is The Most Popular Football League in the United States?" LADS Podcast.

White, James Boyd. *Heracles' Bow: Essays on the Rhetoric and Poetics of the Law*. Madison: University of Wisconsin Press, 1989.

"Widespread Support for Former U.S. International Who Says He Is Gay." Haaretz.com.

Williams, Jean. *The History of Women's Football*. Barnsley: Pen and Sword History, 2022.

Williams, John, Eric Dunning, and Patrick Murphy. *Hooligans Abroad: The Behaviour and Control of English Fans in Continental Europe*. 2nd ed. Repr. London: Routledge, 1992.

Wilson, Jonathan. *Inverting the Pyramid: The History of Soccer Tactics*. 2nd trade pbk. ed., 10th anniversary ed. New York: Nation Books, 2018.

Winrow, Ian, and James Gray. "Players to Wear Black Lives Matter on the Back of Shirts." *I*, June 12, 2020.

Witz, Billy. "Gay Athlete Ready for Role as a Pioneer." *International Herald Tribune*, May 27, 2013.

———. "Milestone for Gay Athletes as Rogers Plays for Galaxy." *New York Times*, May 27, 2013, sec. Sports.

———. "Rogers Says He's Ready for a Role as a Pioneer." *New York Times*, May 25, 2013, sec. Sports.

Woisetschläger, David M., Vanessa J. Haselhoff, and Christof Backhaus. "Fans' Resistance to Naming Right Sponsorships: Why Stadium Names Remain the Same for Fans." *European Journal of Marketing* 48, no. 7/8 (July 8, 2014): 1487–1510.

Young, Jabari. "Major League Soccer Increased Viewership This Season. Now It Has to Convince Networks It's Worth $300 Million Per Year." CNBC, December 18, 2021.

Zirin, Dave. "Soccer Star Robbie Rogers: Out, Proud and Now Un-Retired!" *The Nation*, May 26, 2013.

Index